Praise for *The Ribbon of Road Ahead*

I met Carol while walking through my life crisis in Spain. This fair American lady with her pink cap, passionate love of life, and wise attitude to her Parkinson's put me on pause. She's inspired me to turn my *can'ts* into *cans*—her spirit is infectious. I am lucky she's been my friend ever since. You are lucky she writes so well.

—ALISE AVOTA, Co-owner, Mr Page bookstore, Riga, Latvia

Growing up in the same town as Carol Clupny, I knew her to be a fierce competitor. I wasn't surprised, then, with her response to a diagnosis of Parkinson's. She picked up her hiking poles or got on her bike to tackle paths most of us would not attempt. Carol's story will be an inspiration to anyone facing a challenge in their life, not to mention [that it's] just a great read of one woman's journeys—both literal and figurative.

—SALLY McPHERSON, Co-owner, Broadway Books,
Portland, Oregon

Carol Clupny's personal narrative of her travels since being diagnosed with Parkinson's disease is both entertaining and enlightening. Part travel journal, part education, the two elements combine for a wonderful message to us all to keep seeking new horizons and redefined adventures.

—HOLLY CHAIMOV, Executive Director, Parkinson's
Resources of Oregon

This book is a story of resilience, strength, and belief in oneself. Carol takes you on her journey [of] suffering with Parkinson's disease and her recovery after deep brain stimulation. She never accepts defeat. You will be taken in by her courage and her faith in God. Her book is a message of hope for anyone. It is a beautiful read.

—CLAUDE TRANCHANT, Author, *Boots to Bliss:*
The Intriguing Story of a 21st Century Pilgrim Who Walked
the Way of Saint James

Rather than perching on a pedestal as the perfect person with Parkinson's, Carol slips in the mud and gets up laughing at herself. Walking next to you, she listens carefully, offering her hand or her treasure, un-self-consciously showing how to take the next step along this ribbon of road ahead. Enjoy the trek.

—NAN LITTLE, PhD, Author, *If I Can Climb Mt. Kilimanjaro,*
Why Can't I Brush My Teeth? Courage, Tenacity & Love Meet
Parkinson's Disease

A 425-mile bicycle trek across the state of Iowa in the iconic RAGBRAI can be quite an adventure for most people. For a 50-year old woman diagnosed with Parkinson's disease that recently discovered the joys of cycling, it can an almost insurmountable fete. *The Ribbon of Road Ahead* relives Carol's trying journey that tested her physical and mental limits as she experienced crashing, late night rowdies and a road full of pork chops, homemade ice cream and pie as she pedaled towards the mighty Mississippi River. Carol shows us that determination and indomitable courage can help you through life's biggest challenges.

—TJ JUSKIEWICZ, RAGBRAI Director

To Joyce

The Ribbon of
Road Ahead

Carol Chapny

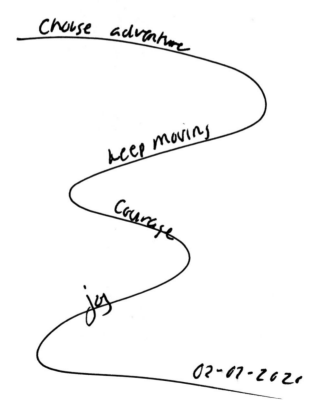

Choose adventure

keep moving

Courage

joy

02-07-2020

The Ribbon *of* Road Ahead

*One Woman's Remarkable Journey
with Parkinson's Disease*

Carol Clupny

UTREÏA BOOKS
Hermiston, Oregon

THE RIBBON OF ROAD AHEAD

Utreïa Books, Hermiston, Oregon

The Ribbon of Road Ahead is a memoir of the time period in the author's life before her diagnosis with Parkinson's through her recovery from a deep brain stimulation procedure. The events are portrayed to the best of her memory. While the stories are true, some identifying details and names have been changed to protect the privacy of the people involved.

Unless otherwise noted, all photos in this book were taken by the author.

Editing and design by Indigo: Editing, Design, and More
Cover photos Karen Lewis with Maryhelen Peterson

ISBN: 978-1-7335524-0-0
LCCN: 2019900422

For Charlie

Thank you for always being my "greatest fan."

Everything I was I carry with me
Everything I will be lies waiting on the road ahead.

   —Ma Jian, *Red Dust: A Path Through China*

Don't give up before the miracle happens.

   —Fannie Flagg, *I Still Dream About You*

Ultreïa!

   —The wish of unfailing courage shouted among pilgrims
   in the Middle Ages

Contents

Chapter 1

This Is Just the Beginning

THE LAST TRAIN FROM PARIS STOPPED IN BAYONNE AFTER MIDNIGHT. Our small band of five hikers straggled off, backpacks slung over shoulders, walking sticks dangling at our sides. We had a name of a hotel, a confirmation number, and the understanding that it was very near the train station. I stayed at the station with our thirteen-year-old son Luke while my husband Charlie, his brother Allen, and our family friend Jeremy walked down the deserted street searching. As I visually scanned the neighborhood from the train station bench, I saw only weathered buildings and a few signs that said *Bar*.

"Here it is," I heard Charlie call to Allen and Jeremy. How he found it, I did not know. It looked like a rundown apartment building. Luke and I grabbed our packs and headed across the street to where all three guys had now gathered.

"Oh shit" was the next thing I heard. "The door's locked." Charlie's loud and insistent knocking woke the night clerk. We could hear the sound of keys jingling as the man unlocked the door from inside to let us into a tiny hallway. The sleepy fellow went through another door and opened an office window. Charlie gave him our names, and he in turn handed out two room keys, pointed to a tiny elevator, and slid the window closed.

Attached to the keys were big numbers *1* and *2*. "Shouldn't be too hard to find," Charlie mumbled as we passed a steep set of stairs and went on to the elevator.

Charlie and I tried to get into the elevator while still wearing our packs. Twisting our bodies this way and that, we soon realized the impossibility of our situation. Charlie stepped out, the door closed, and up I went. I didn't recall punching any buttons. The tiny elevator was encased in glass, and although there were no lights, I could make out the ancient cables hauling me slowly skyward. When the elevator stopped, I saw Charlie, who had taken the stairs, opening our room door with key #1. Luke and the other two guys shared room #2. I was exhausted as I heaved my pack onto a chair and dug out a t-shirt to sleep in. I didn't bother picking up the items that had fallen out of my pack and scattered on the floor.

Jet-lagged and having slept very little, I left everything where it was and lay down on the bed next to Charlie, who had not even bothered to change his clothes. The blankets covered crisply ironed sheets, as if I was conscious enough to worry about the cleanliness of the room. Just as I dozed, my husband of nearly thirty years started snoring. I had learned over time to push him on his side and it would stop, but tonight I had no luck budging him. I had packed earplugs for this exact reason. Out of the bed I went and over to my pack, tripping on the items I had already dug out. Opening the outside flap, I started pulling more and more stuff out.

Where are those dumb earplugs? I thought.

When I had emptied the entire pack, I found them. Back in bed I remembered to warm the earplugs in my hands and then twist them a bit as I pulled my earlobes back. I wanted to get them deep enough into my ears to block out the snores. I glanced at my watch—it was ten minutes after three a.m. Putting my head on the pillow, I finally fell asleep.

There was loud pounding on the door! "Carol, Charlie, are you in there?"

Grabbing my watch from the nightstand, I saw it was eight forty-five a.m. Charlie slowly rolled over and staggered drowsily to the door. Jeremy was standing outside, and it was apparent he was in a panicked state.

"You have to come now! There's only one train to Saint-Jean-Pied-de-Port today, and it leaves in fifteen minutes!"

I looked around the room. My belongings were scattered everywhere. I grabbed a bra and slipped it on under the t-shirt, put on hiking pants, and stuffed everything else randomly inside my pack. I slipped on my sandals and tied my boots together by their laces to carry them. Charlie, still dressed from yesterday, was out the door with his pack, and down the stairs as I headed for the elevator. Pushing the call button, I saw the gears and cables slowly come to life. The door opened, I shuffled inside with my pack, and slowly down I went. As I walked out the front door of the hotel, I was met by an out-of-breath Charlie. He grabbed my pack. "Allen has the tickets. *Run!*"

My run was little faster than my walk, and luckily the train station was less than a block away. I hopped on the train just as the conductor called for the final boarding. The train was much older than the high-speed TGV we had ridden from Paris. It picked up speed, and we were on our way to Saint-Jean-Pied-de-Port.

The landscape was a luscious green and more mountainous than I'd expected. Looking out the train windows, I saw spring grasses sparkling with dew and wildflowers blooming along the tracks. Creeks were raging with snowmelt. White ribbons of waterfalls could be seen on the valley walls. It was beautiful!

We were on our way to hike the Camino de Santiago. I, a fifty-four-year-old woman four years into a diagnosis of Parkinson's disease, was on track to walk nearly five hundred miles on this pilgrimage trail with my family. This trek was more than just a walk across Spain for me. I was on a mission. My entire life had become a mission. I would not give in to this cruel disease. I had seen the pictures of people in the late stages of Parkinson's disease, with a hunched back, only able to take shuffling steps, not able to swing their arms or show any expression with their faces. I told myself, "Carol, you ain't going there." My life took on a different meaning; it became a constant fight against an invisible invader. And I would do anything—try anything—to come out the winner.

The Camino de Santiago, also known as the Way of Saint James, is a large network of ancient pilgrim routes stretching across Europe. These paths lead to the city of Santiago de Compostela, Spain, where it is believed the body of Saint James, an apostle of Jesus, is buried.

Yearly, hundreds of thousands of people from all over the world walk the Camino de Santiago, trudging muddy paths and climbing rocky mountain passes. The most popular route, the Camino Frances, stretches eight hundred kilometers (nearly five hundred miles) from Saint-Jean-Pied-de-Port, France, to Santiago. Walkers are called *peregrinos*, "pilgrims" in English. A pilgrim is a person who travels to a sacred place for religious reasons. Not all walkers set out on the Camino on a spiritual quest. Others walk for a great adventure in another land, to contemplate a major decision, or in memory of a loved one. Pilgrims travel simply, carrying a backpack containing a few changes of clothes,

We collect *sellos* in our pilgrim passport books.

a sleeping bag, and rain gear. Water and snacks round out the contents of their packs.

The infrastructure to support the pilgrims has developed over the centuries. Modern pilgrims now find shelter, food, and medical assistance every few miles. Camino travel can fit anyone's budget. Lodging choices range from the top-of-the-line *paradors* (government or historic buildings remodeled into luxury hotels) to the dormitory-style *albergues*. Food is easily found. Open-air markets and grocery stores provide ingredients for meals cooked in an albergue kitchen, or a simple but hardy pilgrims' menu dinner may be purchased at a restaurant or bar. Many of these trekkers pack snacks and share a picnic lunch with those they meet walking that day.

In the cities along the Camino, pilgrims are distinguished from tourists by a scallop shell dangling from their backpacks. The shell is an important symbol of the Camino. It, along with yellow arrows painted on signs, rocks, roads, and trees, points the way to Santiago. The grooves on the outside of the scallop shell are said to represent the many paths to Santiago. Early pilgrims also wore the shells as a type of identification badge. Their shells were also used as bowls and cups for eating. The modern pilgrim collects *sellos*, beautiful stamps from churches and albergues. These stamps, placed in a passport-type book, become precious souvenirs but also assure the authenticity of their pilgrimage when presented for the *Compostela*, a certificate of completion for walking to the Cathedral of Santiago.

I wished I could have done this walk when I'd had a "normal" body. My diagnosis changed that possibility. Parkinson's disease is a progressive chronic neurodegenerative disorder, meaning I would not get better over time. There's no cure. The doctors don't even know what causes it. They do know it is associated with damage to and loss of dopamine nerve cells deep in the brain, and dopamine is the chemical that helps regulate the body's movements. My most visible symptoms of Parkinson's included tremors, slowness, and stiffness. Other symptoms associated with Parkinson's include a stooped posture, facial masking, shuffling steps, and freezing of gait. In addition to motor symptoms, there are other traits of the disease that may not be so visible. These nonmotor symptoms that have a great impact on quality of life include poor speech volume and production, declining thinking skills, swallowing challenges, incontinence or constipation, anxiety and panic attacks, and difficulty with sleep. Parkinson's was once considered an old person's disease, being identified mostly in people over the age of sixty. Yet now individuals are being diagnosed at much younger ages. I was one of the younger ones.

The train bumped along the tracks, and after a while it would have taken toothpicks to keep my eyes open. My excitement was overtaken by sleepiness, and I laid my head on Charlie's shoulder. It seemed just a few minutes had passed when I was awakened by the screeching of the train's brakes. People around us started to move and look for their belongings. We had arrived in Saint-Jean-Pied-de-Port, France, our starting point for this month-long trek. We gathered our packs from the overhead storage of the train, and our "family" of five walked uphill into the old part of the city.

Locating the building known as the Pilgrim's Office was simple enough as we followed the stream of colorful backpacks and chatty pilgrims. At the Pilgrim's Office, each person walking from this point registered so demographic data could be collected. The volunteers there gave us photocopied trail maps, altitude charts, and lists of possible overnight accommodations in the villages we would pass through as we walked west. From a large map on the wall, we became oriented to this day's walk. We received the first sello in our pilgrim passports and gave a donation for shells to hang on each of our packs to show that we were now official pilgrims.

I asked to use the restroom before we left, and finding it occupied, I sat on a small chair. Waiting there I recalled how we'd gotten started on the journey to the Camino.

I loved to travel and had already been to Europe three times. As our kids were growing up and Charlie and I were nearing retirement, I dreamed of more adventurous treks. Machu Picchu, Hadrian's Wall, walking across Ireland, and trekking the Camino de Santiago had been on my bucket list for years. But when I got this diagnosis of a degenerative neurological disorder, I wondered if I would be able to walk any of them.

I had to try at least one. I showed Charlie my list. "Which one?" I asked.

"It's up to you, princess. Pick one and let's get going."

The Camino de Santiago sprang up off the page. The huge

accomplishment of walking five hundred miles across northern Spain would be like throwing a mud pie in Parkinson's eye.

Hollywood helped fire up that desire when the film *The Way*, with Martin Sheen and Emilio Estevez, came out. Charlie and I saw it at a ten p.m. showing, the only patrons in the theater. We felt okay commenting out loud as it showed scenes I could put myself in.

"I would love to be there, sipping coffee outside that small café."

"That long, straight, dirt road looks like eastern Oregon!"

"I wonder if we'll ever have to sleep outside."

"Look at that mountain village. All the houses are made of stone!"

We'd definitely gotten hooked.

My turn for the restroom came. I would've been more appreciative of the tiny washroom with no toilet paper had I known there was not another restroom for eight kilometers. I returned to the open area and looked for Charlie.

My eyes darted around the Pilgrim's Office. It was busy but not crammed with people at that time. Regardless, I felt the walls closing in around me. I started to hyperventilate and found a place to sit on a bench against the wall. I was very unprepared for this trip. The unknown had me panicked. The other hikers registering at the desk looked so fit in their new hiking clothes. My thoughts turned to my Parkinson's, my braced ankle, the pain I felt when I struggled to get the pack on my back. I was overwhelmed with the thought, *I can't do this!* Tears started falling, and my body started heaving and shaking as I let out the sobs. Thoughts of self-doubt filled my head. *Whatever was I thinking? I have a stupid disease, and it's not going away. These people look so fit and ready to go. I didn't train enough. I know I can't make it.*

This sobbing American woman was drawing attention to herself on a day that should have been filled with fun and excitement. Charlie saw me, and the look on his face was not one of a patient, doting husband. He rolled his eyes and sighed. Charlie just wanted to get going. He always just wanted to get going. Yet even in my early years of Parkinson's disease—called PD by those in the community—he had learned what to do. He had to distract me.

"Hey, are you all signed in? I saw an ice-cream shop just down the street. Let's get a snack." He took my pack in one arm and my arm in the other and guided his still-sobbing wife out of the building. In the fresh air, I started to get myself back together. The ice cream was a great ploy. My mind was distracted by the brightly colored and strongly flavored peach gelato. Ice cream had always been a favorite treat. Charlie knew that with the first spoonful, I would feel better. And I did!

The walk out of the walled city of Saint-Jean-Pied-de-Port and into the Pyrenees mountains was steep. Charlie and his brother Allen chatted with excited tones as we walked alongside couples and small groups of hikers. Luke, full of teenage energy, was already far ahead walking with Jeremy.

The road veered to the right and took us directly uphill, making it even steeper. A farmer herded cows from a side road, yelling in a tone that could be understood in any language: "Get out of the way!"

This was too much! The second panic attack of the day came on. I was totally freaked out!

It started in the pit of my stomach as a queasy feeling and worked its way up to tighten my throat. I tried to ignore the sensation and keep hiking. The trekking pole on the end of my right arm clinked on the pavement. My left foot moved forward. I reached my arm out with the left pole. My right foot didn't want to move. It was as if my foot had been inserted into a boot of quick-dry cement. Not only did my right foot not want to cooperate, but also the sweat on my face now turned into a running stream of sunscreen stinging my eyes. The sun heated up the surface of this black asphalt country lane out of the village of Saint-Jean-Pied-de-Port. The heat was stifling.

A car approached from behind, and the groups of people with their colorful backpacks moved to the sides of the lane to let it pass. The vehicle lost its momentum on the steep incline as it slowed for the walkers, and it had to back down to take another run at it.

My throat felt tight and very dry.

Hot, steep, stinging eyes, leg won't work…

Oh…my…God. If the rest of this Camino is anything like this, I am in for it! There's no way I am going to be able to walk the five hundred miles to Santiago de Compostela.

"My men," as I thought of them, were all ahead of me now. My scream was stifled before it got out of my mouth, but I still had some tears left. They rolled down my cheeks as I tried to catch up with the guys.

"Charlie," I squeaked out, then *"Charlie,"* a little louder.

He turned around, and as I saw him look at me, I crumpled right there on the hot pavement: backpack, hiking sticks, and all. Nearby walkers rushed to me. By the time Charlie got there, I was a sobbing mess of panic. The pilgrims stepped back when they realized he was there to help me. He pulled me to my feet, handed my trekking poles to Allen, and supported me as we walked to the side of the road.

Charlie found a level area, and I lay down, pulling my water bottle off my pack as my body met the cool green grass. He poured water on a bandana and hung it around my neck. I got control

After two panic attacks in one morning, I nap along the side of the road on Napoleon's route.

of my breathing, which with the efforts to cool off, helped me relax. Soon I was asleep. The Camino seemed a little more doable after an hour siesta. I was cooled off, rested, and refreshed when I awoke. Charlie had lain down beside me, and now we chatted pleasantly. I was sure he was wondering if I could go on and what he would do with me if I couldn't. My upbeat mood convinced him I could, and soon we had donned our packs and were continuing the march uphill.

Allen started our little group on another technique of hiking survival: singing to take our minds off our worries. We sang the chorus of "Yellow Submarine" over and over again, as nobody remembered the rest of the song. Singing really helped the rest of the hike fly, and before long we found our lodging for the night at the Refuge Orisson. When we checked in, we were shown around the building and given tokens that would allot us five minutes of shower water each. The cold, quick shower refreshed me, and I was ready to join in the lovely dinner served to all the pilgrims staying there. It started with a hot soup, followed by a crisp salad, and then pasta as the main dish. Chunks of bread delivered in baskets to the tables disappeared as fast as the contents of the bottles of red table wine. These were famished pilgrims. Between bites of food, I made friends with everyone seated around me.

Many of these pilgrims we would meet again and again as they became members of our Camino family. Lights-out was ten p.m., so there was no lingering at the table tonight. We headed to bed.

Excitement, anxiety, and snoring kept me awake most of the night. Shamefully my husband was one of the loudest snorers. I hoped my earplugs would help block out at least some of the sound. In our sleeping area, there were eight bunks. Jeremy, Allen, Luke, Charlie and I, and three people from New Zealand filled the room. I was tired, so I inserted my earplugs and quickly fell asleep, only to be awakened by a very loud snore. I looked toward the sound and saw some movement. Grabbing my glasses, I watched the woman on the top bunk swing her pillow down at the guy in the bottom bunk to get him to quit snoring! I muffled my laughter in my pillow and tried to sleep, but that picture in my mind mixed with my anxiety about this trip kept me awake.

I was out of bed and dressed before the sun, so I climbed up the stairs to the dining room. Ah, breakfast. Toast, butter, and marmalade were set out for us. As I drank my coffee out of a bowl, as they do in France, I did some self-talk. *You can do this. One step in front of the other. All the way to Santiago!*

Soon it was time to go. Charlie helped me get my backpack on, as I always got my right arm stuck. We hiked away from Orisson on the paved lane. It was still steep but not as bad as

I hike away from the *albergue* in Orisson, France, on day two.

the day before. I took notice again of the dew-sparkling grass and wildflowers on the side of the road. Herds of grazing sheep, horses with new foals, and groups of cows covered the hillsides. To walk among grazing animals out on the open range like this was an incredible experience.

A mare with her new foal was on the shoulder of the road. I didn't even think, *Range horse with new foal—possible danger!* I walked right up and petted the baby. The mare turned her head slightly, looked at me with her soft-brown eyes, and put her head back down to graze. These horses had seen thousands of people walk through their grazing land.

After a few hours of hiking the road, we left the roaming horses, cows, and sheep. The path took us away from the road, up over a pass, and down a steep hill on a rocky trail to our next night's lodging. It was treacherous! Loose dirt and rocks required us to watch every step. I don't know how I managed, but I didn't

At the end of a steep downhill, we arrive in Roncesvalles, Spain.

fall. Finally reaching the bottom, Charlie, Allen, and I were met by Luke, who was playing in the creek, and Jeremy, who quickly took my pack and carried it inside the huge stone building. We had arrived at Roncesvalles, Spain. I literally staggered into the albergue to check in.

Chapter 2

Reality Strikes

IN RONCESVALLES, THE FORMER MONASTERY HAD RECENTLY BEEN remodeled into three floors of pilgrim lodging. On the first floor were rooms for our boots and trekking poles. Here we learned another Camino etiquette lesson: boots and poles were not allowed in the albergue. Our bed assignments were in a cubicle of four bunks on the second floor. Lockers were available for our gear, and lovely modern showering facilities were around the corner—no tokens required! After the fixed-menu pilgrims' dinner of trout, spaghetti, and salad, I returned to my bunk in the cubby of four in the lovely new albergue. Earplugs in hand this time, I was prepared for a good night's rest.

In spite of my exhaustion and the use of earplugs to dull the noise level, sleep still evaded me. As I tossed and turned, bits of this and that ran through my head. I imagined my thoughts were a big bowl of spaghetti noodles. I picked up each one, examined it until it was done, then laid it out on a cutting board. This strategy had helped me through many nights before. With the first noodle, I recalled what I had read about this place.

Roncesvalles was formerly an abbey that had catered to pilgrims starting in the 1100s. The church was very ornate due to the number of early pilgrims who passed by making dona-tions. Historically, in a huge battle nearby the present abbey, Charlemagne's army was defeated and his favorite knight and nephew, Roland, was killed. Centuries later, Napoleon and his army traversed the pass we had just hiked. I could not imagine how those big guns got over that steep incline and decline. To this day the main route over the Pyrenees is called Napoleon's route. It's favored by the pilgrims for its beauty.

Even the dullest of historical facts could not help me off to slumberland.

The next noodle was pure frustration! Even my trick could not help me sleep. I was so tired…maybe overtired? Was it jet lag? I had read about insomnia with Parkinson's. Who would think it would start affecting me now?

What I knew about sleep issues in Parkinson's disease is that they are some of the most common and most irritating symptoms. In addition, the medication often used to treat Parkinson's symptoms also contributes to sleeplessness. People with Parkinson's may fall asleep during the day and not be able to sleep at night. They may be woken at night with the need to use the bathroom and not be able to fall asleep again. Disturbances in REM sleep can even result in patients acting out their dreams.

It was one thing to be able to recognize this as a likely Parkinson's symptom. It had been a completely different thing before I knew what was happening in my body.

In my late forties, my body had started demonstrating symp-toms I couldn't explain. Insomnia was one of them. Internal tremors, fidgeting, pacing, feeling anxious, twitching little finger, frozen shoulder, an intestinal illness that would not go away were a lot more. No one seemed to notice some of these symptoms, or they didn't connect them to any significant pathology.

In February of 2008, Charlie surprised me for my fiftieth birthday. He generally could not get anything past me, yet this one he did. My work asked me to stay a little late on a Friday night to meet with some other employees. *Really?* I thought. *What's so important that it can't wait until Monday?* As we had just sat down at a conference table, there was a knock at the meeting room door.

I turned to see nine-year-old Luke standing there with a bouquet of flowers. He had dressed for the occasion—an Indiana Jones–style hat tilted down over his eyes, an oversized tie around his neck, and his shirttails half tucked in. My coworkers, who had been in on the surprise, clapped and shouted, "Happy birthday!" Luke then took my hand and led me outside where a limousine was waiting. I was tickled to see my dad, who had been experiencing health issues, and my sister, who lived in California, seated inside. It was about a thirty-minute ride from my office in Pendleton, Oregon, to the high school commons in Hermiston. Seventy-five friends, family members, and colleagues gathered there to toast and roast me.

Charlie's big gift to me was a three-day women's kayak adventure in the San Juan Islands of Washington state. I had mentioned many times how much I wanted to try kayaking, but the picture I had of my first kayak experience was a two-hour paddle in a secure harbor with a one-on-one instructor. Perhaps Charlie overestimated my kayaking desire and thought I would love this. He may have been getting back at me for buying him a weeklong mountain climbing class on Mount Rainier five years earlier when he turned fifty. Regardless of the reasoning behind the gift, I was not going to pass up this opportunity. I was worried about my strange health issues and increasing tremors, but I didn't want these feelings to interfere with a great adventure. The trip was scheduled for the beginning of July, so I had a few months to prepare. I assumed I would be feeling better by then.

Spring came. I did not feel any better. The strange symptoms continued and increased in severity. It took a game of fetch with the dogs to get me to the doctor. I had played softball for many years and still played catch with our two sons. I could throw the ball fairly far, and the delighted dogs would race each other to retrieve it.

That day, as I wound up and threw, the ball landed a pitiful five feet away. The older dog, who especially enjoyed playing fetch, snatched possession of my poorly thrown ball from the younger pup and pushed it back to me with her nose. She looked up at me, and I imagined her saying, *Lady, can't you do better than that?* I picked the ball up and threw it again. Even with the extra effort I put into throwing it farther, the ball didn't travel any distance. That was weird. It scared me. I decided to make a doctor appointment.

When I called our primary care physician's office, the urgency in my voice got me an appointment the next day. After reviewing my health history and asking some questions, the doctor had me fill out a checklist for anxiety.

"You seem to have a lot of stress in your life. Let's try this prescription and see how you feel in a month or so," he suggested as he handed me a prescription for an antianxiety medication.

The kayak trip date rolled up on the calendar. I convinced my friend Laura to come along as my paddling partner. We left early on June 30 to catch a ferry that would take us to Friday Harbor. A nice dinner and a comfortable hotel room surprisingly resulted in a good night's sleep for me. In the morning I closed up my backpack and walked outside to experience early summer in the San Juans. The skies were blue, the seas were calm, and the temperature was perfect. Laura joined me with her pack. As we walked toward the dock, we spotted a van pulling a trailer of sea kayaks. The friendly guides made small talk as the group loaded into the van for transportation to the launch site.

At the boat launch, guides fitted each of us women with a life jacket and spray skirt. The kayaks were heavy, about a hundred pounds empty. This required teamwork to carry each one to the water. I hadn't thought about how our gear would travel and soon discovered this when we tried to lift the boats. Divided among these eighteen-foot vessels' sea hatches were tents, sleeping bags, food, wine, gas stoves, and the personal effects of fifteen women for this three-day paddle.

Laura had no difficulty following the instructions presented by our guides. She was ready to go when it came time to launch the boats. For me, just getting into the personal flotation device was a challenge. A motherly sea kayaker took over and got it on me, like she was putting a coat on a kid when she was in a hurry. I was a bit embarrassed at this need for help. Then I tried loading my body into the boat. A guide was nearby, and she and Laura held the sides steady while I practically tumbled into the front cockpit of the two-person kayak. The preparations so far had been difficult but snapping in the spray skirt was impossible. I was stiff, and I could not twist my torso far enough for me to snap the spray skirt on the lip of cockpit behind me. The woman loading the boat next to me noticed and reached over to finish the snaps. *Oh my God*, I thought. *They are going to think they have to tie my shoes and wipe my nose.*

We were instructed to paddle out of the inlet and up the coast of the island. Laura and I paddled with the group at first, but soon we were left behind. A guide paddled back to check on us, watched for a little while, then gave me a lot of tips. I could not coordinate my strokes. I could not twist my body. I did not raise my paddles high enough. I pulled when I should have pushed. Laura was having to do nearly all of the paddling. *This is worse than novice paddler behavior,* I thought. *What's wrong with me?* Not only was I worried—I was also embarrassed. Having been athletic and competitive all my life, I did not believe that I couldn't paddle a boat.

The guide paddled away a distance and sat still in her kayak watching us. I was fighting back tears of frustration, trying to follow her suggestions but still not making the boat go any faster. She approached us again and came alongside our kayak. Instead of giving me instructions, she asked Laura and me questions about ourselves. Soon I discovered we were matching her strokes. She wasn't pushing us hard, but her strategy was successful in moving us along faster. We turned north, and I saw the rest of the group landing and unloading lunch supplies from the boats on Posey Island.

After a brief rest and a gourmet lunch on the tiny island, I felt energized. The feeling was short-lived, however. We crossed a wide channel where the currents met the tides, causing waves and whirlpools and all other manner of scary sea stuff. I was frightened at this point. The what-ifs came pouring into my mind. *What if we get capsized by a big wave? What if we don't paddle fast enough and a boat hits us?*

I wanted to call out to the guide who had watched over us during the morning paddle. *I have had enough sea kayaking. Take me home now, please!* Just then the lead called out, "Adventure paddling, ladies. Paddle hard, and don't stop for anything." The guide nearest us showed us how to keep the bow of the boat directed toward a point on a distant island. Maybe that took our

The other kayakers wait for Laura and me during the women's adventure trip in the San Juan Islands, Washington.

minds off the rough waters, and in a very short time, we were across the shipping lane. We traveled along the shoreline of Stuart Island to a beautiful harbor.

Already tired and down on myself for my lack of strength and coordination, I imagined the other women on the trip were talking about my weakness while they waited at the mouth of the harbor for us to catch up. As we paddled into the harbor, they chanted, "C-7, C-7"—our boat number. I took it totally wrong. Instead of thinking of it as encouragement, I imagined I was being victimized by bullying and mean-hearted teasing. Laura, however, was good-natured about it all and joined in the chant.

We disembarked our boats, and the guides had us form teams of six to eight to carry the heavily loaded crafts above the high-tide line. But first I had to get out of the spray skirt. Laura helped me this time, which eased the embarrassment of asking one of the other ladies to help me. I felt especially weary. My insides felt like Jell-O in an earthquake. I asked Laura if she could see me tremoring, but by all outward appearances, I was fine.

At camp, the entire group worked together to unload the kayaks and put up the tents. Afterward the guides prepared a gourmet dinner, and the wine flowed. I tried to relax, but I was worried.

Morning light woke us. After a hearty breakfast prepared by the guides, we lined our boats up in the little harbor and performed synchronized paddle routines for the delighted occupants sipping coffee on the decks of the yachts moored there. We paddled around several small islands, observing eagles, sea otters, and ocean life among the rocks. Laura and I got stuck paddling against the current as the tide changed in a narrow passageway between two islands. Finally we broke through and were met by cheers—"C-7! C-7!"—as we pulled our kayak onto the beach.

The group was consuming another gourmet meal, so we dug right in. Someone served me a crispy green salad with smoked salmon and blue cheese crumbles. At another table were artisan breads, fruits, and cheeses. A small cooler held various sparkling drinks. The effort of the morning had left me starving. After I had gobbled my lunch, I grabbed a bowl of cherries and stretched out in the warm sand to relax. I had just dozed when the lead guide called, "Saddle up. Time to paddle." The paddle back to the campsite was tough, as I was so exhausted from fighting the current. The rest of the group held relay races ahead of us to pass the time as they waited for C-7 to finally catch up with them.

Before we loaded the boats the next morning, I approached the guides with my concerns. They reassigned boat partners so that a guide would be paddling with me. Actually, she paddled *for* me, just as Laura had. We paddled back across the perilous shipping lanes and into Roche Harbor just as seaplanes were ferrying out. Our sea kayaks seemed so small as we maneuvered them close to the docks. No one wanted to be near the spinning propellers and overwhelming loudness of the engines as they taxied for takeoff. My innards trembled even more. I felt an anxiety attack brewing in me. Normally I would have taken an additional dose of my antianxiety medication to help me through such a difficult moment, but that wasn't an option in the kayak. I worked on keeping positive and thinking ahead to what needed to happen next, and I kept the attack at bay. The parking lot ahead was a welcome sight as I spotted the kayak trailer connected to the outfitter's van, waiting to load us up and return to Friday Harbor.

I called my primary care physician's office as soon as I had cell service. During my appointment the following week, he scratched his head and said, "I think a referral to a neurologist is in order."

* * *

Expecting a busy medical center office, I was surprised to find the waiting room empty and quiet. The receptionist desk was dark. *Is this place open?* I thought. I'd driven the forty miles to the larger medical facility in Kennewick, Washington, alone, not wanting to disrupt Charlie's work schedule, though if I could talk to that younger Carol, I would tell her to bring him. I recommend people always take another person to be a second set of eyes and ears when facing a life-changing medical evaluation like this.

I heard footsteps, and the door to the hallway of exam rooms opened.

"Mrs. Clupny?"

There stood an older man who reminded me of my grandfather in appearance: a bald head with white tufts of hair sticking out behind his ears, piercing blue eyes, and a kind smile. A spotless white exam coat, pressed and starched, with slight frays on the cuffs, covered his long-sleeved striped shirt, which was topped off by a solid-colored bowtie. *I wonder if his socks are argyle.* Worn but impeccably polished wingtip shoes slid back as he opened the door further for me to pass. His soft voice was accented. I remembered someone had told me his home country was New Zealand.

"I am Dr. Eisler. Pleased to meet you. Pardon me for the wait. The receptionist is gone today."

Seated in the exam room, I answered question after question. He recorded my responses in precise handwriting on a chart stapled inside a manila file folder.

In his soothing voice, he said, "Now I test your nerves." With a little rubber hammer, the doctor tapped my knees and elbows. He poked and lightly scratched the bottoms of my feet with a safety pin. That tickled a bit and made me jump.

The exam continued with me drawing a two-dimensional box, copying a picture, filling in the numbers on a clock face. I was shocked and fascinated at the same time. My drawing of the box was convoluted. The numbers on the clock face were jumbled up on the right side and looked as if they could fall off at any second. He asked me to repeat series of numbers extending from three to eight digits in a row. I listened to lists of words and repeated as many as I could remember. He asked me to perform large motor movements with my arms and legs and smaller movements with my fingers. My movements were slow, inaccurate, and uncoordinated.

He scooted back on his stool and looked at me.

"Do you have a diagnosis for me, doctor?"

His reply was a little puzzling. "I will give you a prescription for some pills. I don't want to give you a diagnosis yet. We'll know more when you've taken this medication for a few weeks." He walked me to the door of his still-empty waiting room. Putting his hand on my shoulder, he said, "You think you have Parkinson's disease, don't you?"

"I've done my reading," I responded.

"If this medication makes you feel better, we'll have some answers."

I don't remember much about driving the forty miles of freeway home. I was still stunned when I stopped to fill the prescription. The pharmacist used such a quiet and serious voice as she counseled me about the drug, saying, "This medication is amantadine, and it is used to treat the symptoms of Parkinson's disease." She lost me there. *To treat the symptoms of Parkinson's disease. Oh my God.* It suddenly felt real.

I paid for the prescription and walked to my car, my head crammed full of thoughts and emotions. There were so many things to think about! *My family! How will I take care of them? Will they take care of me when I become crippled by this disease? My job! Will I be able to work? I love sports. I love to hike and climb and fish and now kayak. Will I be able to I do any of those things?*

I moved into a temporary state of denial, stuffing those thoughts away as I went on with daily life. It was the beginning of the school year. Fall sports and marching band kept this mom of two active boys quite busy. At work it was a fun time with the staff I supervised, catching up on their news since I had last seen them in the spring. In-service training had to be facilitated, assignments made, materials distributed. It was business as usual at home and at work.

A brilliant late September Saturday morning, the sun shining in the windows and the leaves catching its glow, I woke up in the mood to move! I zipped around the house doing chores and cleaning with a vengeance, when I was stopped in my tracks by the thought, *Crap! I feel really good. No inner tremors, no twitching little finger or pinging legs. The medicine is working. That means…* I had to face the unthinkable. *I have Parkinson's disease.*

Chapter 3

Defining Moments

A Gregorian chant circulated the room: our wakeup call.

Oh, was I dead, dragging tired. The strenuous hiking and lack of sleep had caught up with me. With backpacks loaded, we went downstairs to the boot room and reclaimed our footwear. Just across the road was a sign that read *Santiago de Compostela 790 km*. Pausing for a photo, the members of our group chuckled about the distance. It was just a three-kilometer walk through a dark forest to the small village of Burguete. The cement-cast-feet feeling had returned, and I was struggling to walk even at the slowest pace. Not having had any breakfast, we needed to find some food before we went much farther. Our luck, there was a store open with a wide selection of pilgrim-friendly foods. I chose a few items, and Charlie paid as I went outside, where I laid my head down on a picnic table. Soon Charlie appeared with the food.

"Eat up," he said. "I called you a taxi!"

"You what? And why?"

"Look, you're really exhausted. You can't even keep your head up. We have a very long walk today, and I hear the terrain is challenging."

I was greatly disappointed. I came to Spain to walk! But the adventure of this first taxi ride in Spain soon took my mind off my sadness. The taxi ride was wild, to say the least. Having ridden in a few taxis in the United States, I thought I knew the protocol: get in back, buckle your belt or not, as you wish. When my taxi arrived, the driver opened the front passenger door. With me buckled in the front seat, the driver put his foot on the gas. The taxi passed every vehicle it came up on. The driver even took the chance of going around a string of Spanish RVs, which he called caravans. The road curved through the foothills and made some steep climbs. The driver slowed as we came up to some buildings and stopped in the middle of the village where my group had planned to stay that night. I had no idea where I was, but I did remember the name of the place we had planned to sleep.

After a walk around the village, I found the private albergue. There are several types of albergues; those run by communities are called municipals. Church-run albergues are parochials, and there are also privately owned or chain albergues. Hostels, hotels, bed and breakfasts, and *casas rurales* make up other classifications of lodging. It was still early morning, a time when all pilgrims were out walking and the *hospitaleros*—volunteer caretakers—were cleaning and preparing for the new overnighters who would arrive mid- to late afternoon. There was a bench across from the door to the albergue we had chosen, and I waited there in the sun until I saw activity in the windows.

I found the door cracked open just a bit and let myself in. I explained my circumstances to a woman there, thinking she was an employee, when actually she was a pilgrim granted a second night's stay due to an illness. She found the cleaning person who was employed there. This person called and asked the owner if I could come in and lie down. Permission was granted, and I was

Leaving Roncesvalles, Spain, our group poses at the highway sign.

shown to a bunk where I had several hours of blissful silence to sleep. I lay down and thought about Charlie and how our family had come to be.

When Charlie and I had been married eight years, we started to talk about why we had not yet conceived a child. It was heartbreaking for us to see friends with new babies in their arms. Working with our local church youth group and teens at retreats and camps filled the void for a couple years. Then during an annual exam, my gynecologist pointed the finger at endometriosis. I underwent several procedures to improve fertility. Then, as the suggested procedures became more and more invasive, we considered foster parenting or adoption, even going as far as taking a six-week course and becoming certified as foster parents.

My mother had been battling ovarian cancer for six years, and the pull we felt to have her see our first child was very strong. I never heard my mom swear or use any type of crude language, so I was surprised when my sister overheard her on the phone telling her cousin, "When I get to heaven, I am going to kick some butt and get Carol and Charlie a baby!"

We continued the process of providing a new grandchild for my mom by applying for adoption. The State of Oregon adoption process was quite complicated and intrusive into family matters, so we also got in touch with Catholic Charities. A skilled social worker interviewed us. We filled out a brief application and got letters of recommendation. Sadly my mom passed away before the adoption occurred. She kept her promise, though, as nine and a half months later, we came home from a vacation to a surprise phone call from our social worker. There was a three-day-old male infant needing a home.

Not expecting a baby so soon, we were unprepared. Actually we did not have a single baby item in the house. I called neighbors and friends for some immediate needs. When I picked up the infant car seat from our friend Dana, she had made us a shopping list of newborn essentials too. Stopping at a Kmart in a neighboring community, Charlie and I tore the list in half, each got a shopping cart, and went on a shopping spree in the baby section. By the time we got home with our new son, our house was full of baby items. I could see my mom's face filled with joy at the results of her "butt-kicking."

Loren was a sweet, happy baby. We doted over him—who would get to feed him, bathe him. We even fought over changing his diapers. We involved him in all usual activities: t-ball, soccer, piano, dance. Charlie came from a family with seven kids, and I was sure he wanted more children. It just wasn't happening for us naturally, and we remained in the adoption pool with Catholic Charities, but no birth moms were looking at our file. We had been waiting a long time. I was satisfied with a one-child family and hoped Charlie would be too.

When Loren was eight years old, I mustered up the courage to ask Charlie, "Are you happy with just one child?"

"Why do you ask?"

"I feel like our family is complete. And we probably look pretty old to a teenage girl looking for adoptive parents. Can we pull out of the adoption pool? And how about taking the childproof gadgets off all the drawers and cupboards?" Charlie lowered his head and shook it as if to say, *You're asking me to do more work, and I'm tired.*

"Winter break is in a couple of weeks. Let's think on this and make a decision then," my wise husband responded. "And we can take the childproof locks off also."

December 10, 1998, started out as a typical Friday. Our lives were about to be changed dramatically. I arrived home from work to see Loren playing with toys on the kitchen floor and Charlie on the phone with a very serious and intent face.

"Carol, you need to come here."

He put the phone to my ear. "We have a baby boy, just born. Would you be interested in meeting with the birth mom and possibly taking him home?" the social worker on the other end of the line asked.

Without thinking, we both responded, "Of course!"

"Can you be here tomorrow by noon?"

"Of course!"

I was so in shock as we went to a school faculty Christmas party that night, I could not even talk. Since adoption is such an uncertain process, we didn't know what was going to happen. Charlie and I didn't tell Loren and pledged to keep it a secret from everyone else too. It was difficult to contain our excitement. After the party I went to one neighbor to borrow an infant car seat and another to borrow some cash, as banks were closed and we didn't use a cash card. We found a babysitter for Loren, as we did not know for certain how long we'd be gone or if we'd be coming back with a baby.

On the long drive across the state to meet this baby, we composed a prayer for his birth mom and decided on the name Luke. At the hospital we were taken into his birth mom's room in the maternity ward, and she relinquished him to us. The nurses helped us celebrate by sharing toasts of sparkling cider, providing us a nice meal, and giving us a New Parent class. Before Luke was twenty-four hours old, we had him secured in the car seat and were on the highway home.

Thirteen years later, Charlie and I were planning the Camino trip for the family. Loren had started college and needed to stay home and work, but Luke would join us. From his body language to his silent behavior, though, it was apparent Luke didn't really want to go. He had been to France with us before and felt frustrated in not understanding the language. As I imagined Luke on the trail forging ahead of the group again, as he had done the day before, I thought, *I wonder if he thinks by walking faster he'll be done sooner and can go home.*

Luke, with all his energy and those long legs emerging from his young teen body, could really move out fast when we walked. Charlie and I had both known this would be the case based on the training hikes we'd taken at home. Our favorite training routes included the Hermiston Butte, a 581-foot basalt core of an eroded volcanic flow within a mile of our house. A city water reservoir was hidden under the rocky surface of the butte. Sandy trails helped strengthen our ankles, and steep climbs challenged our calves, hamstrings, and glutes on the way up and quad muscles and knees on the downhill portions.

Another training hike for the Camino was an old railroad grade turned hiking path along the Columbia River, the Lewis and

I train on a fifteen-mile segment of the Lewis and Clark Commemorative Trail, Oregon.

Clark Commemorative Trail. We'd parked our car at the McNary Beach access and walked east about five miles until we reached Hat Rock State Park. Along the way we spotted raptors soaring from nests in the basalt cliffs, clusters of white pelicans floating on the river, barges carrying goods downstream, and deer headed to their favorite riverside watering hole. At the State Park, we cut cross-country with eyes open, ears peeled, and careful foot placements, as spring was time for the rattlesnakes to come out of hibernation. Wildflowers dotted the hillsides, and jackrabbits darted out from behind stands of sagebrush. When we reached another river recreational access named Warehouse Beach, we caught a maintained trail back to Hat Rock. At the small store and grill, we were able to get a drink and a cheeseburger. A nap on the park lawn preceded the walk west and into the setting sun on the return to the car. I remembered blinking into the sun and thinking that on the Camino we would always walk west.

I'd heard that the hike along the Columbia was very like what we were to experience on much of the Camino: gravel and dirt roads with small elevation changes.

On these walks, Luke had run ahead and left notes in the dirt: *I'm bored* and *Hurry up* scrawled with his hiking stick, reminding us of his young age and short attention span.

Other days, when time was short and a long hike was not feasible, I'd taken a quick three-mile jaunt in a neighborhood near our house. Luke didn't join me in this training. At thirteen and with those youthful legs, he would have no problem hiking the Camino distances. Charlie, with his years of backpacking experience, would enjoy this challenge. But I'd wondered, *What about me?* On the Camino, our mileage would average ten to fifteen miles a day. Every day. For over thirty days. *Am I prepared for that?*

* * *

When I woke up from napping on the bottom bunk in the still-empty sleeping room of the Zubiri albergue, I noted someone had come in and placed a blanket over me. Such thoughtfulness.

I looked up and saw a different woman in the reception area and guessed she might be the owner. I wiped the sleep out of my eyes and went to introduce myself. With a few words of Spanish interspersed with my English, I thanked her for allowing me to come in so early. She invited me to share her lunch, and from a small refrigerator on the counter, she removed a jar of white pickled asparagus spears and a can of beer. She was very attentive to me, as if she sensed there was more to what was bothering me than being tired and feeling ill.

In her few words of English and slowly pronounced Spanish, she inquired what was wrong. When I explained my disease and

Allen settles in at a typical albergue.

my disappointment about arriving by taxi, this stranger took my hands and looked directly in my eyes. This is what I understood her to say: "This is your Camino. There is no right or wrong way to do the Camino. Don't be disappointed if it is not as you expect. If your plans are changed, there is a reason, and something good and special will happen."

It already had, I realized.

I returned to the sleeping room and lay back down on my bunk to ponder the words this wise woman said to me. My thoughts wandered around her words, going this way and that, considering the bigger picture of her comment. *If your plans are changed, there is a reason, and something good and special will happen.*

After wrapping the blanket back around my body, I thought back to when I'd received the diagnosis, four years prior, and the second opinion that I'd received from Dr. Hiller at Oregon Health & Science University (OHSU) in Portland.

Dr. Hiller's crisply starched white lab coat had her name embroidered in red over the left breast pocket. She wore knee-high leather boots and a miniskirt topped with a blue sweater. From her seat in front of the exam-room computer, she turned her head toward me, and I saw her blunt-cut bangs and inquisitive eyes. "Mrs. Clupny, describe what you've been noticing about your body."

I heard the speedy tapping on the keyboard as she entered my responses. I told her about the twitching little finger, lip, and eyelid and the intensity of the inward tremors. I recalled the stories of trying to throw the ball for the dogs, the women's adventure kayak trip, and when my arm wouldn't swing. I told her of my disappointment when the first prescription of amantadine actually decreased my symptoms. Recently, my legs began to "ping," as I called it, and they felt as if something was crawling on them. My sleep patterns were becoming more unusual.

She turned to look at Charlie, who was sitting near me in a second chair in the exam room. "Do you snore?" she asked him.

He jerked and sat up tall. "I don't know. I'm asleep."

Dr. Hiller looked at me. I nodded emphatically.

"We're ordering you a sleep study. Your snoring is not contributing to her healthy sleep hygiene."

With her attention back to me, she asked more questions and quickly entered the answers on the keyboard. The actual physical exam started with pokes with pins and bumps with rubber mallets. Next came the testing of my physical movements. I followed her directions to motor movement tasks: touching my nose with my pointer finger and then touching the moving target of her pointer finger, flapping my hands up and down on my lap, flicking fingers at her, getting up from a chair, walking around a cone and hustling back to the chair to sit down.

The next part of the exam was one I've since learned to dread; it's done at each visit and startles me every time. The doctor stood behind me and, when I least expected it, gave a big jerk on my shoulders to knock me off balance.

It did not take her long to come to her conclusion. She looked directly at me, and her face at that moment is forever burned in my memory: "Mrs. Clupny, I concur with your previous evaluation. You have young-onset idiopathic Parkinson's disease."

A few tears escaped and rolled down my cheeks. *Don't lose it, Carol. Don't lose it. Here is the opportunity to ask questions. Keep it together.* I listened to my inner voice and thought about each component individually.

Young onset: Under age sixty. Until recent years Parkinson's was considered an old person's disease.

Idiopathic: Without known cause. Was it hereditary? Possibly. There were a few relatives in my background with suspected PD. Was it environmental? Possibly. I swam in the Columbia River downstream from the Hanford Nuclear Reservation in the 1960s, when no one knew how dangerous it was to dump radioactive material in the river. As a little girl, I'd loved to mix up whatever chemical weed killers and pesticides I found in the garage—and maybe even tasted a few of my concoctions. I rode my horse in pea fields after the crop dusters had spread their herbicides.

Parkinson's disease: A chronic neurodegenerative disease affecting movement and characterized by rigid body, shuffling feet, freezing gait, speaking and thinking difficulties, and tremors.

Having made myself a definition of my diagnosis, I knew I was now at war with a chronic debilitating disease. I asked, "How is this going to affect me in the near future? What do I need to do to take care of myself?"

Dr. Hiller answered, "Keep exercising and taking your meds, and you'll have five to ten years before things get more difficult."

Charlie was very quiet. I was stunned. *Five to ten years? Then what?* It was like an ambiguous timeline looming over me.

Pulling the blanket even closer to provide me an extra feeling of security, I became cognizant of the number of years that had passed. I was in the middle of that ticking bomb's time frame. I was exercising my body, taking my meds as prescribed, and hoping for as much time as possible before Parkinson's would send more challenges my way. And of course I prayed for a cure.

Chapter 4

Moving on Down the Trail

IN ZUBIRI WE LEARNED WE COULD SEND OUR PACKS AHEAD. AN enterprising local person had established a service to deliver pilgrims' larger backpacks to the location of that night's lodging. The pilgrims carried smaller packs with the day's necessities, including something for lunch and, of course, water. It was this day I happily walked out of the village — no backpack, no taxi — and started the trek to Pamplona. Charlie and Allen were at my side. Luke started out ahead of us with a small stipend for lunch and directions as to where he should meet us toward evening.

As we walked toward Pamplona, I reflected with Charlie how simple life had become. "Wake up, eat, walk, eat, walk, find a place to stay, rest, eat, sleep, and do it all over again," I said. "Why did we even worry about buying all this stuff?"

I recalled a blog post I had written:

The 500-mile walk across Spain in the early summer requires different considerations for clothes and gear. Our outdated frame backpacks weigh 5–6 pounds each before anything is loaded. We won't need sleeping bags for temperatures at 0 degrees when we plan to sleep inside each night. Flannel shirts and jeans and heavy leather hiking boots we usually wear backpacking are to be replaced by fast-drying tech shirts, pants that zipped off into shorts, and trail runner shoes.

I loved shopping. Reading the Camino forums and various social media groups had given me a good idea of what we would need. I studied pack weights and sizes. "Should we get lightweight sleeping bags or silk cocoon sheets and flannel liners?" I asked Charlie. He didn't offer an opinion on any of the gear, which gave me permission to have fun shopping.

My love of shopping had come up another time early in my life with Parkinson's. During a conference sponsored by Parkinson's Resources of Oregon, a question was thrown out for discussion at our tables: What was the first thing you did after hearing the diagnosis of Parkinson's?

"Oh, I went out and bought a coat," I blurted out to the seven other people at the banquet table. All eyes darted to me. I was expected to explain. "That coat fit me well. It represented a time and place in my life—a career where I attired myself in professional garb of suits and dresses, a position that changed me into a person I never thought I would be. Some of that was good, some not so good. That coat no longer fits me. I've gained forty pounds since my diagnosis. But it also represents who I was pre-Parkinson's diagnosis. I'm so different now."

I turned to the woman on my right, a college professor with a brand-new diagnosis. As tears rolled down her cheeks, I knew what I was about to say was too raw, too fresh for her to comprehend at this time. Yet I had to say it, because it was that very moment I had discovered it was my truth.

"I'm a much happier person since my diagnosis, and for that I am thankful for this event in my life." Everyone at the table became completely still. I could feel their attention as they listened even more carefully to my words. Lightening it up a little seemed like a good idea, so I planned my next comment. "I've been permanently excused from jury duty! I get to park right close to the supermarket entrance! I have new hobbies, new friends, no responsibility for employees. I feel softer, rounder, stronger, and tougher. The daily stress I once felt is replaced by peace. The anger I once harbored is gone. I find it difficult to get mad or really hurt. I am thankful."

We sat there in quiet for a moment around that table, the four people with Parkinson's and their loved ones or caregivers pondering. I wondered what they thought. I wondered if any of them had come to peace with Parkinson's.

* * *

We met up with Luke a bit sooner than expected as we entered a small village about noontime. He had eaten his way through his money. Instead of handing him more, we all sat in bright-red chairs under a sun umbrella on the patio of a little café and ordered oven-fired pizza. He scarfed his food down and quickly was back on the Camino to catch up with a group of young adult friends he enjoyed walking with.

In the late afternoon Charlie, Allen, and I reached the outskirts of Pamplona and started following the little brass Camino markers embedded in the sidewalks. I suggested we catch a bus, and by asking around we discovered we could take a bus to the city center and the plaza and cathedral where we were to meet Luke.

There I spotted Luke sitting at a table with his young adult friends, a beer in front of him. He did not see me approach, and I surprised him when I sat down beside him, took his beer, and said, "Luke, how thoughtful of you to order a beer for me." I took a big gulp. And then looked at the friends.

My question, "Do you guys know how old he is?" was met with stares.

"He's only thirteen."

"Oh, I thought he was older than that," one of the group piped up. I gave that person my best frown.

"Please keep his age in mind."

* * *

That night, still striving for a good night's sleep, Charlie and I booked into a four-star hotel just off the plaza. Allen, Jeremy, and Luke registered at a nearby albergue. We had a nice dinner in a restaurant purported to have been a hangout of Ernest Hemingway. The author had come to Pamplona from Paris in 1923, arriving during the San Fermín festival, which is world famous now for its running of the bulls. Hemingway was so enamored with the city that he returned year after year, making it the backdrop for his first famous novel, *The Sun Also Rises*.

We rose too early the next morning. There was no hospitalero to chase us out at seven thirty a.m., so we lingered in the luxurious room before we loaded up our backpacks and found the Camino markers leading us out of town. There was a steady stream of pilgrims following the same trail out, all hoping to climb the Alto del Perdón before the noon heat.

The other pilgrims did not seem to notice that I was any different. There were people of all sizes, shapes, and colors walking.

A good number of pilgrims struggled with blisters or tendonitis. I had an ankle support and knee braces, and so did several other walkers. Charlie, who spent the most time with me on the walk, could readily explain how my Parkinson's issues impacted me. It was the nonmotor symptoms of Parkinson's disease, which are less apparent, that set me apart.

Some days my behavior was affected in unusual ways. My slurred speech, incomplete thoughts, and staggering movements might've led others to think I'd had a few too many *cervezas* at lunch. Other times I would become sleepy and walk in a dazed state and not communicate at all. The noncommunicative times distressed Charlie, especially since some of these behaviors were emerging on the Camino. Because I had not experienced them at home, I wondered what was causing them. Could it be that the amount of walking, the altitude changes, and the heat were affecting the way my body absorbed and reacted to the medications?

The amantadine, the medication I took as a part of my initial Parkinson's diagnosis, had been only my start into the pharmaceutical world of Parkinson's. When I met with Dr. Hiller and had my diagnosis confirmed, she prescribed the dopamine agonist Ropinirole. This medication is used alone or with other medications to treat Parkinson's disease. It can decrease tremors, stiffness, slowed movement, and balance issues. Ropinirole is also used to treat restless legs syndrome, the formal name for the creeping feeling and pinging I felt in my legs. Ropinirole acts like dopamine in the body. By prescribing it to me at that point, Dr. Hiller was saving the use of the gold standard medication, Sinemet, for later. Sinemet wasn't discovered as a treatment for Parkinson's until the 1960s. It was and continues to be the most common treatment for PD, and although it helps many of the symptoms of Parkinson's, it eventually starts wearing off before the next dose and causes extraneous body movements, called dyskinesia. Dr. Hiller had explained that Sinemet would be in my future. And by the time I took this Camino walk, it had found its way into my medication regimen.

On the Camino, medication became a headliner issue with me, right up there with blisters and tendonitis. One day a well-meaning helper sent my backpack ahead on transport before I got my day's supply of meds out. On a particularly wet day, I had not closed the containers properly, and my medication was damaged. I asked another pilgrim what I might do, and it was recommended I visit the *farmacia* for advice. The first farmacia asked that we go to the next village, as it was larger and Sinemet would be readily available. There, I showed my prescription bottle and was provided a month's supply for approximately three dollars. However, they did not have another medication I had recently started to assist with the absorption of the levodopa, one of the ingredients of the Sinemet. We called a responsible neighbor with instructions on how to get in the house, where to find my medications, and to send them to a post office in Santiago de Compostela. It was waiting at the post office when I arrived.

Early on in my diagnosis of PD, I had a problem with falling. I was not picking up my feet enough, and my toes caught on bumps or uneven cracks in the sidewalk and especially on stairs. One particularly bad fall resulted in a broken nose, black eye, and bruised face. Charlie was teased a lot about causing these bruises, but we managed to shake it off with comments such as "The darn sidewalk likes to jump and kiss me!" That usually changed the focus.

In the fall of 2009, I fell on a short step while visiting a neighboring school district as a consultant to their Speech and

Language Program. I hit the floor hard—but I had no idea why. I looked down at my painful ankle and noted its awkward position. The superintendent of the school district was present and, as a bonus, was also an emergency medical technician. He said, "We're not going to move you. I'm calling an ambulance and will have you see the doctor at our new community hospital."

That fall resulted in a surgery where pins and screws were used to put my ankle back together. In waiting for the surgery and recovery, I could not move around freely. Nonmovement was detrimental, and it seemed my ankle would not heal. It was so stiff. I was diagnosed with foot drop, meaning I could not flex my toes toward my ankle when walking. My ankle was declared a 7 percent permanent disability, and I received a small check from workers' compensation. How they can place a percentage on a body part, I will never know!

While walking on the Camino, I developed calluses on my big toes. These in turn developed blisters under them. Blisters are a big deal on the Camino. Heat, moisture, and improperly fitted shoes or socks that rub on the foot can all result in blisters. Every pilgrim has a prevention idea, and every sufferer has a treatment to offer. I decided to lance through the callus to the blister with a borrowed needle and left a bit of thread to keep it open for drainage. Covering it with a Compeed plaster, a common European-brand bandage for wounds, I thought I was set. But it hurt like heck. It was supposed to get better, not worse.

After another painful day of walking, I pulled the plaster off in the shower, taking a chunk of skin off. My big toe was red and draining a really bad-smelling liquid. It was infected.

Some of the hospitaleros had developed expertise in blister care. Sister Lucia at an albergue staffed with nuns gloved up like a surgeon when she examined my toe. She cleaned it well and

Sister Lucia, a trained *hospitalero*, cleans my infected toe.

put a proper dressing on it. She recommended I take a few days off for the infection to heal. Charlie helped me investigate the schedule for buses and availability of taxis. We made a plan, and I would be riding the bus out of that village the next afternoon as the rest of the group walked.

I found myself developing quite the expertise on alternative forms of traveling the Camino. Each taxi ride, bus, or train trip continued to bring a little bit of sorrow, as I really wanted to be walking. I wanted my heart to be open to the Camino's plans for me, as the albergue owner in Zubiri had explained after my first taxi ride. Riding in my wheeled modes of transportation, speeding down the highway or slowing through a village, I plastered my nose against the window searching for pilgrims. I watched especially for my own family and for my Camino family, as I had come to recognize those walking the same daily pace by their jackets, hats, or packs. I missed walking with them.

Chapter 5

Miracle on the Meseta

THE MESETA IS A MUCH-DISCUSSED SECTION OF THE CAMINO.
"If I'm running out of time, should I skip the Meseta?"
"Are you going to walk the Meseta?"
"You walked the Meseta?"
It's a high-plain agricultural area in northern Spain between the two cities of Burgos and Astorga. Known on the Camino for its big skies, dry heat, flat lands, and the boredom and loneliness it inspires, many pilgrims decide to skip this part of the Camino and bus ahead. I believed it was a part of the walk I needed to do on foot more than anywhere else. The Meseta called to me strongly, just as I had been called to the Camino as a whole. From my research, I learned that this 232-kilometer section was most likely to test what I was made of. Maybe from this stretch of the Camino, I would gain the feelings of strength and independence I was seeking—the mud in the eye of Parkinson's disease.

We left Burgos early on the morning of June 19. This was a significant date: Charlie's and my thirtieth wedding anniversary. The air was delightfully cooler than usual that morning. We met up with Yvette, Charlie's sister-in-law, and her son, Brandon—making seven now in our Camino family. Adding members to a group always changes the dynamics, and this time was no different. We soon discovered who walked at a fast rate. And as we had ten days' experience, we would have to teach the new arrivals albergue rules. The walk out of the city was pleasant, with lots of chatter and photos at each monument we passed. As we left Burgos behind, we also left the shade trees. The sun climbed higher in the sky, and the morning coolness evaporated away. Our goal for the day was twenty and a half kilometers to Hornillos del Camino. *Hornillos* means "little ovens." The area at one time had been a major bread-making center for the region. I didn't think ovens would be needed to bake bread on a day like today.

As the heat increased, I felt we were walking into one of those huge ovens. No one had thought to carry a thermometer, so we had no way of knowing the temperature, other than hot. The gravel-and-dirt road was almost a straight ribbon stretched out before us. On one side of the road was barren ground with small stacks of hay bales. The other side gave way to acres of wheat, golden heads on barely green stalks swaying in the hot breeze. The guidebook warned that this stage of the Camino was through the fields with no water fountains to refill our supply and no trees for shade. The golden sun scorched through the bluest sky imaginable. Stopped beside a tall clump of grass, I huddled in the tiny bit of shade it provided. I drank long from my water bottle and poured what was left on my pink baseball cap in hopes of cooling my head. My hat dried immediately.

I wouldn't have minded a nice air-conditioned taxi ride at that point. I dreamed of a cold beer in a bar with walls of three-foot-thick stone I could lean against and cool my roasting body. I looked ahead to see if there was an oasis on the horizon. What I saw was a sign. It was a road sign intended for drivers going east. On the back of the sign, facing the pilgrims walking west,

Yvette Clupny and I walk across the Meseta in Spain.

someone had scribbled with a black marker, *Don't give up before the miracle happens.*

What miracle? Don't tell me not to give up. I can give up anytime I want to! I may have felt like quitting that walk right there and then, but what good would it have done me? There was no taxi, no beer, and no shade. I took up behind Charlie, and we walked.

I grew up a cradle Catholic. My parents sent all five of us children to Catholic schools. I learned the catechism and studied the history of the Church. I was no stranger to watching for miracles. The first miracle of Jesus's public ministry, turning water into wine at the wedding in Cana, held many connotations. One I held close was that when I am presented with the opportunity to improve a situation, I will do it. In more modern times, the apparitions of Mary the mother of Jesus were awesome miracles. She chose to visit children and peasants, the lowly and the marginalized, at lonely and humble places such as Fatima, Lourdes, and Medjugorje. I was in awe of the miracle of holding a newborn infant when I could not give birth to my own, of seeing a rainbow shining when I was still in the storm. The miracle of hope my mom modeled when given just a few months to live, and because she wasn't done living yet, she stayed alive for six years. But on this day, as I spiraled down into a sort of despair, I needed to experience a miracle.

I was overheated. Melting, in fact. More than that, emotion had started bubbling up inside. At home the antidepressant citalopram worked with the Parkinson's medications to keep my emotions stable. In fact, I felt a real lack of emotion, without true happiness or sadness, while I took this medication. I realized my body wasn't reacting the same way as I walked the Camino. The panic attacks I had already experienced proved that. This emotion I felt was strange, something from the past, something different than the panic attacks. I held on to it until I could recognize the feeling: anger!

The growing anger started with my feet, which continued to hurt from multiple blisters, and found its way up to my knees, where tendonitis persisted, through my body, where I now felt every little ache and pain or hurt and was looking for someone or something to blame it on.

I started to lay that blame. Whoever last assisted me with my water bottle had jammed it too deep in its pocket, so my stiff arms couldn't reach back to get it. That helpful person who boosted the blue Gregory Jade backpack on had let me buckle up tight before it was on straight. By the time the emotion reached my head, I was blaming my pink baseball cap. I had overpaid for it in a small magazine shop in the Paris subway, and it had to be responsible for this headache I was developing. As my anger grew, I realized I was not going to be able to contain it much longer.

I was angry at Charlie for "making" me walk in this heat. And then I got to the bottom of it: I was angry at God.

In the four years since my diagnosis, I had not gotten angry, or fallen depressed, or lost hope. I had unknowingly suppressed that anger and let medication do its work to chemically reduce my overall depth of any type of emotion. Now the emotion poured out of me. The sweat from my forehead mixed with my tears. I stood out in the middle of the dusty road, the full heat of midafternoon beating on me, and yelled at my God. Charlie stood back and let me have my conversation. The venom that was stored inside spewed out of my eyes and my mouth and my sweat glands until it took me to my knees.

Then I heard a voice, maybe Charlie's, I don't know, as God often speaks through others. I was certain the words were sent from God.

"Look at you. Look at what you're doing. You're in Spain. You're walking out here on the Meseta. How many people are doing this? How many people with a chronic disease do you see out here today? How many of your healthy friends are here walking?"

"Okay, God! I hear you! What am I supposed to do with this…this chronic debilitating degenerative disease?!"

"Do something good, Carol. Find something good to do with it."

I struggled over the dusty road to Charlie. I wondered what he would say after my tantrum and talk with God. He didn't comment about what he'd witnessed but said, "Look," and pointed his walking stick. I looked and saw it too: The ribbon of road that we had been following to the west suddenly dropped down into a river valley. Trees lined the river and surrounded the entrance sign to the village of Hornillos del Camino. Across an intersecting dirt road were a bridge, some dwellings, flowers, and greenery. How come I had not seen this oasis before—was it a part of the miracle?

I arrive at Hornillos del Camino, Spain, after the miracle on the Meseta.

On our thirtieth wedding anniversary, I had my Camino miracle. Walking west through the heat and monotony of the Meseta, I found the suggested direction for the next part of my life. Vague, open-ended, perfect for me: "Do *something* good, Carol."

Unsure what that something would be, for the rest of the Camino, I spoke words of affirmation and encouragement to anyone and everyone who would listen. Sharing my story and attitude of hope and optimism with pilgrims from around the world was to be my *something good* for now.

Chapter 6

You Look Good

WE COMPLETED OUR WALK ON THE MESETA AND STARTED TO CLIMB over another range of mountains. Climbing mountains is the definition of work—at least I think it should appear that way in the dictionary!

As I willed my legs to hoist my body forward and upward one step at a time, I reflected on my life's work. I had just officially finished my last day on the job the day we flew out. Any other year, this journey would have been considered my summer vacation, so it hadn't fully set in yet how much my life was sculpted by my job and how much it would change.

My college coursework had trained me to be a speech-language pathologist. I'd developed a strong work ethic early in life, and in high school I'd worked at my parents' mom-and-pop drive-in restaurant, The Ice-Burg, in Walla Walla, Washington. I had a horse and a boyfriend, and I played sports and maintained a decent grade point average. My full slate of activities continued right after high school graduation in 1976, when I enrolled in summer classes at Walla Walla Community College. I kept taking courses year-round, and in the summer of 1980, I obtained a master's degree from Eastern Washington University.

My professional career began when I was hired as a speech-language pathologist by an education service district that provided special and related services to eleven small school districts in rural eastern Oregon. Continuing education workshops were necessary to maintain my teaching and speech pathology licenses. I also discovered that by taking for-credit college classes, I moved along the salary scale. School Leadership and Administration classes became available on weekends and during the summer. Prior to this time I had not planned on becoming a principal or a superintendent, yet leadership in education became more interesting to me. I learned school law, curriculum development, teacher negotiations, research methods, and budgeting—all topics that seemed a good investment of my time. I designed my academic program carefully, knowing that educational leaders with a background in special education were needed in this rural region, if I should decide to pursue an administrative position. Ultimately that's exactly what I did. I became the director of the Speech, Language, and Hearing Program for the InterMountain Education Service District, a position that challenged me and allowed me to oversee quality services to children in our rural service area.

Stress is a big trigger for Parkinson's problems, so after my diagnosis, medication was only part one of the solution. I had to address the stress. By then I had almost twenty-nine years of work invested toward my retirement fund, which I could draw from without penalty at thirty years. During a counseling session with a Public Employee Retirement System advisor, it was suggested I hold out for another year if my health allowed. Everything within me wanted to be with my family, to have warm cookies and milk ready when my kids got home from school. An hour and a half a day was spent commuting to the office, and much more was spent driving through the rolling gold wheat fields or over the Blue Mountains of eastern Oregon to visit staff at distant locations. I wrote a letter to our superintendent asking to step back from my administrative duties and return to direct speech therapy services to children. With that done I slowly began to tell my relatives, friends, colleagues, and staff of my diagnosis.

Fellow administrators and I met and designed a job where I evaluated preschoolers' communication skills. A five-minute drive from my home, a four-day workweek, and an extended lunch were wonderful accommodations that helped my stress level immensely. I would have more time for my family and spend less time driving across snowy mountain ranges.

During the extended lunch breaks, I would go to a nearby gym to walk on the indoor track or shoot baskets. When the four walls of my little shared office became too much and anxiety would start to overwhelm me, I could go out to my car and listen to music or take a walk in a nearby neighborhood. It was working for me.

Parkinson's symptoms may not always be obvious. Quite often I would explain that I had Parkinson's disease, and the response I would get was, "You don't look sick." Having a comeback for this comment was difficult, as I was really suffering from the disease. One response that seemed to lighten up the conversation was, "I work really hard to be this gorgeous!"

On the Camino, I was receiving some precious comments as I walked, not looking different than anyone else. Most often, when Parkinson's disease entered the conversation, I heard (just like at home): "I wouldn't be able to tell. You don't look like you have Parkinson's." "Wow! You look great for having Parkinson's." "You're too young to have Parkinson's." Then there was, "I am not

I shoot some baskets during my extended lunch break.

complaining anymore. If you can be out here with that disease, I don't have anything to talk about."

My favorite comment was made by a woman who was walking faster than me as we climbed a small hill in a lovely shady area. She decided to slow down, enjoy the shade, and talk a bit.

She picked up her walking sticks and swung them up over her shoulder. I did the same. The absence of the constant clicking of the stick tips on the pavement made it easier to talk.

"Where are you from?" she asked. I couldn't quite place the accent of her English, but it wasn't American.

"The state of Oregon, in the US," I replied.

She slowed her pace and looked at me. "There are a lot of people on the Camino from there."

"Really?" I knew where this was leading.

"Yes, and you know there is a family out here and their mum has Parkinson's disease?"

"Oh?" I held back my smile and let her continue.

"There are many of them, and they take turns walking with the mother."

I paused for a few seconds then said, "Well, that mother would be me."

"Nooooo! You are doing really well, lady."

I was four years into this disease and was growing more and more accustomed to comments like this. But even as I worked hard at physical activities, the disease continued to progress slowly in my body. "Carol, you look great!" was getting old. I started to wonder, *How can I explain that, in this context, it's not exactly a compliment?*

My friend Michael Benton had been chronically ill for a number of years. We were first acquainted while working together at the Catholic Diocese of Baker Youth Ministry camps and junior high camps in the 1980s and early 1990s. Mike was the camp musician, and I held several roles, from camp counselor to leadership instructor to activities director. When we grew up—or grew away from the youth camps—the friendship continued, with visits full of hysterical laughter, sometimes crying, or Mike trying to teach me the eight-bar blues on guitar...which often led to laughter or tears!

As I stepped forward on the trail, I could not even begin to list the illnesses his body had thrown at him. I was quite humbled by my friend, who had maintained his positive attitude and will to live in order to "find out what comes next," as he put it. With each new diagnosis, Mike embraced the treatment and, frankly, just continued on. I, in turn, knew my diagnosis was stable, but to embrace Parkinson's? I tried to make it look like I had, but some days I, too, questioned if I had the disease. Could it be something else?

One day I received a message from Mike that he would be traveling through my area and wanted to know if we could meet.

Mike Benton and I emcee a talent show at the Catholic Diocese of Baker Junior High camp, Wallowa Lake, Oregon.

We decided on lunch. I planned what I would say when I saw him, just to see his response to "Mike, you look so good!"

Mike and I had already started joking and telling stories about our experiences with this common greeting extended toward ill people. People don't know what to say, or they want to give encouragement, or they truly think the patient looks good for a person living in a diseased body. In our dark moments of humor, Mike and I commented (but only to each other), "What are we supposed to look like?" Was Mike supposed to be in a hospital bed, with wires and tubes coming out of a gray, emaciated body? Was I supposed to be using a walker, hunched over, taking shuffling steps, not able to use my right arm except to tremor, having someone feed me? Mike wondered, "Why doesn't someone say, 'You look like crap. Let's see what I can do to help you'?"

During this conversation we decided that people were not

just offering niceties; generally people are afraid of facing the realities of serious illness. "You look great" fits right in with "I'll pray for you." We both appreciated being prayed for, of course. But was it a possible cop-out to say these things? What about coming over and sitting with me for an hour so my spouse could have a break? Another overused but well-meant comment was "If you need anything, just call." I was so bull-headed that when I needed help the most was when I definitely would not call. *A true friend*, I thought, *shows up unannounced with a bag of treats and plans to get my laundry started.* People are good and want to help—they're just scared and don't know what to do or say.

I could understand why a person might say to me, "You don't look like you have Parkinson's," though. My mind turned to why that was true. *Is it because I keep pushing myself to keep moving, to stay active and involved? But the disease is still there, and it affects the activities of my daily life greatly.*

Back at the restaurant with Mike, I ordered a decadent dessert for the both of us: one of those brownies with hot fudge and an extra scoop of ice cream. It was in celebration of our good health, which we both knew would not continue for long.

"Carol, what can I do for you?"

"Mike, you look good. It's not necessarily your handsome physical features that look good. It's your resolve for living well and in harmony with your illnesses that makes you look good. You let me see into your heart and soul, and you look into mine. We share the joys (yes, there are some) and heartbreaks of chronic illness. And you asked me, 'What can I do for you?'"

My eyes teared up as I thought of Mike, the man who had sat across from me at a table in the bar of a restaurant and helped me poke fun at my serious illness. He was gone now, but the lessons I learned from him continued to live strong in my heart.

* * *

The Camino left the Meseta at the city of Astorga, and from there we started the *work*, our slow, deliberate march up the next range of mountains. When we got to Rabanal del Camino, our stop for the night, relaxation and dinner would have to wait until after our pilgrim chores. Tonight the chores included showering—a tremendous chore for me. I never came across what we would call in the United States an "accessible" shower. I was terribly afraid of slipping, and there wasn't a bar to grab. I was so slow at moving that my allotment of warm water ran out, and the freezing-cold water put my body into spasms.

Charlie washed our socks and underwear and hung them to dry in the afternoon breeze. It didn't take long to get them done, so Charlie and I explored the town. There was a line of pilgrims leading into the doors of the small church. Not wanting to miss anything, we joined the line. Two monks sang the evening vespers in a church crowded with pilgrims. Then we looked for dinner and found a bar open. Thinking it would be special, we ordered Italian dishes from the menu. We were served microwaved Italian cuisine from the box to our plate. We curtailed our laughter until we left this establishment so as not to seem ungrateful.

Early the next morning we set out for the highest point on the Camino, the Cruz de Ferro. Our group split up according to speed. Luke went ahead with his cousin and aunt as Charlie walked at my pace. The wind came up, and rain mixed with sleet began to fall. Temperatures dropped. I remembered that Luke had left his coat somewhere and was really without any protection from the elements. The last I saw, he was wearing a t-shirt and shorts. He was like that, leaving stuff behind. A few days before, he'd left his MP3 player on a bus. The honest bus driver turned it into the station's lost and found at the end of his shift, and Luke was able to collect it. Now I worried about his exposure to the elements.

The gradual incline of yesterday's walk was replaced by a steeper trail through the forest. Around the corner we could see it…Cruz de Ferro, the "iron cross." Our advanced group of hikers was huddled together, sheltered from the wind at the side of a small building. "We're freezing! Where have you been?" Luke complained. Digging through our backpacks, we found a sweater and another t-shirt for Luke to layer for warmth.

It is tradition that each pilgrim carries a small stone from home to represent a burden they carry through life. They place the stone at the foot of the cross, representing the release of this burden. The mound of rocks was tremendous, as it had been accumulating for a while. Each of us took a turn climbing this mountain of cast-off stones to lighten our own personal load. Luke reached out and took my hand to help me get closer to the top.

It was not so much leaving a rock behind that I'd remember about this place. Luke's gesture of kindness brought tears to my eyes.

The cold wind became stronger, and it started to rain harder. The others in our group went on to try to get to a lower elevation before the weather became even worse. Charlie went to his pack and brought out a rosary that a friend had made. He and I stood huddled together at the bottom of the mound and started to pray, "In the name of the Father and the Son and the Holy Spirit. Our Father who art in heaven…"

The rain was driven sideways now by the increased wind speed.

"Hail Mary, full of grace, the Lord is with thee…"

The rain hitting the hoods of our coats and the wind in the trees created a tremendous sound.

Luke helps me climb the mound of rocks at Cruz de Ferro, Spain.

We started yelling back at the storm, "Glory be to the Father and to the Son and to the Holy Spirit."

The more the weather tried to drown our voices, the louder we shouted back at it. The hot tears that streamed down my cheeks mixed with rain.

"My sweet Jesus, forgive us our sins, save us from the fires of hell." I didn't feel cold, or wet, or tired, or in pain huddled close to Charlie holding tight to the rosary. I felt like Charlie and I had been thrust into this spiritual battle. We were battling against Satan, who was prowling in this sacred place, watching out for people who had opened their hearts here, left their burdens but not refilled those spaces with peace and goodness and love. We had to be strong warriors. We prayed with such purpose, now shouting out intentions: "For all who have lost a loved one. For all who are imprisoned. Hail Holy Queen, Mother of Mercy. Our light, our sweetness, and our hope…"

The wind let up momentarily. Charlie's brother Allen was there. He'd gone a little way and come back for us, watching quietly, not wanting to interrupt our fervent prayer. We three hugged hard. I felt peace. The war against evil spirits was over for now. It was an emotional and very spiritual moment.

We had a choice of walking routes. Yvette and the boys chose the trail that progressed steeply over rain-slickened rocks. Allen stayed with Charlie and me, walking the highway to the next village. Soaked and trying to keep warm, we sang songs and told jokes until we arrived in the small mountain village of Acebo at a break in the downpour.

Yvette found us wonderful lodging in private rooms over a bar. Showered and with dry clothes on, I wandered down to the common area, where a roaring fire blasted heat from a huge stone fireplace. I made myself comfortable and was soon mesmerized by the flames.

My mind took me back again to those early days with Parkinson's, before I knew a neurological disorder had hijacked my body. Charlie and I had registered for a speech and language pathology conference in Orlando, Florida. We were taking our two boys, who were now old enough to entertain themselves while we participated in the workshops. It was a trip Charlie was especially excited about. His favorite theme park was on the list: Disney World.

The flames danced in front of my eyes.

I now was sipping a warm drink and had propped my feet on a chair in front of the fireplace. A long way from Florida... I was in that very comfortable place where I could fall asleep but really wanted to just be there with my thoughts.

Our boys—Luke, then nine, and Loren, then seventeen—played in the many theme parks and water parks while

Charlie and I attended the conference sessions during the week. The conference came to an end, and our family "work-cation" was in its final hours as we walked to the EPCOT Center for dinner and the light show. The boys were walking with me when we noticed Charlie got ahead of us—quite a bit ahead of us. He was excited and looking ahead at all the attractions. He must have thought we were right there behind him. I was angry, feeling he was inconsiderate for taking off. Luke ran to catch up with his dad, and they waited for Loren and me.

We set out again on what I thought was a brisk walk, trying to swing my arms to give me more speed, a tall son on one side and the younger one on the other. I noticed then, my right arm wasn't swinging. Charlie, who had set out at the same time, was now far ahead. I felt frightened with the knowledge now that something was wrong. My right arm did not swing, and my walking pace had slowed.

Loren received a text from a friend asking why there were fire trucks at our house. We called neighbor after neighbor until we were able to find someone who answered. They were all at our house! Nine fire trucks protected our property from a field fire gone wild in a high wind. Our homeowners' insurance agent was there and sent us pictures from his phone. Our shop, fence line, and pump house had been destroyed. Thankfully the home had no damage. Neighbors and strangers saved our dogs and moved the cows and horses out of harm's way. Someone with a tractor had pulled the barn wall down in an attempt to save the winter's supply of hay. Some of the hay had already ignited, and the fire crews sprayed the rest with retardant, making it not consumable by the animals.

This commotion at home exasperated my unusual symptoms. I felt so odd, so strange. Slow and stiff body movements made me feel like gravity was pulling me closer to the earth. It was so hard to think and move quickly. Something was really wrong with me.

Early the next morning, we caught our flight home from Florida. Arriving at the house just at dusk, Charlie opened the front door while Loren and Luke went to check the animals. The electrical feed to the well pump had been damaged, and we had no water. The house didn't smell bad to me, although Charlie and the boys thought it was horrible. *Loss of smell or taste is an early indicator of Parkinson's disease*, I thought back now. It had never occurred to us we should not sleep in the house that night, so we did.

We'd pulled together as a family unit to assess the damage. The greatest loss was the shop. The shop had stored tools, supplies, old textbooks, tack for the horses, hay we had just purchased for the winter, and an accumulation of various things from the twenty years we'd lived at this location. It was also jammed full of candy machines from a newly purchased vending machine business.

Our neighbor, owner of a fire and water restoration business, helped Charlie and the boys drag those items not totally destroyed out of the burned shop. My job was to write down every item and a possible value for the insurance claim. The inward tremors multiplied in strength. My body seemed to move only in slow gear as I walked up to the main house for water or a bathroom break. The tiny scrawl I'd used to record the damaged items was barely legible.

Hypnotized by the flames in the fireplace, I didn't notice Charlie. When he came up to me, I was startled and almost fell off the chair. He knelt down and hugged me.

"Hey, Carol, there's a great menu in the restaurant." I was reluctant to leave the fireside, but I was famished! It could have been bologna on dry white bread and my tummy would have been thrilled. The gourmet dinner and the ever-full glass of wine warmed me inside and out. I climbed the stairs to our room, and Charlie and I snuggled into the clean, crisp sheets of the king- size bed. I cherished alone time like this on the Camino, where often there were ten or fifteen other pilgrims sharing the room.

This day had been amazing. Although slow, I had done the distance up- and downhill. I had joined with my husband in prayer and turned a spiritual battle into victory. I had cried and sung and laughed. I had moved my arms well with the trekking poles. The panic attacks I'd had in the first days seemed so far away. Was there more to this Camino miracle?

* * *

Guidebooks suggest stages for walking the Camino. The walk facing us in the new day was long, across a populated valley before a steep climb up to the high mountain village of O Cebreiro. We were on a distance-per-day schedule to greet some more family members who were flying in to join us for the final six days of the walk. Charlie and Allen huddled up to make a plan to ensure we'd make it in time. I saw them talking with the bartender. As a result, Charlie hired a taxi.

This was not your average taxi—it was Taxi Luis! Taxi Luis had a big van to fit us all. Charlie had called him on the bartender's recommendation, not aware of Taxi Luis's claim to fame as a favorite driver of pilgrims and locals alike. Charlie arranged for Luis to tour us around some of the significant sites on the way. Luis was quite a character and spoke in rapid Spanish, laughing as he took corners at twice the recommended speed. Charlie held on for his life in the front seat, trying to translate for us in the back what he understood Luis to be saying about the countryside.

Everyone was ready to walk when the taxi stopped on the other side of the valley. Luis dropped us off, and I gave him a ten-euro bill as a tip. He declined (tipping is not a common practice in Spain), but I told him not to think of it as a tip, but that we were buying his lunch. He drove off as we waved and shouted our goodbyes.

Now that we'd jumped ahead 23.3 kilometers, we were ready to begin the day's trek. But one of my trekking poles had come apart, so Charlie left to ask a local resident about a tool to repair it. The rest of the group and I were standing there waiting for Charlie's return when Taxi Luis drove up with one woman passenger. He opened the door, and she looked right at me.

"Luis wants you to get in. He says it is very steep and he will give you a ride."

"Me?"

"Yes. He insists."

"Okay, but not all the way. I want to walk some today."

Allen shoved my pack in the van as I hopped into the second-row seat. The smiling Luis slid the van door closed, and up the rough mountain track he drove, slower this time, as there were many ruts and bumps. He stopped at little villages of four to five houses to see if there were any more riders. But it was just the woman and me sharing Luis's taxi until O Cebreiro. When I got out, I realized I did not have any more money, and we had taken a long, expensive cab ride. I started to tell the other passenger, and she said, "Luis heard of you, walking out here with Parkinson's disease. He told me how excited he was to learn he was going to pick up your family. And he was honored to take you the rest of the way. You're a bit of a Camino celebrity."

I thanked Luis, and he grinned from ear to ear and bowed to me. What a guy!

My fellow rider said, "Wait here a minute." She took her pack around a wall and came right back.

"I just left my pack at the hotel. Told them I'll be right back."

Then she walked with me to find the municipal albergue. There was a line of at least fifty backpacks leading from the door around the building. The sign on the door said simply *15:30*. The doors would open for registration at three thirty.

"Guess my family isn't staying here tonight," I commented. Walking back toward the village shops, I saw a sign that said *Casa Carolo*.

"Hey, it's Hotel Carol," I joked. "I'm going to check this out." My pilgrim friend stayed with me as I explained to the clerk how many rooms I wanted, but I couldn't pay for them now because my husband had my money and he was coming later. I'm not sure how much of this she understood, but she put her hand out and said, "*No problema*. Passport."

I reached for my pilgrim's passport.

"No, no. Passport. I copy give back." Oh, she wanted my US passport. This was an unusual request from a pilgrim, yet we were in a touristy place, so I thought it must be standard here. She took some keys off a hook and showed me the rooms we would be staying in. Simple but very lovely.

When my friend said bye, I called back, "See you for dinner?" but I didn't think she heard me as she walked past a group of chattering scouts eating ice-cream cones.

I never did learn this woman's name. And I didn't see her again that night.

When Charlie, Luke, and the rest of the crew arrived in the village, they were exhausted. After some refreshments purchased from the village bar, we got everyone checked into the hotel and set out to explore the small village. The Santuario de Santa Maria Real do Cebreiro is one of the oldest churches on the Camino Frances. It is especially fascinating in that a Eucharistic miracle occurred there.

In a side chapel we found the reliquary that holds the evidence of the miracle. We read the story of a priest who was saying the Mass by himself in the church. It was very stormy, and he did not expect any parishioners to attend. As he rattled through the prayers, a peasant farmer arrived. The priest belittled him for walking through the snowdrifts just to partake in eating bread and drinking wine. It was apparent to the peasant that the priest did not believe the bread transformed into the body and the wine into the blood of Christ. As the priest elevated the Host during the consecration of the Mass, blood dripped out and onto the altar cloth. The priest was shocked and knelt in honor of the miracle he'd observed.

That evening we attended a pilgrims' Mass. When Charlie and I turned to offer a sign of peace to the person seated behind us, the hand reaching back was someone we'd met earlier on the walk. Dinner that night was at the Casa Carolo. We had a fine meal served family style, and my passport was returned!

The morning dawned cold and crisp, reminding me we were high in the mountains now. Our trail went down steeply only to climb back up a rough track. Crossing a highway, we saw a huge bronze statue of a pilgrim fighting the wind. We each related to his situation and in turn posed for pictures to remind us of the challenges of earth and wind.

Chapter 7

I Arrive

IN SARRIA, SPAIN, WE WERE JOINED BY ALLEN'S WIFE, DELORA, THEIR adult son, Joshua, and Charlie's sister Cece. From there, the distance to Santiago is one hundred kilometers. A completion of this segment, documented with passport stamps, is the minimum a pilgrim can walk to receive the coveted certificate of completion. We stopped at the hundred-kilometer marker for pictures. I found it unfortunate that people covered these milestones with graffiti. We were now a fairly large group walking together, and we took over the space around the marker. Pilgrims passing by cheered as we took pictures of husbands and wives, parents and kids, sibling pairs, and our whole group.

After Sarria, the Camino became more crowded, plus our group had grown to ten people. If we wanted to stay together, we had to reserve lodging ahead. Charlie found a chain of private albergues that would take a reservation. With that, everyone knew where they would be sleeping the next night, so that allowed for freedom in walking at our own paces. Charlie stuck with me most of the time. One day I walked for twelve hours to reach the destination. The family had spotters out, and when Charlie and I walked into town, they directed us to a bar where the bartender had just pulled for me the biggest, coldest beer he could sell.

After the young adult group Luke had been walking with had moved on, he walked several days with his cousin and aunt. Then the last two weeks of the trip, he stayed close to Charlie and me. As far as I knew, nothing happened to cause this change. We chatted and teased each other as we walked along through the fragrant eucalyptus forests. Our conversations were mostly surface level until the day I asked him, "Do you remember the day I told you and Loren I had Parkinson's disease?"

"Yeah. Well, sorta." A typical Luke response.

"This is what I remember," I told him. "It was time to tell people about my diagnosis, and after Dad, you boys were first. I asked you and Loren to come into the living room. You and I sat on the blue couch, and Loren sat in my favorite leather-covered rocking chair." Walking beside Luke, I felt a change, like his body stiffened.

"You never liked it when we sat in *your* chair."

"I know, but it was okay in this circumstance. As hard as I wanted not to cry, those big tears rolled down my cheeks. Loren came around the coffee table and put his gangly teenage arms around me. You stood up, and your eyes got really big, and you had a look on your face like you didn't know if you should cry too, or maybe laugh… I could tell you thought something bad had happened, but you didn't really understand."

I slowed my pace, and Luke shortened his steps to match mine. I glanced over at him and saw he had tilted his head and his ear toward me. He was listening with intent.

"I remember the last thing I said was, 'I am not going to die of this disease, you guys. I am just going to get old sooner.'

"Looking back, Luke, I should have had some information for you to read in your own time. There must have been something available for children. I didn't even think to look. I'm sorry."

Members of the Clupny family walk to Santiago, Spain.

Shaking his head, he responded, "No worries."

"Have you ever seen a person with Parkinson's disease— besides me, I mean?"

"Mom, I know what Parkinson's people look like." And he took a couple of giant steps to get ahead of me on the trail. I surmised he had become uncomfortable with this topic.

According to the Parkinson's Foundation, approximately sixty thousand people are diagnosed with the disease in the United States each year. Ten million cases have been identified worldwide, with many more underdiagnosed or misdiagnosed. Luke was nine when I broke the news. Had he even heard of this so-called old people's disease? Had he truly seen a person with Parkinson's? I saw more and more people in our community who had the disease as I became more familiar. I wanted to continue this conversation with Luke to find out what he knew, what he felt. It wasn't to happen.

I pose in front of the Cathedral of Santiago de Compostela.

It took us five days to walk from Sarria to Santiago. I insisted that I walk the entire way. It was rainy and cool as we passed through a lovely forest of eucalyptus trees. On the last day of trekking, my two nephews were assigned to keep an eye out for me, so they moved ahead and stopped every once in a while to see me coming up from behind. Other family members were scattered along the path, ahead of and behind us.

My nephews and I had stopped for a hamburger and were eating inside because of the rain when I glanced out the window to see Charlie walking by. I had to run out the door to even catch a glimpse of him. I yelled as loud as I could, but he continued at his usual fast pace. He had no idea he was passing me. He was playing catch-up to a Carol he thought had arrived in Santiago by then. I found out later that he'd stayed behind to help his sister send her pack ahead.

As I drew close to Santiago, I stood on the hillside above the city and saw the Cathedral of Santiago de Compostela in the distance. I could feel my heart start to pound with excitement. When I got into the city, the walk through the streets seemed much farther than it had appeared from the hillside. I came from the back of the cathedral through a tunnel, like an athlete might enter a stadium. Instead of cheerleaders and marching bands to greet me, there was a man playing bagpipes. I still felt like a celebrity. I followed a path of stone to the center of the large square and sat down directly in the middle, where I could view the cathedral and the incoming pilgrims.

There were family members waiting for me. They had already experienced the thrill of arriving at the cathedral, so they gave me a little time to soak it all in. My pack and shoes came off. I sat on the hard cement, marveling at the wonder of the moment. The outside was not as beautiful as I had imagined. But it wasn't all about the architecture. It was about the place, the arrival. I observed the pilgrims walking in, by ones and twos, in groups. Some were streaming tears, others with laughter and cheers. Pilgrims with suntanned faces, scraggly beards, sun-faded back-packs, and treasured wooden walking sticks contrasted with the neatly dressed tourists who had arrived not by foot, but on the little white-wheeled tourist train.

While I sat, I took a good look at my feet; the feet that had caused me so many issues with blisters and infection were almost healed.

My family gathered around, and we took pictures with the cathedral in the background. These cherished family moments come to mind first when I think of Santiago de Compostela.

We went on to the Pilgrim's Office and waited in line to receive the coveted certificate. As we approached the service counter, I heard a variety of languages spoken by the volunteers there. They all asked the same thing: "Where did you begin your walk? And your reason for walking?" After a brief look at my collection of stamps in my pilgrim's passport, I was given my

My certificate for completing the Camino lists my name as *Dnam Carolam Clupny*.

preprinted certificate, with this handwritten Latin inscription: *nam: Carolam Clupny, die: 10, mensis Julio, ano dni 2012.*

My walk on the Camino de Santiago was over. I felt as if this battle with Parkinson's symptoms and the rigors of walking the Camino had helped me understand myself. When the volunteer at the Pilgrim's Office asked me, I had answered my reason for walking as "spiritual." I did have significantly strong spiritual experiences on the Meseta and at the Cruz de Ferro. My soul was impacted by this walk. What was different about me now was that I had a purpose; that purpose was to figure out what "Do something good, Carol" meant in relation to my disease and get working on it.

Chapter 8

Learning More about PD and Me

Charlie, Luke, and I headed out on an Air France flight from Madrid to Portland, Oregon, stopping over in Toronto, Canada. The plane was late, so we missed our connecting flight and had to stand in line to reserve another flight. There were no more flights that evening. Air Canada provided a food voucher and a van ride to a lovely hotel.

As we got to our room—tired, hungry, and upset—I snapped at Charlie. He yelled back, and we had a screaming match. Luke just watched us with his head going back and forth, looking at me as I shouted, then at Charlie as he yelled. It was a senseless exchange of meaningless jabs.

"You should've gotten us some food!"

"You were more interested in looking at your phone!"

"Didn't you wash out our underwear last night?"

"It was your turn!"

"Why did we even bother to come here? We get three hours to sleep."

"You wanted to sleep on the airport floor?"

I turned my back and walked away from Charlie, locked myself in the bathroom, and took a quick shower. When I got out, he was snoring heavily from the far right of the king-size bed. I crawled in on the left, as far away as possible. In the morning I woke up snuggled against his back, remembering we had a fight but not remembering what it was about. The airline sent a van to take us back to our morning flight. They even provided more food vouchers than we could use.

Just before I'd left for the Camino, I had started a small fundraising effort. It was a last-minute thing. I wasn't sure exactly how to do it or who the money should go to. I'd started contacting some foundations, but I had only a few days before we were leaving for Spain and none had returned my calls yet. It was a coincidence that I had an appointment for the clinical study I was participating in at OHSU the day before our flight was to leave Portland for Paris. The research assistant and I had spent hours together at each visit and were getting to know each other well. I mentioned my frustration with the foundations, and she said, "Why don't you give it to us?"

"'Us' meaning...?"

"Parkinson Center of Oregon here at OHSU."

Duh! was my thought. That should have been a no-brainer.

She put me in touch with the OHSU Foundation, and I quickly put together an online fundraiser page. When we returned to Oregon, I was surprised to find that through social media, my connections with OHSU, and the online fundraising page, my friends and family had donated $7,000 in my honor to research for a cure for Parkinson's disease. Another *something good* had started, even without focused effort.

Oregon Health & Science University acknowledged the gifts submitted on my behalf at their annual Parkinson's conference in September 2012 in Portland, two months after my family's return from Spain. I put together a slideshow and a poster about

I present a poster at the Parkinson's conference sponsored by OHSU.

my walk on the Camino. Charlie helped me carry everything in and then took a backseat and allowed me to enjoy my two minutes of fame.

Standing up near the podium while the slides were showing and then hearing the audience applauding made me again feel that celebrity status people had bestowed on me on the Camino. The professional presentations at the conference were very good. But I learned more from the people with Parkinson's who came to see my poster, talked to me about their aspirations for travel, and marveled at my backpack and trekking poles.

Someone asked, "But where are your boots?" I had everything else displayed, this astute person noticed.

"They're in a dumpster in Santiago, the wicked things."

* * *

In August of that year, my inner body had been winding up to return to work. But I was retired! Late in the month, I sat in my living room watching Luke run out the door to catch the school bus. *School. I should be at school.* I had spent the last thirty-two years of my life at work on this day. By the end of September, I was bored. I approached the local hospital HR department and found that they needed some part-time, temporary help in their speech therapy department. I would be limited in my hours per week—perfect for the once-workaholic.

And so I rejoined the workforce, but I still had days without work and without company at home. On non-workdays I tried to keep as busy as possible. I wrote a blog post once from the perspective of an outsider looking in at my life on a typical Thursday, covering what they might have seen:

> Got up, took 7:00 a.m. meds, ate breakfast, took my kid to school, rode my bike three miles to the gym, worked out thirty minutes, rode bike home, put a load of laundry in the machine, showered, took meds, went for a massage, went to friend's house, practiced styling my hair left-handed, drove to another friend's house, practiced church music, drove home, took meds, ate dinner, got guitar and went to assisted living, played guitar in jam for two hours, went home, snacked, took meds, fell asleep on couch.
>
> Can a person with Parkinson's do all that? That was a pretty busy day. But here are some punctuations you don't see in that description. When I got up I was frozen to my bed. I could not move my body. I called for my husband to come and help me out. I leaned against the wall for support and just barely made it to the toilet without losing the contents of my bladder. After my son got out of the car at school, I sat in the parking lot trying to figure out where I was and

how to get home. I couldn't carry the full baskets of dirty laundry, so I split the dirty laundry into manageable loads. It took me three tries to get my bra on straight. It felt great to ride the bike, there was no pain in my hip or back, but to get on and off my bike I needed to lay it down softly on the road, so as to not scratch it, and step across the frame. My right foot froze, and so I had to lean on a telephone pole to pick it up and move it across the bike to step on the pedal. In the shower I held onto the bar for balance, and reaching the bottom of my feet without letting go was impossible! A sheet shielded my body from view as the massage therapist struggled to roll me over on the table. It was great fun to play the guitar and practice church music. Then, getting ready to go to the music jam, I couldn't zip up the little side zippers on my boots. I wanted to put on a little eyeliner and mascara. What a joke! The eyeliner went on zigzagged, and the mascara applicator missed my eyelashes altogether.

My arrival at the assisted living center where the old-time fiddlers were performing was announced when I dropped my overstuffed guitar bag. Capo, tuner, picks were under my chair, under other musicians' chairs, and some picks even escaped into the audience. I was so exhausted, I played only every other song. When my hand trembled badly, it was a good time to just tap along on my guitar like it was a drum. The stiffness from sitting made me feel the forces of gravity a hundredfold as I tried to get out of the chair. It took con-certed effort to get everything packed up in my guitar case backpack, get the zippers closed on it, swing it on my back, and stand up straight. I had to move slowly from table to table, grabbing for balance, until I could walk and get out the door. At home I put my guitar bag down by the piano and collapsed on the couch, falling into a deep sleep. Charlie tried to wake me for my meds. I was so deep, he couldn't get me to move, so he set the medicine down on the coffee table and gently tucked a blanket around me. When I woke up in the middle of the night, I was in pain. I sought comfort food. Ice cream? Potato chips? Leftover pizza? It couldn't be found there. Comfort, that is. The craving for junk food...it only makes it worse.

Connecting with others with Parkinson's was a big part of coping with the disease, I'd realized early on.

In our town, there wasn't an active support group to turn to. Charlie and I researched conferences and workshops for both patients and caregivers and found several offered throughout the year within a day's drive. The first gathering we attended was in nearby Kennewick, Washington. What surprised me most—and should not have—was meeting so many people who had the disease and lived within thirty miles of me. I was particularly inspired by Jenny Davis, a speech pathologist who had Parkinson's disease. Jenny was able to continue to provide therapy to people with PD.

When I became a patient at OHSU, I started receiving mailings for publications and workshops. We traveled to Portland to attend a one-day conference sponsored by OHSU. Lectures from nationally known researchers and local experts filled the day with valuable information. But there were two personal experiences that were more significant than all the great information we received about the disease.

Parking was a challenge, and we arrived at the conference room just as the first speaker was being introduced. I scanned the audience for two open seats, and what I saw were hundreds of people who were somehow affected by Parkinson's. Seated around tables of ten were caregivers, allied health professionals, doctors, students, and patients. The patients were of all ages and stages of the disease. There were walkers, wheelchairs, crutches, canes, and even a service dog or two. I had the thought, *Hey, a lot of these people look just like me. I'm not alone!*

Near the back of the audience I noticed some people waving at us. There were two spots at their table, and they were inviting us to join them. As the speaker had started, we did not have the opportunity for introductions. Water glasses and a pitcher were near the center of the table. I reached for a glass, and the man directly opposite of me stood up, took the pitcher, and poured the water into my glass. I smiled and nodded in appreciation, and then caught the look on the faces of the others at the table. They looked shocked, or maybe just surprised.

It was later at a break time that I started to understand. His wife wheeled him out of the conference room in a very specialized wheelchair. It must have been quite a feat for him to get up and pour water into my glass. At the end of the conference, Charlie and I hastily said our goodbyes and turned toward the conference room doors, as we had a long drive back to eastern Oregon. As I walked away, the gentleman who had poured the water called me back.

"Sit here by me," he said. "You are newly diagnosed, aren't you?"

"Yes. Well, sort of."

"I need to tell you something." And he proceeded with this story: "I have been a farmer all my life. I love to farm. I love to be out on my tractor tilling or seeding or harvesting. It became harder for me after I was diagnosed to get up on the big tractor.

So I worked with a smaller tractor and stayed closer to the house. But then it was hard to manipulate the controls. So I worked with a simpler tractor in the barnyard. Not too long ago, I couldn't get out to the tractor, so I had the kids park it up close to the house. I can sit on the porch and look at the tractor and recall all the beautiful sunrises and sunsets I saw from the cabs of my tractors. Do you understand what I am getting at?"

"Yes, I think I do."

He continued, "Parkinson's can take a lot. But don't you let it. Continue to enjoy what you love however you can."

Chapter 9

I Plan Another Walk

I MUCH PREFERRED TO HANDWRITE THANK-YOU NOTES. AS I TRIED TO do that for the contributions that had come in while I was walking the Camino, I saw that my writing looked like chicken scratch. *No one will be able to read this*, I thought as I twisted the ends of my hair around my fingers.

I walked down the long hallway of our house and into Loren's old bedroom. Since he'd left for college, it had become an office/storage room/hangout for me. I turned on the computer and sat in the big office chair, spinning myself around and around, not able to get focused on typing the thank-you notes. Something wasn't right. I felt restless. It wasn't Parkinson's symptoms—it was different.

Around I went in the chair, again and again until it hit me: I needed to return to the Camino. I still had something to prove to myself. I needed to know that Parkinson's had not taken my independence, that I could travel without someone tying my shoes or sending my pack or dispensing my medications. Deep inside I felt a bit of anger; the anger I thought was gone was not. There was still more in me that required a long walk to vanquish it.

The list of donors set aside, I typed in *PDX to MAD*, airport codes for Portland, Oregon, and Madrid. So began the research of airfares and ground transportation. *Hop, skip, and jump. That's what I will do*, I thought. Within a couple of hours, I developed a general plan that had me walking where I had ridden buses, taxis, or trains, and riding where I had walked. In this manner I would cover in 2013 what I'd missed walking on the first Camino in 2012. And I would go solo. Getting there, finding transportation along the way, taking care of my belongings and medication—I was sure to get the feeling I was looking for: independence.

How will I break this to Charlie? The timing would have to be perfect and come with a well-prepared plan.

In the meantime, my thoughts turned to how I would prepare myself physically, mentally, and spiritually for this solo endeavor. I thought about an encounter Charlie and I'd had in 1989 with some climbers. We were day hiking toward the Inter Glacier on Mount Rainier. Wearing shorts and tennis shoes and carrying day packs, we climbed over boulders and through scree fields alongside creeks roaring with milky glacial waters. We happened upon this group of serious climbers, the youngest age sixty-five, resting at the base camp before their summit attempt that night. Some of the men were checking their equipment; others were lounging about on the foam sleeping pads. The sole woman in the group was happy to talk with me.

"When did you start climbing?" I inquired.

"I retired at age sixty from teaching and decided to try something new."

This is something all right, I thought. "How do you train?"

She examined her crampons as she spoke. "The best way to train for anything is by doing it. I walk several miles each day near my home. On weekends I hike steeper and longer trails.

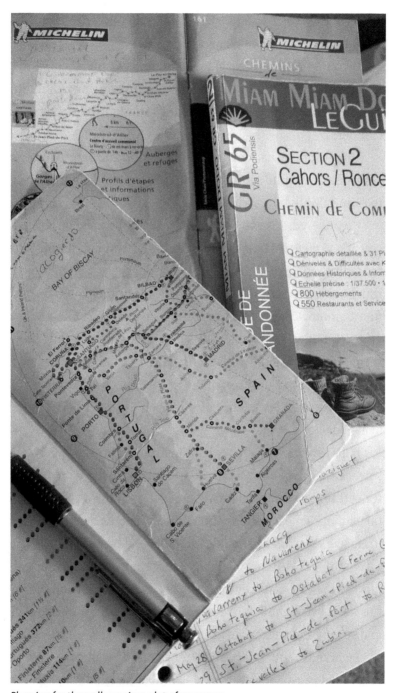

Planning for the walk requires a lot of resources.

Sometimes we get together as a group and practice technical skills for the terrain we'll encounter."

"No cross-training? Weights? Swimming? Cardio?" I inquired.

She nodded her head as she continued checking her equipment. "I just walk" were the words from this experienced climber.

Now, thinking back on that conversation and, later, the view of the massive white summit glowing in the moonlight, I resolved to train to walk by walking.

I wondered, *Does my condition require I do more or different exercises to prepare?* Having had encounters with fatigue, blisters, tendinitis, and generally dealing with a degenerative neurological disease on my first Camino walk made me think. On the first Camino, Charlie and the rest of the family had helped me quite a bit. It was easy to let the sympathetic friends and family members help when I was stiff, in pain, tremoring, or fatigued. As a person with Parkinson's traveling on my own, I would need to be able to take complete care of myself. *Yes, there's more I need to do*, I decided.

I spoke with Tom, my tai chi instructor. He was a problem solver who was skilled in identifying what muscles were needed for certain body movements. I showed him how my right arm tangled in backpack straps and required outside help to remedy it. He had me work on shoulder mobility and core strength. Once I had stronger muscles, I practiced loosening my pack straps almost to the end, carefully inserting my right arm first and getting the waist belt tight before boosting the pack higher on my back and setting the pack straight.

I worked on my agility and strength, and I walked daily with my loaded pack. The wise woman climber had had it right: "The best way to train for anything is by doing it."

My confidence bolstered with these stronger muscles and my daily walks, I carefully approached Charlie with my idea, and he agreed that I could go to Spain and walk the Camino alone. He appeared to be supportive and trusting, but I was sure he had to be very anxious on the inside. I needed to make my plans as safe as I could for myself as well as for him and our two boys.

Using the American Pilgrims on the Camino's (APOC) website and forums, I sought out other travelers who would be on the route at the same time. I found several Americans who were volunteering as hospitaleros, taking care of the albergues and the pilgrims who slept there each night. Researching bus schedules, I discovered the availability of long-distance buses across Spain and the local buses that stayed within each state or region. Taxis were everywhere, expensive but a great source of point-to-point transportation. Train stations could be accessed along most of the Camino. Luggage transfer was available. Charlie watched the hours I put into planning a safe trip. He knew I was a great planner, and he also knew I needed his support to be successful.

I had just finished telling Charlie my plans to fly by myself to Madrid in mid-April when I returned to the computer and saw a forum posting about a different Camino path. The Chemin du Puy (French hiking route GR 65) is one of four main pilgrimage routes through France that connect with Spanish paths leading to Santiago de Compostela. Beginning in Le Puy-en-Velay, France, it follows the route Bishop Godescalc of Le Puy took in the winter of 951 AD on his pilgrimage to Santiago de Compostela. The scenery was purported to be magnificent, and the trail passed through four of the most beautiful medieval villages in France.

I became enthralled with the idea of changing my route. Linsee, a friend I met on APOC, would be walking this route from Le Puy. Her itinerary showed she would join the Camino Frances near Saint-Jean-Pied-de-Port and cross the Pyrenees on her way to Santiago de Compostela. From Santiago her walk would continue on to Finisterre—which in olden times was considered the end of the world—on the western coast of Spain. Linsee's total distance walking would be about 1,100 miles!

The more I studied, the more I knew the Le Puy route was for me. Unfortunately my purchased tickets had me flying to Madrid on April 17 and returning on May 30 and would not allow me to walk the entire route with Linsee. By mid-April, she would be in great shape and burning up the trails, but I would meet up with her in Montcuq, France, a little more than midway on her path to Saint-Jean-Pied-de-Port. We planned to cross the Pyrenees together, and then I would have to go home.

Linsee and I had a common bond. We both experienced degenerative neurological disorders. I speak for myself, but I sensed she felt the same. We were gasping for air—for life, really—gulping in every experience of the senses, planting them so firmly in our memory banks that when our bodies could no longer move us to those places, our minds would take us there.

After her mid-March flight to Barcelona and some brief organized tours in Spain, Linsee emailed me that she had arrived in Le Puy-en-Velay, France. So far she had traveled by plane, train, taxi, and bus. Prior to the trip, she had shared an extensive itinerary she'd developed on an Excel spreadsheet. From our occasional email interactions, I could see that she appeared to be consistent in following it. When she discovered internet cafés, where one could have fifteen minutes of computer time for a little more than a euro, she jotted off emails on a more regular basis.

When her itinerary date to start walking came, I started too. I hoisted my loaded pack daily and walked on steeper trails on the butte near my home. My body hurt some, and my steps seemed short. I wondered how the Parkinson's would affect this journey. I had learned on the last Camino that I could distract myself from pain using a mantra, singing, or praying a repetitive prayer in a chant-like format. Thinking of the songs I would sing and the stories I might tell helped me ward off the discomfort I felt on my training walks. *Hey, I can do this thing!*

Charlie was silent about my plans. He never came out and said I couldn't go or that he was worried sick about me. I had completely abandoned my original well-thought-out agenda of walking on the Camino Frances in Spain, instead planning to walk in France with someone I'd met on the internet. That didn't sound good even to me when I told my friends. I was an adventurer but not a risk taker.

I had done most of the travel arrangements and planning throughout Charlie's and my married life. Sometimes I would get off track and come across a neat travel blog. I would dream about it and develop ideas that I would say out loud—"Let's take Luke out of school and travel through South America on mini-bikes." This sometimes got us into fights, as Charlie thought my out-loud thoughts were what I wanted! I imagine he thought I was crazy at times. When I told him about this new adventure, it probably sounded like I was saying, "I'm going to escape to France by myself to hike because the Camino just didn't do it for me. I'll be going on this really cool trail you've never heard of and meet up with a woman I found on the internet." Charlie had always been supportive of me. I knew he wanted me to have the life experiences I dreamed of while I still could. This had to cause him some concern. Yet he continued to nod his head in approval as I chose to follow this new friend's itinerary.

My goal to prove I could travel independently was good—I was sure of it. But the *something good* God had asked of me out on the Meseta the summer before was yet to be disclosed for this trip. I thought maybe my example of hope that one can live a fun and adventurous life while battling an incurable disease was the something good.

Before Linsee embarked on her thousand-plus-mile Camino in mid-March, she and I had chatted on the phone and Skyped several times. In one conversation we were discussing how we'd meet up, and I said, "Why don't I just meet you wherever you are on April 17 and walk with you until I have to go home?" Quickly checking her itinerary, she replied, "Montcuq. See you there."

I did not realize the logistical travel nightmare I'd created for myself until I found the tiny Montcuq, France, on the map. My research showed I needed to get to Toulouse to get to Montcuq. I reviewed and researched what I thought my options were: I could hire a taxi (very expensive), take a bus (none went in that direction on that day), or board a train (there was no nearby train station). I shared my dilemma with my sister Beth, who had traveled extensively. She happened to have a dear friend, Jane, who was currently residing in Toulouse and graciously offered to pick me up at the Toulouse airport and drive me to Montcuq.

I managed to make all the connections and arrive in Toulouse to catch my ride with Jane. Jane took me to a sports store, where I purchased trekking poles. From my first Camino, I already knew that trekking poles were very helpful for support and propulsion. Similar to ski poles in appearance, their length was adjustable for up- and downhill navigation, and wrist straps helped the hiker and her poles to stay together. Their lightweight durability removed some of the stress from my knee and ankle joints while hiking. I found them essential for balance. Rather than fly with them, though, I thought it would be easier to buy some in France for this trip. Around the corner was a mall with a food court, where I grabbed a bite to eat. I loaded my backpack in the "boot," or trunk, of Jane's little car, and she sped us away on the freeway, on a highway, and then on some backcountry roads.

Jane was a fascinating person. I wanted so much to talk with her and see the French countryside as she drove, but I could not keep my eyes open. In the past twenty-four hours, I had flown from Pasco, Washington, to Seattle to Philadelphia to Madrid to Barcelona to Toulouse.

She woke me up, saying, "Montcuq. Where do we go now?" I didn't know where to find the *gite*—what albergues were called in France. I was about to suggest we find someone to ask when right in front of us appeared a tiny sign that said *Lestos*.

"Lestos!" I shouted to Jane. "That's it. This is where I meet Linsee. Gîte de Lestos." She turned her car down a small gravel drive into the Lestos property. I'd learned online that like the albergues in Spain, gites had beds with sheets and blankets, sometimes in open-room dorms, other times in more private accommodations, and often towels were provided. A home-cooked dinner and breakfast were included in the modest price.

I recognized Linsee immediately, sitting outside in the lovely yard, her long hair down, her feet up, sipping a cool drink. Instant friend. Patricia, co-owner with her husband, and Linsee came over to Jane's car. Introductions were made, and the chatter started. A bystander would have thought we'd all known each other for years.

It was unfortunate that Jane had to return to Toulouse. I would've enjoyed spending more time with her.

Patricia showed me to my "room," which was in what had to be the most creative use of a cow barn I had ever seen. Each stall was curtained with heavy drapes. Inside each one, there were one or two single beds. The hay trough became the shelf for clothes. The floor had been cemented over and was covered in a throw rug that coordinated with the bedspread. The wood of the barn walls was sealed. Over the stall entrance for my room was a sign with the name of a previous resident: *Daisy, Melody, Mari-Lou*. It was spick-and-span clean. A bathroom at one end also held a shower. Over a small kitchen area was a loft that one could climb up for some quiet time. *What a cute place.*

There were only a few other guests at the gite, so Linsee, Patricia, and I talked and played card games and ate and drank for two days. Patricia took me on an open-air jeep tour around the village and told me the history of the area.

Whenever it appropriately fit in—such as when she won a hand at cards—Patricia would say, "Don't worry, be happy, like Snoopy."

Linsee was an astute observer about Patricia's interactions with her husband; he often put Patricia down. He didn't want her to speak English with us, and he was adamant that only French be used in conversation at the dinner table. I didn't really notice how rude and abrupt her husband was. But Linsee did. Between Linsee and me, we had maybe six words of French. Our end of the dinner table was English speaking, with our co-host sending glaring looks our way.

On the third morning after my arrival, Linsee and I pulled on our boots, donned our packs, and—after finding the red-and-white blaze that marked the way—walked on GR 65 toward Spain. We left a sleeping Patricia, not wanting to wake her for what would have been an emotional goodbye. I carried in my heart fond memories of those few days of rest and fun after my flights.

When Linsee and I arrived at our lodging that night, there was a message from Patricia. Thinking it must be because we had forgotten something, we were surprised to read her favorite phrase: "Don't worry, be happy, like Snoopy."

Chapter 10

I Can Talk and Walk
at the Same Time

WALKING WITH A PERSON FOR HOURS RESULTS IN CONVERSATIONS on many topics. As Linsee and I became better acquainted, we let some of our guard down, and our talks went deeper into matters that were important in life. I also found myself imitating her swearing, a habit I knew I'd have to carefully leave behind when I returned home. As the kilometers passed underfoot, I felt safe in sharing some of my deeper thoughts…and swearing about them!

Linsee did not know me or anyone I knew, and it was unlikely we would ever see each other again after this trip. One night I took a risk—I told her I wanted to be a writer, something I didn't share with many people. I'd just started blogging about Parkinson's and asked Linsee if she'd like to hear a bedtime story. The story I read was one of my blog entries:

> I have been looking at a lot of guitars lately. As in many aspects of life, I need "accommodations" (or so I think). Parkinson's disease has made me "special." I was looking for guitars with a bit shorter neck, a bit narrower body. I looked at my first acoustic guitar. It was my brother's. He sent it to me for my 16th birthday. There was a lot going on in my life

at that time. And not all of it was happy. The guitar gave me joy and helped heal some of the wounds. Music does that to you, you know. That guitar is no longer playable. But I remember its first major scar. We were at Meadowood for a SEARCH retreat, staying in a small lodge which has a sleeping loft. Someone knocked a pop bottle off the balcony and it skidded across the face of the guitar and left a long scar. Funny, I remember that incident so well, and that it left a scar. I don't remember the songs I played that weekend.

Fred, playing his jazz guitar, wears a bracelet bearing his son's name. His beautiful teenage son died in a swimming accident. The loss of a child sucks the breath out of the parents. Fred works on those wounds through writing jazz. His wounds are still open and bleeding. Someday they will heal over...into scars. The music helps him through the dark nights.

The old guitar maker called and invited me over to try out some guitars. First he had me play the first guitar he made for himself. It was full of scratches and dings...much like himself, who for so many years had toiled and labored to make a living. This guitar has autographs. The autographs of friends, bluegrass and country artists...autographs on his heart...memories of good times that more than erase the scars on his arthritic hands.

The young man guitar player let me try his cherished guitar. It has been replaced for daily playing, but he will never part with it. I felt honored to place my hand and around its neck and feel where the oils of his hand had worn into the wood. Holding the guitar I could see the dings on the face and scratched-up pick guard. Scars you would never notice from a distance...scars that are apparent when you are close enough to embrace.

I looked at my current guitar. It has some dings in it that I put there. It's just starting to develop its character. The scars aren't deep. They are not obvious unless you get up close. They are my scars. I think I will keep my guitar...I don't need to play others' guitars. I don't need to take on their scars. I have my own scars.

I didn't think this story was very good, but Linsee loved it!

With that encouragement, my writing became more frequent. I began to develop a discipline about it, spending a little of the downtime before dinner each evening writing. I knew Linsee would ask me to read it right before bed.

The topics I wrote about changed. I became more honest about the disease and its invasion of my body. I wrote about dark moments and challenging times as well as the accomplishment I felt as I walked through the forested rolling hills of this part of France. I posted my writing on the blog and used social media to draw people to each new entry—I copied part of an entry into my Facebook status and then would leave a link to the rest of the story. My stories included a way for the readers to be introduced to my challenges on the trail. Yet I wanted readers to see how I worked through the challenges to make each day a success.

One particular story about a day near Manciet in France became a popular post and a story I have told over and over again: The morning started out with me a little off-kilter. I got up in plenty of time to be ready to go by eight thirty. Then I noticed a couple of hot spots on my feet, which could become blisters.

I worked on them as quickly as possible, loading stuff in the pack as I went.

Linsee called, "Carol, Carol! *Carol!*" from somewhere below or outside. We were catching a ride into town with a friend of the owner of this gite who had a car. I had to hurry! My fingers felt fat and stiff and didn't want to move as I tried to secure all the openings on my pack. Finally everything was closed, buckled, velcroed, or zipped and ready to go. I should've been downstairs with my pack and strapping up my boots ten minutes ago. Ready to pull myself up off the floor, I glanced around for anything I might have left in this three-hundred-year-old barn loft. My eyes caught a quick glimpse of my feet and went on…only to return for a more careful look at what seemed wrong. There were my feet, yes—they were neatly wrapped up in blister-protect mode. Then it hit me!

Socks! I didn't have any socks on. There were no socks to be seen, in fact. I thought they might be in a zippered bag near the bottom of my pack. For some reason this brought tears to my eyes. I am sure this is the first time ever I have cried over packed socks, but probably not the last.

"Caroooooool!!!!"

The gite owner, Elizabeth, came up the steep stairs of the barn loft and into the room to try to help. There I was, a sobbing mess sitting in a pile of all that had come out of the pack, every bit of clothing I had, finally finding my socks. Of course, I wore toe socks. Toe socks are a little harder to put on than regular socks because they're like gloves. I had to position each toe and slide the sleeve for that toe over it. Basically having five toes means it takes five times longer to put a toe sock on than a regular sock. Finally, I stuffed my spoon, comb, garbage, bandana, and money in my pockets and shoved the rest of my belongings back in my pack. *Suck it up, Carol*, I said to myself. *Get going.*

I did suck it up. After the short car ride into the village, Linsee and I were walking again, following the GR 65's red-and-white stripes. That day, as every day on this trail, we had to keep an eye open for the markings. We didn't know where they would appear. We had found these stripes painted on trees, telephone poles, corners of buildings, and sometimes on the road. There were times when we would spot the red-and-white stripes with a big red X over them. That told us we had gone the wrong way and needed to look around some more for the correct trail marker.

As we meandered through the village, the conversation between us centered on the different colors representing the GRs in France. There are approximately one hundred of the Grande Randonées across the country. The French people have a love of hiking and are known to take walking vacations. From my previous walk, I knew we would no longer see so many red-and-white stripes when we reached the border of Spain but would watch for yellow arrows. Then the arrows would be supported by shells, which changed slightly with each region across the country. If the hiker is a careful observer, there is no need for maps or guidebooks.

When Linsee had agreed to have me to hike with her, I'd adopted her agenda. I hadn't brought so much as a map. She had purchased a Michelin guide and a Miam Miam Dodo guide. The advantage of the Michelin guide was in its map of the nearby roads as well as the trail. I laughed out loud when I heard that *miam miam dodo* was French baby talk for "eat eat sleep sleep." This guide was written completely in French but was easy to follow. Although we could ask our hosts to suggest the next night's lodging or visit the visitor's office in many of the larger communities, the Miam Miam Dodo became a favorite tool for finding the next stay. I liked taking advantage of local wi-fi (pronounced "wee fee" in France) to email ahead for reservations.

I point to the red-and-white stripes marking the French GR 65, known to pilgrims as the Chemin du Puy.

These walking routes in France and Spain are quite safe. Yet I was careful to be aware of what was going on around me, and I never wore headphones when walking and always kept my head up.

There were cars parked solidly along the street we followed to get out of this village. In spite of the sock incident, it was still early. Not too many people were driving yet. I noticed a small, dark-colored car coming toward us. Suddenly it pulled over and parked right alongside another car. We would call it double-parking. The tall, handsome driver got out and approached us.

"Clupny?" he asked.

I was shocked, but I responded, "Yes."

"What the f***? You know him?" asked Linsee.

"I am Mathieu. You stay at my gite tonight." His French accent sounded seductive.

Oh wow, I thought. *What is this about? Who is this guy, and how does he know my name? We are not staying in this village tonight. Where is the nearest convent? We would be safe there.*

Then he leaned down and kissed me on both cheeks like I was his long-lost favorite aunt. "Carol Clupny, yes? You eat dinner. You like ice cream."

Now I knew. A few days prior, it had been my turn to find lodging. I'd emailed ahead for reservations, writing, "Need two beds for American women." The gite owner responded, "You want eat?" referring to demi-pension dinner and breakfast. I wrote back jokingly, "Yes, and I like ice cream!" Mathieu was the gite owner, yet how did he pick me out of hundreds of walkers he might have seen going to Manciet that day?

"See you two hours. I go get ice cream now." He got back in his car and drove off.

Puzzled by the awkward interaction, Linsee and I walked away from the village streets and out into the countryside. There was so much mud. We took a wrong turn and walked an additional muddy kilometer or more out of the way, meaning we had to walk that distance back to find the correct route. We walked along rows of Armagnac grapevines. More than once we were doused with whatever the farmer was applying to the grapes from his large spray rig. There was no way to avoid the tractors. I hoped the drivers would shut off the spray for just a few seconds—that didn't happen. On one slippery slope, Linsee fell, and a nearby walker—an elderly Frenchman—raced to help her up. It looked like they were mud wrestling! I didn't want to laugh as I waited for the take-down. There were also cultural considerations. I did not want to insult the French hikers. She managed to not take him down into the mud. Shortly, she fell again and, as a result, added five pounds of mud to her fifty-pound pack. Trying to keep

Linsee's weighty pack made even heavier by mud.

our spirits up, we chatted about cute Mathieu and speculated about how he'd identified me.

More French-speaking walkers joined the mud path as we were descending another hill. Glances kept coming our way from their side of the trail. I realized they were talking about us, yet not knowing their language inhibited me from comprehending what they were really saying. With context as my guide, I was fairly certain these experienced French hikers had commented on my muddy pants legs and Linsee's mud-covered clothing, worn-down trail shoes, and overfilled pack.

"Perhaps a few changes would make your hiking experience more pleasurable, madame," I imagined them saying to her.

"I am fine!" my imagination had Linsee snarl back.

I'd had some suggestions for Linsee from the very start—I'd done long-distance walking before, after all. But it didn't take long for me to get it that Linsee had planned her trip and wasn't

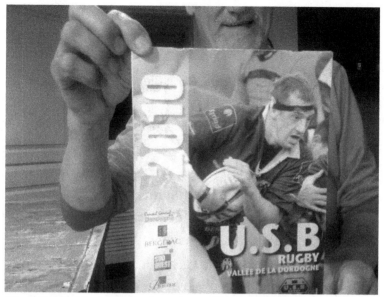

Gîte de Chez Mathieu in Manciet, France is owned by a former professional rugby player.

changing anything just because I mentioned it. I took to saying, "This is a suggestion. It's only a suggestion. You can choose to follow my suggestion or not. In fact, you don't have to listen to my suggestion. You can pretend I am talking to myself, because that's what it feels like when I make a suggestion."

We arrived in Manciet late afternoon. Mathieu's gite was hidden down a back alley, and we asked for directions to find it. He saw us coming and opened a window to yell, "You are here! The famous Carol Clupny is here!" We walked around to the front of the building, which now faced a blocked-off street.

Behind the nondescript door in an old *boulangerie* (bakery) was his gite. He showed us where to put our muddy boots and hiking poles. Then he grabbed my pack and took it to a bedroom. Linsee was left to carry her own. As I followed him up the wobbly set of stairs, which would not have passed any inspections in our country, I heard music, very familiar music. In fact, it was one of my favorite walking songs: "The Road Goes Ever On." I became even more freaked. It was way too weird. Mathieu could tell I was uncomfortable.

He laughed and said, "You, Carol Clupny, are famous. I watch your movie on YouTube."

Further discussion in broken English revealed that, when I'd made the reservation, he thought the name Clupny was unusual. It did not sound American, so he Googled it. My Camino slideshow, *C-Team Walks*—the one I'd shown after the previous year's walk, at the Parkinson's conference—came up. He knew I had Parkinson's disease and that I moved slowly. He had watched it and enjoyed the music. In fact the music I had heard was playing from the video on his handheld device. That explained part of the mystery. His identification of me walking along the street was yet to be solved. I asked to see his phone and looked at the tiny pictures of my slideshow whipping by, and then I looked at myself in the mirror.

I was wearing the very same clothing combination: pink hat, tan long-sleeved shirt, red t-shirt, green shorts, and blue backpack, same as one year ago on the Camino Frances. No wonder he had known my name.

Chapter 11

Breaking the Trust

CHECKING IN WITH CHARLIE VIA EMAIL FROM A GITE THAT HAD WI-FI, I learned that home was experiencing significant windstorms. This was not unusual. We had taken to calling this windy period at the end of March and into early April the season of *winder*. Anytime we expected rain, we knew that it would be windy both before and after any precipitation.

Walking this section of the Chemin du Puy was lovely. No mud! An unblemished blue sky was overhead with not a wisp of wind. The grass along the trail was a deep green, as if it had all been specially irrigated for our delight. Wildflowers dotted the hillside. The path was hard-packed dirt, and Linsee and I were making jokes and kidding each other, cheered by the good weather and great hiking.

We were surprised to come upon a steep downhill of about twenty-five yards with loose dirt and pebble scree. Linsee took to the left side and was about three-quarters of the way down when I started my descent. I chose to head straight down the middle of it when—*womp!* I found myself flat on my butt. I tried to get up, but dirt and rocks were sliding out from under me, making little avalanches that slid to the bottom of the hill. I quoted the famous commercial for the emergency buttons for the elderly: "I've fallen and I can't get up." The comment put us both into hysterical laughter, which meant I was not going to be able to do anything until I regained control.

The laughter finally abated. Instead of doing the sensible thing and removing my pack to get up, I decided to scoot down the scree-covered hill, my poles held across my body like an ice ax in a glissade down a snowy slope. I began to narrate my actions, as if I was making a how-to video to inform others who might find themselves in this same predicament.

"Always attach your panic button whenever you may travel." If I had heeded my own advice, I would push the magic button and hear some man's sexy voice say, "This is Life Alert. How may I help?"

Looking up, I saw that I was being videoed by my companion, who could hardly stand—if not for the steepness of the slope, then for the hysterical laughter my narration brought about.

"Okay, Lady Bird. Get up!" Linsee hollered.

Where did that nickname come from? I'll have to think of one for her. "Don't you worry, Girly Girl. I can do this."

These nicknames stuck.

* * *

The not-so-perfect days did exist. Linsee and I had walked together for nearly four weeks and got along well. We had talked about almost every topic under the sun. She revealed she'd "ditched" other walking companions. I laughed, surprised she'd kept me on this long. Our conversations ranged from very shallow goofiness to deep and honest sharing. I trusted the character of my fellow pilgrim. Yet the scaffold of experiences that formed this fun, beautiful friend also created a puzzle with pieces missing that I would not be able to place. Having a childhood so different from hers, I could not achieve any level of understanding. I just accepted her incredible stories as truths.

As we came into a cluster of houses and small businesses, we realized it was not the village we had intended to stay at that night. For reasons unknown to me, Linsee was really pissed off about that. We'd walked only half the day and had already put nine and a half kilometers under our feet. The walk had started out all right, but when we arrived at this village, something changed. I felt a strange sense of impending doom, and Linsee was not talking.

The sky became gloomy, and the humidity was smothering. My stomach started to hurt, and Linsee was moody and pensive. There was a picnic table in the village square, and I suggested we stop for a bite to eat.

But I didn't have an appetite. The sky started spitting rain. My stomach had started to rumble like the thunder in the distance, and now my mouth had that dry sensation, like when the dentist fills your mouth with cotton.

"I think I'm getting sick," I mumbled. "I need a bathroom." Two places I learned to look for bathrooms in a French village were the church and the city hall. The city hall was across the street, and I spotted the small *WC* sign partially obscured by a bush of purple hydrangeas. A few stone steps led down to an ancient door. Underneath the building was a very clean, white porcelain toilet. So thankful that it wasn't the kind of toilet made of two porcelain footprints positioned to line oneself up over a squat hole, I undid my clothing to do the business I came for. I expected a huge diarrhea blowout, yet the discharge was quite normal, and I actually felt better when I was finished.

Being midday in a small village in France, the shops and even the pharmacy were closed. We looked for lodging, but the only building resembling pilgrim accommodations appeared to be permanently closed. Linsee and I were standing in the middle of an intersection, looking up and down the empty streets, when she let out a stream of expletives.

"What's wrong?" I asked, thinking she was sick or had gotten stung by a bee or something at least worth these strong words. She was crying. Big tears rolled down her cheeks.

"*What's wrong?*" she repeated, and then, with more words than I had heard from her all day, "I don't know where I am or where I am supposed to go or where I'm going to sleep tonight. I am lost! I don't know what to do." The tears kept coming.

Where did this come from? I wondered. I was glad my trip to the bathroom had calmed my stomach, because I was getting shaken up by her strange behavior.

"Let's go over here and sit down." We sat down on the slightly damp cement sidewalk with our backs against the white picket fence of the flower garden of a darling cottage.

"Okay. I see you are really upset. Let's work this out." The first thing that came to my mind was a five-step problem-solving process I'd used with language-delayed students in my former work as a speech-language pathologist. Why this came to mind at this moment, I didn't know. Sometimes it just happened that tools from my chosen profession became personally useful in another context.

"Have you ever learned a problem-solving process?"

"What's that? No."

I wasn't sure what was going through her head when I introduced this process. It seemed odd to me have this conversation with an adult. Linsee was a competent person who'd been successfully traveling in a foreign country for almost two months. Why this meltdown now? Had she had them before? All I knew was that I had a choice in how I reacted to it—to get pissed off myself and walk away, or to try something that might be useful later.

"Well, first we identify the problem. You said you're lost and you're worried about where you're going to stay tonight. Okay. So let's use that as the problem. What are some resources that will help you?"

"What do you mean *resources*?"

"Things or skills available to assist in solving the problem. I see you have a guidebook. There has to be a police station here. I went to the bathroom at the city hall, and this town may be big enough to have a visitor's bureau. We just haven't explored enough yet. And there's me. I can be a resource. Let's think of some possible solutions." Linsee had stopped crying at this point and seemed almost curious to see me in my teacher problem-solver role.

The problem-solving lesson continued until we had a mental list of ideas to try. By this time, the clouds had moved on, and the sun warmed the sidewalk and the fence we leaned against. The situation was looking more positive. Moving into action, we started walking and saw a sign advertising a market.

As we walked along the sidewalk in the direction of the store, a voice said, "Linsee?" with a heavy accent. Linsee looked around and through a gate spotted a French woman she'd met a few days ago sitting in a chair by a swimming pool.

"I'm looking for a place to stay. Is there room here?"

"I know deez geet iz full, but I will azk dee owner."

We stood by the gate until the owner could be found. Coming down the steps in her apron, she called, "Hello, hello! How are y'all doin' this fine afternoon? Rain's gone away for today. It's gonna be a lovely evening. How can I help you?"

South Carolina has come to southern France!

To my surprise, Linsee took charge of explaining how neither of us had felt too well earlier and we'd spent a lot of time in this town when we should've been walking and now needed a place to stay.

"You girls stay right here, and I will go make some calls." She went back into the house, and we could overhear her now speaking in rapid French.

The owner reserved us two beds in another house and chatted nonstop as she walked there with us. She'd been born in France to an American soldier and his French wife. They'd moved to South Carolina when she was a baby, and her mother had taught her French while her father addressed her in his booming Southern American dialect. This house had belonged to her mother's parents, and when they passed, she saw an opportunity. She lived here spring to fall, running this bed and breakfast, and wintered in South Carolina.

After a short walk, she stopped at a nondescript house. There was no sign advertising it as a gite, but our guide reached behind a downspout for the key and opened the massive front door. She explained that the proprietor of our lodging was working and would not arrive until later that evening. We entered the house and were shown a bedroom on the right with six beds and a bathroom. The beds were so lovely, with crisp green sheets and spreads in shades of red, all impeccably color coordinated with the other furnishings. To the left of the door was a dining room and lounge and then a kitchen that led out to a beautifully manicured garden and yard. *Wow.* For being lost, we had found heaven.

My spirits were raised, and I felt physically better. The touch of the United States from Mrs. South Carolina had warmed my soul. Linsee and I chose our beds, and I decided on a shower and nap. Linsee said she wanted to check the market to see if they had some items she needed. As I napped, four other women silently slipped in and chose beds. When I awoke I was surprised to see all the beds had been claimed. They had been so respectful and quiet.

In the early evening, a young woman opened the big front door and stuck her head in, saying, "Eat. Come." I trusted that this was a representative of the owner. She showed us to the restaurant in the center of the village that had been closed earlier. Here we would get drinks and dinner. I felt refreshed, and Linsee appeared much cheerier than when she'd left for the store. The group of six from our gite had met up with Linsee's friend the Frenchwoman and her companions just outside the restaurant.

We seemed to be the only customers at this early hour because in France the mealtime was later in the evening. This always threw me a little, but we settled in to eat. We were to be served a special pilgrim meal arranged by the gites. I ordered a beer, and Linsee, who preferred hard liquor, ordered a mixed drink. She sat at the other end of the table with her French acquaintances, and I sat with two blond, pigtailed sisters from Switzerland and two other women.

I had discovered in my travels that Europeans usually spoke their home country's language, English, and maybe another language. I was like many Americans and knew only English, with just a little Spanish and even less French. They agreed to speak my language for table conversation. One of the women in my group was a plant scientist. My end of the table engaged in a conversation about medicinal purposes for a variety of plants. I was engrossed in the conversation as first soup and then salad were placed before each person. A lovely pork cutlet with gravy and tiny potatoes came next. It seemed simple, but it truly was a gastronomical delight. I wanted to lick my plate but instead tried to be polite as I took the last piece of bread to capture the delicious gravy.

I noticed Linsee was talking loudly. I wasn't used to hearing her over the regular table conversation. Then I heard her say, "I love you. And you too. I love you guys so much," as she stood up, walked around to her dinner companions and planted a kiss on the top of each of their heads. Linsee's French acquaintance had an odd look on her face. I watched this for a moment before I noticed several empty cocktail glasses in front of Linsee's seat. *Hmmm*, I thought. *I wonder if my walking companion is drunk.*

Our time at the restaurant concluded. We only had to pay for our drinks as the dinner was part of the demi-pension, which translates to "half board," meaning a bed, dinner, and breakfast. The pilgrims who'd gathered in the restaurant stood to say their goodbyes and exited in twos and threes. I asked the Swiss sisters to engage Linsee until I returned from the restroom. They were successful in keeping her there but quickly left when I returned.

"Linsee, let's go."

"Where?"

"Back to the gite."

"Okay." She went out the door and weaved back and forth across the street to a public bulletin board on the edge of a parking lot.

I kept vigil from the sidewalk. She looked around for me. "Carol?"

"I'm over here."

"What's all over your face? Your face is all red. You're bleeding!"

"There's nothing wrong with my face."

"Yes, there is, it's bleeding." I knew it wasn't bleeding, and yet I wiped my hands down my cheeks to be sure. She insisted again that my face was bleeding, so I took a light-colored bandana out of my pocket, wiped it all around my face, and showed her.

"See? No blood."

No response from Linsee, so I started walking on the narrow sidewalk, and she followed me. Between the cars parked on the street and the buildings, there was not room for us to walk beside each other. She came along behind me, sometimes stepping off the curb into spaces between the parked cars and then back on the sidewalk. *Oh brother*, I thought. *Hope she doesn't hurt herself.*

Still on the narrow sidewalk, I felt a sudden *wham* on my back. Linsee had shoved me. I stumbled a few steps forward and managed to regain my balance when—*wham*—she shoved me again. This time I stayed completely upright, and I whipped around to face her. Standing just a few feet away, I finally got the words out: "Linsee, what the heck are you doing?! You don't shove me. You don't shove anyone, especially your friend who has Parkinson's."

I quickly walked ahead to the gîte and went to the sleeping area, where the Swiss sisters were preparing for bed. Linsee came in the main door behind me, but instead of coming into the room, she went through the kitchen to the lawn and gardens in back of the house. I sat down at the foot of a bed and told the sisters that she'd pushed me on the walk back from the restaurant.

"Do you know her well?" They seemed very concerned.

"I've been walking with her a couple of weeks."

"Do you know she was drinking rum with Cokes all afternoon?" That explained a lot. With the amount of alcohol at dinner, and the mixture of any medication she may have taken during the day in her bloodstream, she was really plastered.

"I don't know if I can trust her anymore. I mean, well, I haven't seen her this impaired before. Who knows what she'll do next? I could have been seriously injured if I'd fallen on the street or against one of the cars."

I made this decision on the spot, without really thinking it through. "I think I'll get up early and walk on without her tomorrow."

The pigtailed sisters nodded in agreement.

I put on the hiking clothes I planned to wear the next day and packed up my bag. What I wanted right then was to be wearing freshly washed, right-out-of-the-dryer cotton flannel pajamas in these sheets. My dreams for homelike comfort were wasted. To facilitate a quick getaway in the morning, I crawled under the sheets in my hiking clothes.

Somewhere around midnight I awoke to a sense of movement going past me and out the door. I looked across the room at Linsee's empty bed, then around, to see all the other beds had sleeping bodies. *Uh oh*, I thought again. *What's she up to now?* I felt some responsibility for my walking partner's well-being. In the condition I saw her earlier, she was very vulnerable to injury or possibly an attack. Swiftly I was up and out the bedroom door, through the common area and kitchen, and I just caught sight of the back screen door closing before she was gone—disappeared into the darkness.

I went back into the common area and saw there was a couch with a blanket folded across the back. I was part angry for having my sleep disrupted, fearful for her safety, and then curious about her strange behavior and what might happen next. I thought I would purposely startle her a little when she came back in by popping up from the couch. I stretched out on the couch and started to nod off. Almost asleep, I heard jingling of keys at the front door. *Who could this be?* Again I was up on my feet and to the door, where I met a woman with her arms full of grocery bags. She introduced herself as the owner. She had just gotten off work and had come to set out breakfast items so she could sleep in. I chatted with her for a minute and then asked if she had seen my walking companion, Linsee.

"Why, yes. She must have been the woman laying on the grass in the side yard when I came into the house. Just now as we were talking, she went behind you to her bed."

I looked in the door, and sure enough, she was there, under the covers, motionless. I crept back into the bedroom and slipped under the sheets of my bed again. I whispered over to her, "Linsee?" No response. The rest of the night, I tossed and turned, restless and afraid she would wake up before I could make my getaway. Just as the first light was hitting the horizon, I drifted to sleep.

The vibration of my phone alarm going off against my chest jolted me awake. Never the first person up in the morning, I nonetheless moved fast to be ready and out the door before Linsee awakened. I gulped some coffee from a bowl, as the French did, and bolted down jam and bread. Darn, there was a line for the bathroom, and I had to wait. Finally I got back to my bed and slung my pack over one shoulder so I could get outside, adjust it, grab my trekking poles, and go. Just as I was about to ditch my walking companion, she sat up. Her long hair, which was usually kept tied up, was loose around her shoulders, like a shawl. She looked at me with her morning smile and her usual singsong greeting.

"Whatcha doing?" Then she looked at me harder. I was fully clothed and ready to go. The realization that I was ready to walk hit her, and the smile dropped away. "What are you doing? Were you going to leave without me?"

"Yes." My heart was pounding with anger.

"Did something happen last night? Please tell me."

Is she toying with me? She has to remember something. "You don't remember?"

I sat at the foot of her bed and told her what I had experienced…from her vision of my red, bloody face to the pushing incident, to the sneaking out of bed, to her sneaking back into her bed. I emphasized that I saw a side of her I had not known existed, and I was really uncomfortable with it. Why she would shove me, no matter what state she was in, was beyond me. Physical violence was not something I was accustomed to.

"Will you wait for me?" she asked.

Anger ran through my veins. Yet compassion and understanding were in my heart. I was sure I'd done some strange things sometimes while under the influence. Could I forgive what she had done, especially if it was alcohol that had been driving her behavior? And did I really want to walk alone? We had been a good team so far. I was intrigued that she hadn't ditched me like she had some previous companions.

Conflicted by my previous decision and now wanting to give her another chance, I waited. She got her gear together and, without breakfast or coffee, walked out of the house and onto the trail. There was no conversation between us.

I kept a fair distance behind. Around noon she stopped and waited for me to catch up. For the rest of the day, we walked in closer proximity, but still in silence, not enjoying this beautiful French countryside.

Amid that silence, I entered into some deep thinking about how I had been raised.

I wouldn't describe my childhood as happy, but it was not unhappy either. It was safe. I'd always had food and clothes and books—tons of books—to read and a warm bed to snuggle with my teddy bear. Although having nuclear disaster drills at school, hearing on the radio about race riots in the cities, and watching the death count from the Vietnam War on the evening news were scary, they were far away and never came close enough to physically hurt me. I grew up safe.

For Linsee, I'd learned, growing up had not been a happy time. It had been an experience of survival. I put together snippets of conversations we'd had earlier in the walk. It sounded to me that there were times when her parents left her unprotected from the world. Times when there was nothing to eat in the house and the heat had been turned off. Warmth meant another body in her bed. Sometimes that body was an "uncle" or an adult male party guest. As a little girl, Linsee had to endure pain that she didn't understand. She just wanted to be warm, to have something to eat. Fear became the constant emotion. Unlike my big faraway fears, fears of war on a different continent and riots in big cities on the east coast, her fears had been daily realities: close enough to harm her physically, sexually, and mentally.

People walk the Camino for many different reasons. I came to prove to myself that, even with PD, I could manage independently. I wasn't sure if Linsee knew why she'd come to walk the Camino. She told me that after seeing the movie *The Way*, she knew she had to do this walk. I believed that each step on the Camino was healing for her. This journey was one where she faced the fears of her childhood—where she herself would find the way, choose what to eat from a plentiful table, and sleep undisturbed in beds with crisp, clean sheets.

The "I don't know where I am" fear and the "I don't know where I'm going to sleep tonight" fear that I'd heard her cry in the middle of the street that day—she could put behind her. No longer did she need to push to get away as she had pushed me in the street. She was leaving that behind in exchange for other tools.

This resilience came from deep inside. She had survived to adulthood. This beautiful place, this wonderful time, the goodness she experienced from people who cared, overwhelmed any horror of her childhood. The old faces and places that once loomed large now stood down. They were diminished to a size where, if they raised their ugly heads at her, she could control them.

And here I was, for some reason, drawn to walk with her for part of her journey. In the early planning and first few days of walking, when I'd accepted and joined her itinerary, I had no idea what was to come. As we walked the Camino together, I learned to love a stranger unconditionally and to receive nothing in return but the gift of being allowed to be present with her. Linsee, broken, spilled out, filled up—and I had been there to be part of her healing.

Chapter 12

From France into Spain

I REMAINED VIGILANT OF LINSEE'S BEHAVIOR AFTER THE PUSHING incident. After a few days more of walking in the French countryside, I relaxed. I let myself enjoy her company again, and the fun, goofy times returned.

While out walking these long distances, I could also empty my brain. I called it "nothing walking," and it became particularly useful when someplace on my body hurt. I put away my awareness of the here and now, left thoughts of home and responsibilities behind.

In my nothing-walking state of being, my bodily functions still required attention. I felt tremors, and my leg would jump, telling me it was time to take my medicine. Hunger and thirst could not be ignored. So I would come back to reality to eat and drink, and usually after a sandwich and hydrating my body with liters of water, I had to defuel. As a person with Parkinson's, I had started to develop some issues with bodily functions. It's hard to pee and poo in the great outdoors under any circumstances. I had experience from years of backpacking, but the comfort of a bathroom, especially a clean bathroom with toilet paper, is always more desirable. My body just didn't have the muscle strength to squat to pee and squat even further to poop.

There was another skill I'd learned in the tai chi class I took back home. I didn't remember how this subject came up in class, but we talked about lot of things there. This skill would be very useful on the trail. I'd said to the instructor, "Tom, how am I going to go the bathroom outside, where there's nothing to hold on to?" Tom had a background in anthropology, and so we students endured a ten-minute review of the human body's waste disposal system over the ages.

"In our first-world nation, we have forgotten how to squat. If you go to China, you will see people in the parks or on the stoops of buildings, squatting and smoking." He grabbed a pile of tumbling mats and stacked them against the wall. "Start with something about this high," he said and demonstrated how to retrain my muscles to sustain that position while I relieved myself. *Hope I'll be strong enough to do this when I'm out walking in France*, I'd thought.

On one particular day when we were walking in France, I HAD to defuel *now*! It came at the most inconvenient time. There were no rest stops, bars, or city halls to scurry into. I had to pee this very minute. We were walking a fifteen-kilometer stretch of gravel road and had not seen a bush or tree in hours. Linsee and I had discussed our personal challenges when relieving ourselves in the great outdoors before this day, the number one difficulty for both of us being balance. Now, of course, it was on my mind, and we started talking about how hard it was to pee outside, which made me have to pee even more!

This seemed to be a busy stretch of the trail. There were many pilgrims walking that day, which was unusual for the Chemin du Puy. At our last water break, we had noticed a group of male pilgrims, including a Catholic priest, identifiable by his Roman collar and black shirt and pants, walking a short distance behind us. I worried about them on the trail behind me as I spotted two trees just up ahead. I knew it was my only opportunity for any kind of protection from view. I did a half jog ahead, simultaneously preparing to defuel by unbuckling my pack and loosening my belt. I dropped my pack by the first tree and pulled my hiking shorts and underwear below my knees, so that now I really was exposed. I knew the group of male pilgrims was speedily approaching from the "south," so to speak, as I stepped to the edge of the field.

Beyond my control, the defueling process began. I was creating quite the puddle when I lost my balance and ended up nose first in the freshly plowed field. The men were in view. I saw them slow their pace but soon they'd pass right by me. I hoped they would be gentlemanly enough to divert their gaze away from me, as I was facedown and, you know, the other end up, right there in front of them. When I finally got on my feet and started making quick clothing adjustments, I saw that Linsee had put a ground cloth down to sit on and was now getting her video camera from her pouch. The situation was becoming more comical by the millisecond.

Here I was pulling my pants up, yelling at Linsee to put the damn camera down, and watching the approaching men out of the corner of my eye.

No one would have guessed I was a fifty-something-year-old woman with Parkinson's disease. In the quickest flash of my former lightning speed, I was partially put together and heading toward Linsee.

I slid myself under a corner of the ground cloth. I put my elbow in my lap and partially covered my face with my hand, pretending nothing had happened. As the men passed by, we tried not to make eye contact, but it was very hard. They were trying not to look at us, either. But their faces revealed what they had observed between the two trees.

On the trail the next morning, we saw these gentlemen again. They grinned in recognition as they passed by us. We politely nodded in return as we attempted to suppress the hysterical laughter boiling inside. Some women might have been aghast at this situation. I was gaining a better understanding of my physical circumstances and tried to poke fun at the challenges—like outdoor bathroom procedures—that it brought up. Linsee ribbed me about this for a few days after. I laughed hard imagining what those men were seeing and thinking. It was such a funny story that I wanted to tell it to other pilgrims, maybe around the dinner table at night as everyone shared the happenings of the day. But I didn't know if I would offend anyone whose culture was not as open to discussion of bodily functions. I wrote it instead, and it became one of the bedtime stories I read to Linsee.

* * *

At three a.m., I was awake. I could not get back to sleep. My brain was busy thinking about the distance to our next lodging. The section of trail through rolling hills would be longer than we'd walked in one day, and the map showed a significant elevation gain. That worried me. Sixteen kilometers a day was a good distance for me. More than that and my feet would start to drag, which placed me in danger of tripping and falling. I'd handled the slight elevation gains so far by playing the mantra over and over in my head: *One foot in front of the other. It's not a race. One foot in front of the other. It's not a race.* I had heard it said that your first ten days on the Camino are about the walking: getting your body used to the day-in, day-out schedule and carrying your belongings on your back. I had passed the ten-day mark. Why was I worrying so much?

I drifted off to sleep just as it was time to wake up. I started out the day with my long pants on. In the Pacific Northwest, when it's raining, it's usually cold. But the temperature outside was very warm for as hard as it was raining. I was hot and uncomfortable, and walking the muddy trails was like walking in a sweltering rainforest. It wasn't long before I told Linsee to hold up while I sat down on a stump, removed one boot, unzipped the leg of my convertible hiking pants, pulled it off, put that boot back on, and repeated the process on the other side. I tucked the pants legs in the side pocket of my pack. Now I was walking in shorts in the rain, which seemed silly, but I felt much cooler.

Late in the afternoon, the rain turned cold. I was still wearing the shorts portion of my pants and a light fleece under my Gore-Tex raincoat. Gore-Tex, or any other waterproof breathable fabric, can only take so much immersion in water before it fails. My jacket was at the failing point. My clothing was soaked, and I was chilled, which caused my Parkinson's tremor to begin in my right arm. This tremor was generally well managed by my medications when all was going well. Other than being slow at any motor task, from tying my shoes to walking along, I felt as if I was doing well on this walk, so I was alarmed to feel the tremor kick in.

The path continued through the lush green countryside. We came to the sign announcing we were entering Miramont-Sensacq. What a relief! I was glad our shelter was only a little farther and I could get warm and dry soon. The sign was deceiving, though, as we walked another forty-five minutes to find our lodging.

It was late afternoon when we arrived at the Gîte des Pelerins. The building was at the far end of the village. The cottages were

I am soaked as I enter Miramont-Sensacq, France.

covered with climbing plants, some of them blooming. Window boxes were full of colorful flowers, and the shutters were painted in pastels, my favorite being the blue. We entered the building through an open door off a patio into a dimly lit room. Three kind male hospitaleros greeted us warmly from behind a counter. I took off my pack and plopped down on the bench. Two of them came to me directly.

My tremors had taken over both arms now. I looked like a soaked, shivering puppy. Even before they signed me in or took my payment for the lodging, they were assisting me. One of these kind fellows, an elderly gentleman, took my coat outside to shake it out and brought it back to be hung on a hanger. The other had me stay on the bench, where he untied my muddy boots, removed them from my feet, brushed the worst of the dirt off, and stuffed newspaper inside of them to absorb moisture.

To have these muddy boots that had carried my tired body throughout this long, wet day removed by a stranger in kindness, welcoming and hospitable, was an intimate gesture of care that I graciously received—a Camino lesson to allow someone to serve me.

Linsee had quickly removed her own boots and stuffed them with paper, checked in with the third hospitalero, and was led around the corner into the sleeping area of the building. One of the other gentlemen who had greeted us showed me into a small room with five bunk beds and pointed to an empty bottom bunk. Linsee was housed in a different room, and she had already settled in. I didn't know if the gentleman had offered her the same special treatment of boot removal or coat shaking, but she appeared content when I walked by the door to her room.

I put my wet pack on the floor, as usual, and set myself on the bunk to open it and look inside. Packs can become transportation for hitchhiking bed bugs, so this was one small precaution I took. Some gites wouldn't even let the *pèlerins*—the French word for "pilgrims"—take their packs into the sleeping area, providing bags to carry your essentials instead. There were usually a few chairs scattered here and there in the dorms. I kept my pack on the floor. *Chairs are for sitting,* I said to myself when I came across someone else's pack on a chair. I dug into my pack for some dry clothes. Although the pack cover had been on all day, the pack was wet, as were most of the clothes inside.

One of the hospitaleros said something in a language I did not recognize. I thought he was saying, "I will show you the shower." I nodded and said, "Oh yes!" and grabbed the driest clothes and my shower bag and camp towel. He had a strange look on his face and then put up his hands in an "oh well" gesture and led me to the shower room. I knew something was not quite right, but the inviting shower outweighed the need to figure it out.

When I returned to my assigned room, my pack, coat, and clothes were not there. I stuck my head outside the door and caught the eye of the gentleman who'd removed my boots. He read my worried face immediately and took some keys off a hook, gesturing for me to follow. He unlocked a door to a room that looked like the dorm, but instead of bunks, it had multiple drying racks. Socks, shirts, pants, and jackets were hung on the racks. It was warmer here, and there were fans circulating the air. Now I understood what the first man had said when I thought he was asking if I wanted a shower. That gentleman had asked if he could hang my clothes to dry.

This gite provided a warm dinner. It filled my belly, yes, but more than that, my heart was warmed by the conversations around the table. Linsee left for bed early, as usual, and did not experience the evening activities provided at this gite.

The first couple of nights we'd traveled together on this journey, I tried to convince her how fun the after-dinner gatherings were.

She said, "I don't know the language."

"Neither do I, and that's what makes it fun!"

I figured out that each day's walk was really exhausting for her. Whereas I was energized by the people, she was tired and needed some quiet time as she prepared for sleep. I couldn't blame her for that. But this was one of those special nights when the after-dinner interactions were magical. I wish she would have stayed up to join us. One of the hospitaleros directed the group of pilgrims to form an inner and outer circle facing each other. We were told to give certain information to the person opposite us. I likened this to speed dating. We each connected with our fellow travelers, and by the end of the evening, we were no longer German, French, English, Dutch, or American. We were just pilgrims, with hearts, souls, stomachs, and feet warmed by the kindness of these three hospitaleros.

* * *

The late May rainstorms continued as we walked through the lowlands, and we heard reports of wintry storms in the higher elevations. I spotted snow in the mountains as the route of GR 65 led us to Saint-Jean-Pied-de-Port, a major starting point for the five-hundred-mile Camino Frances. We stopped there, at the same Pilgrim's Office where I'd had my first major panic attack less than a year ago. We wanted to get our pilgrim's credentials stamped and find out about the weather. An advisement had been issued to choose a lower route through a village called Valcarlos due to extreme winds, fog, and snow conditions at the higher elevation.

"We are going the high route," Linsee insisted.

"I agree," I said. "I think we'll be fine. As long as we don't get blown off the mountains by high winds or hit with a blizzard, we can do this thing. Let's check the weather again in the morning."

"You can check the weather, but I'm going the high route."

Wow. I could see Linsee was adamant that we take Napoleon's route, the higher path over the Pyrenees. I would not throw caution to the wind. I thought we could do it—the trail was well marked, and I had walked the same route last year on June 4 and 5 in beautiful clear weather (having panic attacks the entire way). But now I was different. I was confident and strong and had been walking five weeks in rain and mud.

Outside the Pilgrim's Office in Saint-Jean-Pied-de-Port, France.

After checking in at the albergue, L'Esprit du Chemin, which was conveniently across the steep cobblestone street from the Pilgrim's Office, we made preparations for the next day. Doing laundry, packing lunch, getting cash, and lightening our packs by sending items ahead on a luggage transport were on the list of chores for the day. Saint-Jean-Pied-de-Port was a fair-sized village with banks with ATMs, sporting goods stores, grocery stores, and many different types of lodging. Tourists and pilgrims alike enjoyed the beauty of this medieval walled village.

We'd made reservations for the next night's lodging at the popular Refuge Orisson. This was the same place where Charlie, Luke, the rest of the crew, and I had stayed the previous summer. It was only eight kilometers away, but this eight-kilometer stretch was the steepest on the Camino Frances. Sending our nonessential items ahead made sense. At a market we purchased a bright-green zippered bag. Back at L'Esprit du Chemin, we sorted through our backpacks and filled the green bag with the items that were not needed. We marked the envelope, put seven euros inside, and set it out to be picked up by luggage transport. Our lightened backpacks now contained only our cold-weather gear, first-aid supplies, sleeping bags, and hearty snacks.

A great camaraderie developed that night as the Dutch hospitaleros at L'Esprit du Chemin led the pilgrims in a get-to-know-you activity. A ball of yarn was tossed around the room. When I caught the yarn, the group was surprised to hear me say, "I've already been walking almost six weeks. I actually will be ending my Camino in three days."

Linsee, who had for the first time stayed for the structured evening activities, informed everyone, "I started on March 17 and have already walked five hundred miles. I'll be walking on to Finisterre." We became pilgrim celebrities.

The next morning I ducked into the Pilgrim's Office across the street to check the weather. The advisement was still posted. I asked one of the workers, "Is it really that bad?"

"We must depend on the locals who know the weather and the terrain. Are you reserved at Orisson? You can walk to there and get recommendations for continuing the route."

I reported this information to Linsee.

"I don't care. We are going the Napoleon route."

"Okay, we may or may not be able to do that. They may close the route. Who knows? Let's take it one day at a time, okay?"

It was raining hard when we left Saint-Jean-Pied-de-Port. I had a green poncho over my pack, and Linsee had her black one. We looked a bit like camels as we marched up the steep one-lane paved road.

Probably one of the few personality traits Linsee and I held in common was our bull-headed tenacity. Anyone who told me,

"No, you can't," found me becoming rather defiant, and the next thing they knew, I was doing just that thing I was told I couldn't do. Of course, I could be sensible too. At this point my senses were telling me it was just going to be a wet and foggy climb. We talked about the hike for that day and the next day's longer hike. As we talked a pilgrim walking nearby joined in the conversation. "I went by the Pilgrim's Office, and there was a new sign out that said the trail was closed past Orisson."

As expected, once there was a roadblock, Linsee became determined to go around it. She also wanted to take the challenging descent through the forest to Roncesvalles, the large abbey just over the border in Spain, even though a safer route was available. More pilgrims clumped together now, and everyone had a little piece of information to share as we walked. The more that was said about the dangerous trail situation, the more adamant Linsee was about her chosen route. I thought I might have to just let her go on by herself. My thoughts at this moment were to let the officials and common sense guide my safety. Besides that, I had done the route less than a year ago in good weather. It had been tough then, so I only imagined what it would be like in snow.

Glad we had reservations at Orisson, we trekked the eight kilometers and gained a lot of elevation.

"Frickin' steep," Linsee said. "Steeper than anything in France."

It was steep, but I was pretty sure there were steeper sections she had walked on the Chemin du Puy before I joined her. I thought I would try to distract her with anecdotal remarks of what we were seeing and stories of my first walk last June.

"This is where I stopped to pee in the barn and the dog let me know that was not okay."

Silence. She didn't respond.

"We stopped for ice cream here.

"Where this road crosses, the cows came running down, and the herders yelled at us to get out of the way.

"This is where we leave the road for a while and climb straight up.

"Aha, I laid down here and took a nap."

"I could take a nap right now," she finally responded.

I struck something. "There are some switchbacks here.

"We are almost back to the road.

"Look back now—the fog has cleared. See how far you've come. Be amazed, Linsee. You are amazing. Be amazed with what you've done."

"I am not amazing. Stop saying that!" she said.

"There's a water fountain coming up.

"When we got here, we started singing 'Yellow Submarine.'"

And finally, "*Voilà!* Orisson."

We'd made it to Orisson in a little over two hours. Last June it had taken me six to seven hours to complete the eight-kilometer climb. I was ecstatic. I couldn't wait to tell Charlie! We checked in, were given tokens for the showers, and found our bunks. Orisson was known for its pilgrim dinner and the experience it provided for people to get to know one another, so that evening we had a belly-warming meal and met many pilgrims who had just walked the first day of their journey. After dinner everyone was expected to stand up and say their name and where they were from. Linsee stuck around for this but set off for bed immediately after.

Then an announcement was made that, in the morning, the cook would meet those who wanted to walk the Napoleon route at the point where the Camino left the road and the trail over the Col began. Some hikers had recently gotten lost by missing this important waypoint. After one more glass of wine with the group of Canadians I was sitting with, I was off to bed also. I discovered that now Linsee and I shared a room with four other people. By the time lights were turned out at ten p.m., the man in the bunk overhead was already snoring loudly. It was almost as if an avalanche was rolling down a nearby the mountain. I reminisced about the night I'd stayed here only eleven months ago, then put in my earplugs and tossed and turned myself to sleep.

I woke up and looked around. Our roommates were gone, but Linsee's pack was still by her bunk. Glancing out the window, I saw that dense fog surrounded the building, so I stood up and got dressed. Linsee walked into the room from the restroom, and we took an inside staircase down to the kitchen. It looked like a swarm of locusts had been through it. Drink cups, jam and butter wrappers, plates with leftover bits of bread were scattered across the tables, left by the pilgrims who'd made it out to follow the cook/guide. I walked to the back of the kitchen to inquire about the guide, only to find the cook had left about thirty minutes prior. There was no catching up. We could, however, have a bite of bread and jam and some coffee from a bowl while a lunch was prepared for us to take along on today's hike. *Great. At least we'll have something to eat while we wander around lost in the fog*, I thought.

There wasn't much to pack, since we'd sent the majority of the backpacks' contents ahead to that night's lodging at Roncesvalles. Out through the big wooden doors and up the hill, we started along the paved single-lane road. I remembered the spot where we were to turn off the road, and as we hiked up, we met the cook coming back down the trail, so I knew we were on the right route. The climb was less steep than the previous day's, yet the wind, fog, and sleet brought out a higher level of difficulty. Walking ten feet apart was nine feet too much. It would be easy to miss a landmark or lose each other. Suddenly, I saw my walking buddy sit down on the trail in front of me.

"What's wrong?" I asked, thinking maybe she had a cramp or had tripped.

"That's it. I'm not going on."

"What are you saying?"

"I am not going on."

"What happened? Did you fall? Are you hurt?"

"No. I am not walking anymore in this weather."

Crap! I thought. *What is she thinking? It could be dangerous for us to just sit here in this wind and sleet. I have to get her moving.* "You aren't hurt, and I am not calling a rescue team here. Get up." She did! I was really surprised. "We just need to put one foot in front of the other. We'll stay close."

I tried to sound encouraging. "Good. I see a big rock up there. Let's walk to it." We walked to that rock, then the next rock, then to a bush. We walked ten steps at a time, then twenty steps. I kept this cajoling up, and she didn't say a word. But we were moving in the right direction, and that's what mattered at the moment.

A figure came toward us through the fog. That was unusual, as most everyone walks from east to west on the Camino. He stopped to talk with us. He was an American teenager and as cute as could be. What he was doing out here walking a reverse Camino was a mystery. He was so sweet when he told us, "I've just come up from the other side. If I had to do this over, I would take the road." For whatever reason, his pleasant smile warmed Linsee. She chatted with him for a few minutes, and we both wished him well. Walking on, Linsee had a completely different attitude than she'd had not so long ago when she sat down on the trail. Inspired by this Camino angel, she had new life!

We kept climbing, and soon we were walking along a level trail. It divided, and when we looked up, we saw a small wooden building. I had a flashback of stopping there last summer. It had been locked then, so I didn't know what was inside. Charlie, Allen, and I had gotten our sleeping bags out of our packs and laid them out on the meadow grass. The three of us had napped there in the warm sunshine. The picture in my mind was so different from what we were experiencing right now.

I reached the door first. It was unlocked! The wind ripped the door away from my hand and flung it open, revealing three young people from Great Britain huddled inside. Five pilgrims was almost the capacity of the little place. I looked around. It truly was a shelter. There were sleeping shelves built into the walls. Worn ground pads were rolled up on the shelves, and there was a pile of heavy wool blankets in a box on the floor. There was a stone fireplace but no wood. No matter, this humble building was a pleasant reprieve from the wind.

We shared snacks and stories. One of the young people said, "If we are to make Roncesvalles by dark, we need to get going." They donned their packs and went out the door, the wind chilling Linsee and me still inside. We headed out too, but the Brits were able to move much quicker than we were, and we lost sight of them in the dense fog.

This part of the trail was on a mountain road, so we could walk side by side. Looking ahead, I saw two shadowy figures coming at us through the fog. I called out to them, and they responded, "Hello!" They were Americans also. I guessed that they were related to the young Camino angel who had changed Linsee's attitude just a bit ago. These people were not happy. They looked exhausted, and streaks of dirt and mud layered their pants up to their knees.

"We have to warn you, the next three kilometers are wretched mud," they said as they passed.

Their description was accurate. It was some of the worst we had experienced. There are several landmarks in this section where the Camino passes from France into Spain. We trudged past the border marker, Fontaine de Roland, and along the path with its closely set numbered markers so that travelers would not stray in a whiteout. This mud was embedded with oak leaves that had blown like snowdrifts. I had to pick up my feet in marching fashion to get through it. I was sweaty, so I removed the rain poncho and unzipped the armpits in my jacket to allow some ventilation. Finally we reached a trail sign. The sign indicated that the path went down to the right, which—as far as I could see through the fog—was a steep snowfield. To the left was a road that appeared to curve back to the right. We had the choice to continue down through the snow or take the more exposed road and hope it would connect back with the trail. Linsee did not argue—the road it was.

We stopped at the crossing to watch pilgrims behind us struggling down the snowfield. After falling, one person tumbled head over heels a few times. They regrouped, and Linsee and I joined them to discuss the next choice of routes. I was able to report from experience that the trail down was steep. We could see that it had recently been closed and roped off. All decided on the road. These pilgrims had younger legs; they took off at a fast pace and left us in the fog.

The road cornered many switchbacks, and those strong-legged hikers cut directly down to save time. When we reached the bottom, Linsee and I could not find the trail to Roncesvalles. Heading to walk the highway, we heard shouts from the pilgrims ahead calling us back. We found the trail we'd missed meandering along a creek bed, and we followed the voices of the ecstatic pilgrims ahead. A very large stone building appeared in the mist ahead of us. We had made it to Roncesvalles!

Unlike the year before, I carried my own pack in.

* * *

I registered and ordered my dinner, took my boots and hiking poles to the boot room, and climbed up to the second floor. I found my bunk a few cubicles away from Linsee's. The abbey was warm and filled with excited pilgrims just starting out. A dinner of trout and wine was served in a restaurant. Linsee recovered the green bag full of our extra clothing we had sent ahead two days ago. I stayed awake until lights-out and then drifted off into seamless sleep. Gregorian chant music piped in over speakers as the morning wake-up call. Looking out the window, we could hardly see the pilgrims walking the path below. It was snowing hard.

Out of the blue Linsee said, "It's crappy weather. I am not walking today."

Now my stubbornness surfaced. "Surely we've walked in worse weather than this! And I have only today and tomorrow left to walk. I had hoped we would make it to Pamplona. If we don't walk, it's the end of my Camino. I'll have to try to find transportation from here rather than from Pamplona." I was disappointed.

"You go ahead and do what you want. I am not walking in a frickin' snowstorm."

In my mind, I ran through all the reasons why I should not walk in a snowstorm. *If I got extra cold or wet, my tremors would kick in. I would take smaller steps and might get worn out easier if I have to pick up my feet to get through the deep snow.* These seemed almost lame excuses, but I let them convince me to just take a bus or cab.

As pilgrims are allowed only one night in each albergue, we booked into the posh hotel next door for our last evening together. I asked the desk clerk about transportation, and she let me know the bus schedule. The day dragged on as we waited to be allowed into our room. I went to the bar and met up with pilgrims who'd come in to warm themselves. One woman told me a member of her group had fallen in the snowfield coming down into Roncesvalles and broken her leg. I was glad that we'd chosen to walk the paved road. Another woman was walking with her elderly father and was looking for warmer clothing. I gave her my rain poncho.

Linsee and I were finally allowed into our room at three p.m., and the only dinner reservations available were for five o'clock. A great meal was followed by a somber evening. Linsee was very quiet. Trying to get some interaction going, I asked if she needed me to take anything back to the US for her. We went through our belongings, and she had me take her heavy sleeping bag and a trail cook kit home. I gave her my silk sheet and camp towel. I also gave her my white bandana as a memento and asked her to leave it at Finisterre, as I would probably never make it there.

I wanted some sort of closure to our time together, to make plans to meet up back home or to promise to keep in touch. I wanted some feedback from her—that she had enjoyed walking with me, that I was such a good companion that she hadn't ditched me like some of her other walking buddies. I wanted some insight about the night when she'd pushed me, to have her say, "Hey, I'm really sorry about that. It was the alcohol." It wasn't to be. When I brought up a topic, she looked up from her book momentarily, made a response like "I don't know" or

"You were fine" and went back to the book. Her body language definitely said, "I don't want to talk." Linsee read her book and, about nine o'clock, put her glasses down, turned off her light, and said goodnight.

The bus out of Roncesvalles was set to leave at nine a.m. Linsee and I packed up our belongings and had a *café con leche* and a croissant in the bar. I knew she wanted to get on her way, so I didn't want to delay her by trying again to get more answers or closure. Slinging my pack on for the last time on this Camino, I walked with her out to where the Camino left Roncesvalles. There, where the highway sign reads *Santiago de Compostela 790 km*. I took her picture and said goodbye to my Camino sister.

I turned and walked toward the bus stop and started crying. Soon I could hardly breathe for sobbing so hard. I yelled out one last, "Goodbye, Girly Girl."

I heard her call back, "See ya, Lady Bird!" as I boarded the bus to Pamplona.

I tried to gain my composure, but the tears would not stop. *Why are you crying so hard?* the little voice inside my head asked. *She was ornery and shitty to you at times. Yet she listened and challenged you to be the best you could be. Is that it?*

In one of the few times Linsee had revealed her future dreams, she'd told me of her desire to complete some of the long-distance treks in the United States, such as the Appalachian and Pacific Crest Trails. I'd kept my thoughts silent. *How cool is that? I wonder if I could do something even more demanding than the Camino. Maybe we can buddy up.* Now those thoughts returned.

The bus started rolling. Linsee was still there, and I saw her pointing to the highway sign with her trekking pole. Entering the highway, the bus gained speed. I pushed my nose against the window glass to watch her. The familiar shape of my walking companion was soon out of sight.

I carried that image of her pointing to that sign in my mind while I traveled home. As I returned to home life, I often wondered how she was doing. Late that summer I saw a post about her on someone's social media site. She'd made it to the coast of Spain and then home safely.

In reflecting on this journey, I realized that I had accomplished my goals. I got myself to France to meet Linsee. I walked about 250 miles from France into Spain and made it home. It was not without challenge or incident, but I had taken care of myself, carried my backpack, tied my shoes, and taken my meds on time. No blisters and no major panic attacks (except the meltdown over the socks). Parkinson's disease had affected me minimally. Shorter stride length, moving slower in the mornings, increased tremors when I was cold and tired; did any of these symptoms impede me or take from the joy I felt? No! I had beaten back the disease. It felt good.

Chapter 13

Bicycling Mitigates the Symptoms

AFTER THE TWO CAMINO EXPERIENCES, I CONTINUED TO SEARCH FOR activities and exercises to slow the progression of Parkinson's disease. The physical therapist at my former workplace sent articles from her professional journals for me to read. One article especially caught my attention: it said that "riding a bicycle, dancing, tai chi and kayaking help relieve the symptoms of PD." *Hmm, bicycling.* That sounded great.

In my garage, under several layers of dust, was my ladies' Peugeot cruising bike. I hadn't ridden it for several years. Taking it for a ride meant cleaning it off, checking the tires, and being sure the brakes worked. Completing my check, I got on it for a spin. Getting on shouldn't have been hard, as it was a women's model with the lower center bar, but getting my right leg through to the other side was a challenge. After I got on, I pushed it a bit with my left foot as I started to pump with my right. It was so hard! It felt heavy and wobbly. I felt off balance. *Am I that out of shape? How can cycling help Parkinson's symptoms if you can't even pedal?* I thought as I parked it back in its spot.

In another corner of the garage, I spotted my son's Bianchi road bike he had outgrown. It looked perfectly my size. I picked it

My first road bike, a Bianchi, passed on to me by my youngest son, Luke.

up; it was so light. I pushed it down our gravel lane to the paved road and tried to get on it. It was a men's version, so the bar was higher. Leaning the bike against the mailbox, I figured out that angling the bike and stepping over the bar was easier than trying to swing my leg over the seat. It didn't feel clunky, and I wobbled a bit less. I got up the courage to go out on the paved country road that ran in front of our house. The bike moved well, and talk about speed—I felt like I was tearing up the road. Freedom was mine!

I was determined to learn how to ride this bike so that it would help my PD symptoms. I wanted to be using proper riding posture, shifting to my advantage, climbing, and turning. I wanted to learn from a female cyclist, and I wanted this woman to have firsthand knowledge of Parkinson's disease. Using my favorite search engine, I typed in *women with Parkinson's disease who bicycle in the Pacific Northwest*. The first name that appeared was Dr. Nan Little, Seattle, Washington.

There was an email address for Nan Little. I wrote a note of introduction, to which there was an immediate reply: *Call me.* On the other end of the line, I met the down-to-earth and easy-to-talk-to Nan Little. Nan had recently returned from an adventure on Mount Kilimanjaro, where she'd summited with a team of other Parkinson's patients as well as some with multiple sclerosis. Also on her adventure vita were a trek to the Annapurna base camp in Nepal, a hike to Machu Picchu in Peru, and many fly-fishing trips to blue-ribbon trout streams. In addition to this adventure travel, Nan gave me a rundown of her other physical activities, including swimming, hiking, kayaking, and of course, cycling. Nan was just the type of person I needed to meet: someone who would encourage me and tell me about opportunities to improve my physical abilities *and* feed my love of adventure.

We'd been talking for quite a while when she said, "But you called about cycling."

"Yes, I did!"

Nan had already been into bicycling when she heard about a report on the *NBC Nightly News.* She told me about how she'd watched Dr. Jay Alberts from the Cleveland Clinic talk about his research on bicycling for Parkinson's patients and the outstanding preliminary results. She'd called him and learned about his initial research, which included high-cadence cycling. Several months later he had official results from his study and a protocol for people with Parkinson's to follow.

By that point, Nan told me, she was not only riding outside, but she had also worked up to riding her stationary bike three times a week for forty minutes at a cadence of 80 to 90 rpm. It wasn't much later when she felt her body changing. One day out walking her dogs in her Seattle neighborhood, she noticed that her shuffling steps had been replaced by longer, more normal strides. Her arms, which had stayed closed to her body, now swung freely. She turned her head from side to side without stiffness or pain. Her hands had come unclenched.

"I stopped right there on the sidewalk and cried while the dogs looked at me and wagged their tails. There was something I could do about this diagnosis of Parkinson's," Nan told me. Over time Nan was able to reduce her medication while she kept on this bicycling protocol and increased her activity level.

As the conversation continued, Nan invited me to ride with the Pedaling for Parkinson's team in the Register's Annual Great Bicycle Ride Across Iowa, known by its acronym RAGBRAI. Since 1973, cyclists from Iowa and around the country have gathered in the western part of the state with their rear tires dipped in the waters of the Missouri River. They take off riding east, and seven days later, the swarm of nearly twenty thousand riders stops pedaling with the front tires of their bikes in the Mississippi River. Camping along the way in designated communities provides an opportunity to experience small-town Iowa.

I found out that Dr. Alberts was originally from Iowa, and it had been on RAGBRAI in 2003 that he'd discovered a possible connection between cycling and Parkinson's treatment. A woman in his group joined Jay on his tandem, and after a few days of riding, said, "When I get off the bike, I don't feel as if I have Parkinson's." She also noted improvement in her handwriting, which previously had been illegible. Later, Nan and her husband, Doug, an attorney, helped set up the foundation, and from then on the Pedaling for Parkinson's team had raised money each year to sponsor spinning classes for people with Parkinson's at YMCAs across the country.

I responded to Nan's invitation of riding 450 miles across hilly Iowa in the heat and humidity of late July with a solid *yes*.

Charlie said he'd go with me. I had no idea what we were getting into when we started training.

* * *

March in Hermiston is very windy. Out on the open road, we could have gotten blown over, so Charlie and I started to train in town, riding a ten-mile route on our road bikes. On less gusty days, my friend Anne took me on longer rides of eighteen to thirty miles. With a sudden new interest in cycling, Charlie and I noted across the gravel driveway our neighbors had a garage full of bicycles and tools. Charlie had noticed a bright-yellow tandem bike hanging on the wall. I had ridden tandem with Charlie before—and I swore I would never do it again. But Charlie took a chance. He went over to see if we could try out the tandem. Scott, our neighbor, was helpful in getting the bike ready, changing out the pedals and lubing the chain.

Scott took Charlie out on a ride so he would know what it was like to be in the back. With this introduction, Charlie understood why I never wanted to ride tandem again—he couldn't see, he didn't know what to expect ahead, and he had to try to guess the next moves initiated by the pilot of the bike, seated in front of him. Unbeknownst to me, Charlie researched more on his own about how to make this experience more predictable and pleasant for the rider in back. When he told me all this, it really pleased me—I'd often felt with several things in our life that I had to be the one to find all the information.

The day came when I was to get on the tandem. Riding a tandem bike seemed like such a romantic activity. In the song "Daisy Bell," the lyrics "you'll look sweet upon the seat of a bicycle built for two" made me dream of date night. But in my spandex shorts, cycling jersey, gloves, glasses, and helmet, I looked anything but sweet.

Charlie was great as he clearly explained how a tandem crew worked together. He rode up front in the captain, or pilot, seat. His duties were to drive the bike, controlling the direction of the bike, shifting the gears and brakes through the levers on the handlebars. The job of stoker, in back, is to provide power by pedaling. The stoker cannot usually see to the front and has to trust the captain. Hitting a pothole, making a quick turn, or braking unannounced can throw the tandem crew off balance. That meant Charlie and I had to work on communication.

We developed cues. Stopping at an intersection, he'd put both his feet down on the pavement to balance me and the bike. When I'd roll the pedal into position for him to immediately put his foot on when the light changed to green, I'd say, "Pedal up." I followed with "Ready," and, if I didn't say it quickly enough, he'd ask, "Ready?" Then I'd respond, "Ready," telling him my feet were on the pedals and in position to go. Out on the road, he'd forewarn me of upcoming hills (up or down), gear changes, and bumps. He asked me what ring the chain was on. When it came time to stop, he'd say, "slowing," followed by, "gliding," and then "stopping," which was when he'd actually put his foot on the pavement. Out in the country, where there is seldom need for these commands, we had marvelous conversations that we would not have had at home. The value of this time together was immeasurable.

Charlie's favorite line became: "Wherever you are in your relationship, riding a tandem bike will get you there faster." Our good relationship was made even better as we learned to communicate on a tandem bicycle.

The second week of July, we loaded the camper on Charlie's big pickup truck, which he called Gertrude. The tandem rode inside on the over-cab bunk and the road bikes in a bike rack mounted on the front bumper, where we could keep our eyes on them. My cousin Patty from Iowa had flown out to Seattle to visit my oldest brother and his wife and then ride back to Iowa with Charlie and me. Our plan was to camp overnight in scenic areas along the drive to Iowa. Having someone to share the adventure with was really fun. We laughed and joked and told family stories.

We reached Hull, Iowa, where we were to meet the team, late the night of July 18, 2014. Not knowing where we should park, we looked up the support crew leader's address. I remembered that his name was Jason. Parking the truck and camper at the curb of a tree-lined street, Charlie and I got out flashlights and started looking for Jason's house. There were no numbers that we could see! We aimed the lights on the houses and, on the curbs and still no house numbers came in view. I told Charlie, "If we see a bunch of tables and chairs, I bet we've found the place." Sure enough, the next house had a glass window in its garage door, and I could see cases of soda and water, tables stacked against the wall, and folding chairs. This had to be the right place. Charlie knocked on the door, then pounded loud enough to wake the neighborhood. A very tall and sleepy man opened the door.

"Jason?" I asked.

"Yes." He rubbed his eyes.

"I'm Carol. I know we're here a night too soon. Where can we park our truck?"

"Go around the block and park anywhere in that church parking lot. See you in the morning."

We climbed back into the truck and told Patty the plan. Once we'd parked, Charlie took the big tandem bike off our bed and locked it to the single road bikes on the front of the truck. Exhausted, we were asleep in no time.

Saturday morning came around, and so did people. First, Jason appeared and welcomed us to his home for breakfast. After breakfast I decided to clean up my bike. Patty needed to pack her belongings, and Charlie made a trip to the store on his bike. The church pastor came to assure me it was okay to park there. The chair of the RAGBRAI committee and the mayor drove up in a four-wheeler to welcome me. Then they sent a newspaper reporter to interview me and take my picture.

Later in the morning, Charlie, Patty, and I took a drive to some small-town cemeteries where my ancestors were buried. At about three o'clock, we returned to Jason's house, in time for the team bus to arrive. Other team members had met up on the east side of the state to leave their vehicles at the finish line and then ridden this chartered bus to the west side, where the ride would begin tomorrow. Charlie and I waited to meet them as they gathered up luggage from underneath the bus. Parked behind the bus was a long white trailer with the Pedaling for Parkinson's logo painted on the side and back. The trailer was full to the brim with neatly packed bicycles and crammed-in bike gear, ice chests, and tents.

We unloaded our tent and luggage from the camper onto the asphalt parking lot and found room for our bikes in the Pedaling for Parkinson's trailer. I took a big gulp as Patty drove off in our truck and camper to park it at her house near Orchard, Iowa, farther east. No longer would I have the luxurious surroundings to protect me from the elements. Our main transportation now would be our bikes, and our housing would be our tent. Cousin Patty would pick us up at the Mississippi River in seven days.

Charlie and I found a place to put our tent in Jason's shady backyard. Tents of all sizes and colors were being erected everywhere,

Charlie, my cousin Patty, and I visit the graves of our ancestors.

right up to the edge of the church parking lot. Excitement rang through the air as old friends greeted one another.

There were Pedaling for Parkinson's team riders of all ages. The youngest rider was a kindergarten-aged girl who rode on a tandem with her mom, and the oldest were Nan and her husband Doug in their late sixties. What struck me the most about each and every one was that they were not only cycling buffs but also buff cyclists. Some members of this group were elite cyclists who rode on teams back home. I was surprised to find out that among the fifty members of the team, there were seven with PD.

At the team meeting that night, as one of the riders with PD, I was asked to introduce myself and tell about my experience with Parkinson's.

"When Nan asked me to ride, I responded with a confident *yes!* But actually I didn't know what the heck I was getting myself into. So when you pass me out there, please call out, 'Go, Carol!'" The team started chanting, "Go, Carol," and that became my nickname.

The other people with Parkinson's riding on our team were Nan, John, Cidney, Doug, Mike, and Bill. Later that evening, we attended a local PD support group meeting, and each of us gave a brief talk. I hadn't expected this talking commitment and being unprepared made me nervous. The enthusiastic audience of people with Parkinson's (whom we call PWPs), care partners, and members of our team made it fun, and I relaxed. I learned that there would be a few more opportunities to share our stories of the effect of exercise on the symptoms of PD as the week progressed, so now I knew and was prepared. The meeting dispersed, and I was surprised at how quickly everyone found their sleeping arrangements in the mass of tents. This was a group of serious and experienced riders. Some were tired from riding their bikes back to the starting of RAGBRAI and dipping their tires in the Missouri River. It was a fifteen-mile ride, and we decided not to use the energy. They all knew what the next day would bring. I really didn't have a clue.

* * *

Sleep deprivation for PWPs is detrimental to functioning for daily activities. I'd learned this on my first Camino. Camping in a tent, and the sounds of the night that go with it, is comparable to the snoring in an albergue!

It was one a.m. Charlie and I were in a tent in Jason's backyard, and I was freezing. Thinking Iowa was warm and humid in the summer, I had brought only a light blanket to cover me. The breeze outside would have been a pleasant refreshment most days, but its whistling through tree limbs, paired with Charlie's snoring, added to my discomfort. I heard raindrops tapping on the top of the tent.

Whenever I woke up in the night like this, I would usually need to visit the little room down the hall. This particular night I had a choice of two little rooms: One bathroom could be reached by maneuvering around tents, up a small incline out of Jason's yard, and across the parking lot of the church where we had slept so peacefully in our camper the night before. Option two was to go around a cluster of tents, up a set of stairs to a deck, through the sliding door into Jason's house, and downstairs into the basement. As if on cue, a group of people some blocks away let out a huge laugh in unison. I wished their comic relief would relieve some other things. I was so tired! In a few short hours, I would be donning my official Pedaling for Parkinson's "kit," as I learned bike clothes were called. The big yellow tandem would carry us sixty-nine miles to the next host house.

Argh, now firecrackers! It seemed the rest of the cyclists camping around the small Iowa town were not as serious about sleep as the Pedaling for Parkinson's team was. I made my choice, opting for the warmer of the two locations, and made my way to the bathroom downstairs in the house. At the bottom of the stairs, I nearly tripped over a snoozing body half out of his sleeping bag. As my eyes grew accustomed to the darkness, I saw several more sleeping bodies sprawled on couches and La-Z-Boy recliners. Ah, I saw the door to the bathroom, and oh, what a relief that was. Upon my return to the tent, I ever-so-quietly zipped the door closed. I'm not sure why I tried to be quiet with all the partying around us. Wrapped up in my blanket and trying to sleep, I thought, *Brrrrr! I want my nice warm camper.*

* * *

Day one of RAGBRAI dawned crisp and windless. The previous night, with all the sounds, had been much too short. We packed the Bianchi next to Charlie's bike in the support trailer

The map of RAGBRAI 2014 shows a northerly route across Iowa. (Photo credit: *Des Moines Register*/RAGBRAI)

for possible use later in the ride. Straddling the big yellow tandem, Charlie and I reviewed the communication commands from our tandem training: pedal up, ready, going, slowing, gliding, stopping. There were several other words that were most often spoken to other riders, and we both needed to know when to use them: bike on, bike up, clear, on your left (or right), hold your line, and—most important—rumbles (to warn about upcoming speed bumps before a stop sign). After a few blocks of quiet, tree-lined streets, we turned left to join the mass of humanity cycling into the sunrise. RAGBRAI. *This is RAGBRAI!*

My heart skipped a few beats in excitement. My Parkinson's-induced apathy was gone. I laughed and grinned from ear to ear. I actually felt some real emotion. We were out on the road with sixty-nine miles to the next lodging site.

When Charlie and I pulled into the first town, it was a confused mess, and we had to walk the tandem. For me it was like being dragged through a throng of people by a big, yellow praying mantis. The city park was full of people, music, food, and games. We stopped at a pink-painted hay roll made to look like a pig for

Charlie and I pose with the Big Yellow Mosquito Eater at the first pass-through town on RAGBRAI.

a photo and then got out of there as soon as possible. The noise and confusion were too much for me. I felt much safer and more comfortable on the bike.

We rode among so many excited people from all over the world. At small towns we stopped for snacks and to rest our weary legs and butts. Our itinerary showed us that the night's lodging was a private home near Okoboji. After sixty-some miles of riding past humid cornfields and up steep hills, Charlie and I were enjoying the speed of a long downhill glide. The heavy tandem and our extra-weighty bodies followed the laws of physics, and gravity propelled us at 25 to 30 miles per hour—that slow only because my wise husband kept us under control with good use of brakes.

Unbeknownst to us, we sailed right past the street to the night's lodging and into town. Charlie pulled our yellow beast up in front of a young local family who was enjoying the never-ending stream of cyclists. The kids were thrilled with our strange bike as the parents gave directions. We turned around and headed back uphill against the speeding downhillers. The faster riders hogged the entire side of the road we needed to travel on, just as we had a few moments earlier.

"Bike up! Bike up!" we both shouted. Earlier that day we'd learned the warning call to clear the path as a cyclist pedaled against the flow like a salmon swimming upstream. We were ever so glad to get across the lanes of bike traffic and onto the right road—and extra glad to find the home that we'd been looking for.

The riders kept pedaling by. With the estimated number of participants over twenty thousand, it was going to take some time for them all to find their housing for the night. Every hotel room, spare bedroom, tent spot on lawns, and driveway that could fit an RV was occupied that night.

There was a line for the shower in the basement of this house. A crew of teammates was collecting our riding kits to run them through a cycle in the washing machine. Another group was making sure the bathroom was stocked with soap and toilet paper. I was impressed at this organization. The team even had its own massage therapist who had traveled with some riders from Colorado. Having a massage after a ride like today was an amazing perk. While I was being pampered, Charlie found our big orange roller duffels that held our tent and camping gear, nicely stacked with other luggage outside the equipment trailer. He got our night's accommodations arranged.

Without a thought about his own needs for relaxation after the day's big ride, Charlie then worked on getting the tandem stored away in the trailer. The tandem was half again as long as a single bike, so storing it required removing the front tire to fit. I sat on the patio and waited for him, and when he joined me, we shared the last barbecued burger and some sort of fruity alcohol drink that did not agree with my stomach.

Then it was dark already! Off to bed we went, discovering our tent door had not been zipped closed and the tent was full of buzzing creatures. Drifting to sleep I dreamed our yellow tandem had taken the form of a praying mantis—the same praying mantis who had pulled me through the chaotic small town that morning—and was in the tent, eating up mosquitoes. The mosquitoes were so big, Charlie called them Iowa's state bird. It was that thought that led me to nickname the yellow tandem the Big Yellow Mosquito Eater. My second restless night in the tent was spent dozing, slapping at mosquitoes, and scratching itchy bites.

On the second day, I planned to ride with sixty-eight-year-old Nan. Nan was the diva of our team. She had ridden RAGBRAI four times, taking last year off to climb Mount Kilimanjaro. I left a few minutes before Nan, as I was unsure how I would do descending and climbing a huge hill on my single road bike. I waited at the top, when Nan came speeding by. In a few minutes I was struggling to keep up as we rode into the sunrise.

Nan disappeared into the crowd of cyclists. I scanned for her ahead instead of watching the road immediately in front of me. My bike left the pavement. The front tire dug into the soft dirt shoulder forcing my bike to flip in front of hundreds of riders. My head hit the pavement hard, bashing in the side of my helmet. The warning cry "Rider down!" seeped through the throng of cyclists behind me. Tears streamed down my cheeks. Not only had I lost control of my bike, it was bigger than that. I was losing control of my body and of my life!

Charlie was pedaling right behind me and was off his bike in an instant. It would be tragic to cause a pile up in this crowd of cyclists. After a quick check to see for injuries, he moved me and the bike back over onto the shoulder that had caused my demise. A nearby cyclist stopped and offered me her clean handkerchief with fresh, cool water to wipe the blood off my leg. Nothing seemed broken, except my helmet, my bike, and my pride.

A squadron from the Air Force Cycling Team swooped in and, after a quick "Are you okay?" started work on my bent-up bike. Another contingent of the Air Force Cycling Team, this time women, stopped and immediately attended to me.

"Honey, have you eaten this morning?"

"Let me see your leg."

"Can you move your elbow?"

"Do you have a headache?"

"Eat this."

"Now drink."

The guys got my bike in riding condition, and my helmet would be usable until the next town. There really wasn't much choice—I couldn't just stay on the side of the road—so I mounted up and re-entered the line of riders. Charlie stayed with me and helped look for Nan but, as she knew nothing of my wreck, she had ridden on.

Amazing how word spreads, though; when we pedaled into the camp that night, the group already knew. Several teammates stopped by to see how I was. Nan told me she had wondered and worried about me all day until she met up with someone who'd seen me wreck. I learned that Elise, one of Dr. Alberts's research assistants, had a more significant crash that morning that required an ambulance ride. She experienced deep road burns that had to be cleaned out and bandaged. My injuries were insignificant compared to those Elise had received.

All around camp that night, the cyclists told stories of bike wrecks. I sat with Nan for a while. She did not have a story of a

Iowa is famous for its pie, and RAGBRAI riders love it!

significant fall. But Cidney, another rider with PD, did. Last year her husband made a mistake stopping their tandem. The bike fell over with Cidney clipped in and she broke her arm. I had been lucky.

The next day, Charlie and I rode the big yellow tandem forty miles. We found my cousin Ann in Titonka, Iowa, helping with a community booth. We learned we'd just pedaled past her house. This little town smelled so good. The street was lined with vendors. Delicious food of all types was readily available and served up by firefighters, churchwomen, and Cub Scouts. There were chicken sandwiches, cherry pies, Beekman's Homemade Ice Cream, and bottles of water and Gatorade. We rode on from Titonka with bellies full of sandwiches and pie.

That night, I put my cot in an unused room at a retirement home. The Pedaling for Parkinson's team planners had contacted facilities like this months ahead to arrange lodging, even if it was just the use of their lawns for tents. If there were open lobbies or resident rooms, we were allowed to inhabit them in this order: people with Parkinson's, drivers and crew, then riders. Charlie was stuck in the tent. He slept very well there, while I did not sleep well in my room. My next-door neighbor was a permanent resident of this home. The unfortunate fellow cried all night, "I am dying. Come help me!" I heard assistants trying to calm him. I inquired about him the next day at breakfast.

"The poor man in the room next to mine was so miserable last night. Is he still alive?"

"Oh, yes, he has a hard time at night. His body is healthy, but his mind is gone."

Not all towns had such nice facilities, but here we'd found a gem. This nursing home had provided us a home-cooked dinner and breakfast, done our laundry, offered us electrical outlets and showers, and some of us even got to sleep indoors! As if taking care of our basic needs was not enough, they provided a fire and s'mores too.

The next afternoon we pedaled into the back parking lot of another town's care center. There was one porta-potty for all of us, and it was located about a football field away. The men were told they could go in the bushes. Showers were at the swimming pool down the road, and dinner was downtown about eight blocks away. Our water supply was limited to one hose. The camp crew didn't have much to work with to wash our kits, but they made the best of it. Any protuberance became decorated with towels, and our riding kits hung on impromptu drying racks made from bicycles, tents, and railings. The bikes were lined up against the wall. Residents peeked out of their windows at the unusual camp in their yard. We were not invited in to interact with the residents. Grateful for the space to lay our heads, though, none of us complained.

RAGBRAI cyclists demonstrate Iowa is not "flat." (Photo credit: *Des Moines Register* / RAGBRAI)

I should've foreseen that this would be an interesting night. I was really tired from the day's ride and didn't feel like walking into town. Some snacks were available at the camp, but my body needed more fuel. The camp emptied out as my teammates headed to the line at the pool for showers or to forage for food.

Charlie went for food, and I waited at the tent. I had been cold and went to Nan's van to see if they had any extra blankets. Nan provided me with one and then announced she was going to sleep. One hour went by. I was hungry and started to get angry. Charlie is really social and can get into a conversation and not get out for a long time. A second hour went by. I couldn't imagine what he was doing, and I unzipped the tent door and crawled inside, laying down on my cot with Nan's blanket. The evening's entertainment was just a few blocks away. I could hear the music as if I was there in front of the speaker, and I knew every song. There was no sleeping, even with my earplugs in, so I sang along. The band stopped playing briefly, and Charlie arrived with the food. I wanted to bite his head off for taking so long but was interrupted by a woman at the music venue singing a beautiful rendition of the national anthem.

Charlie said, "Do you remember when we were kids, the national anthem was played on TV at sign-off time?"

Speaking with my mouth full of food, I managed to say, "I was too young to stay up that late." We both laughed.

"What took you so long?"

"The food booths nearby were sold out. I walked an hour across town, and then it took an hour to get the order, and then I walked back."

"Oh my. Thanks, Charlie." I gave him a swift kiss and stuffed more food in my mouth.

It was quiet outside our tent. Charlie took the food wrapping to the trailer, where there was a garbage bag. He came back, zipped the tent closed, and lay down on his cot. "I'm so tired. I'm going to sleep."

Almost immediately, there was a great roar from the crowd at the music venue, and then the band started up. "Sweet Caroline," the crowd yelled. This turned out to be a thirty-minute encore by the band...and the audience sang so loud, that was all I could hear. There was a moment of silence, which I hopefully anticipated was the end of the noisy festivities, then *kaboom!* Charlie and I both sat up. It was firework time. *How can these cyclists party so much and ride so well the next day?* Charlie lay back down and put a pillow over his head. I put my earplugs in and finally fell asleep.

The route for day four's ride looked fantastic! We pedaled through fields of tall green corn to our left and soybeans to our right. The sky was clear, and the wind was light. Charlie and I continued to develop our tandem pedaling skills, and we moved faster. We started meeting up with teammates who had stopped at favorite vendor carts, such as Mr. Pork Chop and Beekman's Homemade Ice Cream, which moved from town to town with the riders. We cycled around a beautiful lake, along tree-lined streets, with families cheering us and children handing out Popsicles. I thought, *The perspective from a bicycle is so different than a car, as you can see and hear and feel the environment, not just pass it in a blur.* Experiencing Main Street Iowa and miles of corn and soybeans was exhilarating.

Chapter 14

Ride On

One day while pedaling behind Charlie on our tandem bike in a crowd of bicyclists, my body made a big jerk. It was telling me to *wake up!*

I realized the possible implications of falling asleep on a tandem bike. Not wanting to alarm Charlie, I decided I wouldn't tell him about it until later. But after a few miles, I couldn't contain it.

"Charlie, guess what. You may not have noticed, but I fell asleep back there."

"You *what?*"

"I fell asleep."

"Don't do that again."

He was quiet for a few minutes. I imagined he was envisioning a massive wreck from Carol falling asleep at the stoker position.

We turned off the highway and entered a town to the sounds of children singing. Schoolkids lined both sides of the street, singing their town's theme song. The tandem took us past a motor home factory and then a giant industrial plant with the word *Jell-O* painted on the side of a building. It was like being in a commercial: "Made in the USA."

After this long but pleasant ride, we arrived at the night's housing. It was sponsored by another care center. They had ten spare rooms provided for our PD cyclists and drivers, and seven shower rooms were opened up. Dr. Alberts gave a lecture, and five of the cyclists with PD, including me, stood up to share their experiences and stories...right into a TV camera. The other riders had such inspiring stories, especially Nan. I felt that what I had to say was of less interest. When I expressed this to Charlie, he said, "Your greatest fan loved it."

The TV crew moved outside to film Nan as she rode her bike around the parking lot, her long, silver hair flowing free. We watched the interview and Nan's cycling around the parking lot on Mason City's KIMT News. A teammate called out, "Nan, where was your helmet?!" She had broken the cardinal rule: *Never* get on your bike without a helmet.

We were fed a satisfying dinner and snacks. Breakfast was scheduled for five thirty a.m. Again the dedicated Pedaling for Parkinson's team gathered their belongings and found places to sleep inside. This night I was given an actual bed, and Charlie brought his cot in to share the room with me. I didn't see Nan inside. She and her husband, Doug, had their bed fixed up in their van and had turned in early.

The five o'clock alarm woke me out of a deep sleep. *Time to get moving!* Then I felt something welling up inside me. Anxiety! *Why this day? Yesterday and last night were so comfortable!* The anxiety grew.

Charlie turned the bike out on the highway, and we were headed east into the rising sun. We rode past crowds of people, and I heard multiple calls of, "Hey, there are the Clupnys." "Carol Clupny! Hi, Carol Clupny." Only a handful of the estimated twenty thousand riders knew us, so my intellect told me I was hearing things. Each time I heard my name called, I asked Charlie, "Did you hear someone yelling my name?" His response was always no. There was too much time for worrying as we pedaled for hours between the corn rows and the soybeans. I recalled the time Charlie and I had walked into a Walmart looking for books on tape for my dad. We walked back to the music and video section of the store thinking we would find them there and were redirected to the magazine and paperback section near the front. While looking through this section, I heard the conversations of other shoppers: "Books on tape?" "Have you seen any books on tape?" Over the intercom I heard, "All associates, find books on tape." Surely "books on tape" was not the topic at Walmart. Back then, too, I'd asked Charlie, "Do you hear anyone talking about books on tape?" "No," he'd responded, and knowingly, he took my hand to distract me with a display of Oregon Duck merchandise.

Hallucinations—particularly visual illusions—are another nonmotor symptom of Parkinson's. Auditory symptoms—such as my hearing people calling out my name, as I experienced at RAGBRAI, and the voices in Walmart—are less frequently reported by patients. On the ride, my hallucinations had been only auditory. At home it was different. I had told Dr. Hiller about the images I saw fleeting around the house. Sitting in my favorite chair, I sensed someone was nearby. In my peripheral vision, I would catch shadowy figures darting out of my view. Dr. Hiller suggested I visit a mental health professional.

I learned that hallucinations were much more common in Parkinson's disease than people talk about. I could understand that. Who wants to tell people they are seeing things? Patients more advanced in the disease are more susceptible, yet these disturbances can also affect the newly diagnosed when they are introduced to certain medications. I was taking a fairly heavy dose of Ropinirole at the time, one of those medications with hallucinations listed as a side effect. With counseling and medication adjustments, I was able to reduce the auditory and visual hallucinations dramatically.

All that worrying and overthinking did not help my present anxiety levels on the ride. Loud noises unnerved me. Groups of cyclists passed with music blaring from large battery-powered speakers. Emergency vehicles approached on the left shoulder with a siren or horn, and I came unglued. I started to hyperventilate. My heart raced, and I got very quiet; silent tears streamed down my face.

When I became conscious of my overly tight glute muscles and hamstrings, I intellectualized about what I needed do to relieve that and I could continue riding. But I could not get control over the anxiety. I was freaking out on the back of a tandem bicycle in the middle of thousands of cyclists. Charlie checked in with me.

"Carol, you're pretty quiet back there."

"Next medical-type facility, please stop," I managed to squeak out.

We rode into a town, and he stopped the Big Yellow Mosquito Eater in front of the white RV that was a mobile medical unit. A medic was right there to help me off the bike. I was sobbing and gasping for air. Wrapping his big burly arms around me to help me up the stairs, he said, "Okay, girl, tell me what's up."

"Parkinson's disease. Anxiety attack, " I said.

There was just no way I could think my way out of the panic—so I thought about its cause. On the Camino, it had been all about fear. I'd felt afraid I wouldn't be able to walk those hills. I was embarrassed that I had planned the trip and then it appeared too difficult for me to complete…and I had just started! Now on RAGBRAI, I felt I had no control. I couldn't control the direction of the bike, the people around me with their noisy boom boxes blaring, the sounds of the ambulances and police car sirens. I needed to get a handle on these things.

The medic took me inside the air-conditioned RV and sat me down in one of the captain's chairs up front with a bottle of ice-cold water and a wet towel. "I'm going to talk to this guy with chest pains, and then I'll be back with you."

Charlie returned from securing the bike outside and sat in the other captain's chair in the front of the RV.

The cool air and drink, the relative quiet, and the distraction as I eavesdropped on the other patient helped me settle down. When the medic returned, I was calm enough to talk, and to listen.

He said to me, "You're doing the best thing you can do for your health. You are out here riding in the fresh air, exercising, socializing. Let yourself enjoy it. Have fun. There are no pressures here. Go out and ride."

Charlie brought the Big Yellow Mosquito Eater around to the front door of the medical unit. I threw the medic a kiss and climbed into the stoker's position behind Charlie. It was only twenty-five miles to our host house. In a little over two hours, we were there.

As we pedaled along, I aimed my thoughts in a positive direction: the medic's advice. Why had I let fear rule? Why had I let it ruin my day and concern my husband? This was a challenging but very cool event. I was determined to relax and enjoy.

That night, the team hosts gave Charlie and me a bedroom to sleep in. I was emotionally and physically drained, so I fell asleep quickly. I didn't even wake up when Charlie crawled in next to me and snuggled his warm body close to mine.

On the sixth day I was dressed and ready to ride. A storm had rolled in. It had rained all night, and the tent dwellers were quite soggy. Many were gathered in the garage of this house, putting on raincoats or fashioning protection out of garbage can liners. Lightning lit the morning sky, and the immediate thunder told us the storm was directly overhead. The downpour left streams of water running along the road. If I was to get wet and cold, I knew the Parkinson's would revolt, making my arms tremor so it would be difficult to hold on to the handlebars, and my body would get rigid and stiff. I only imagined what it would be like to be out in the open cornfields with lightning striking all around, and I could feel the anxiety rising in my throat.

These powers of nature decided for me—my riding that day would be inside a support vehicle. Charlie decided to ride his single bike. This would have been wonderful for him on a good day, to ride without having the responsibility of caring for me. The weather did not show any signs of improving. I worried. He didn't have any rain gear, not that it would have helped in this monsoon. The Pedal for Parkinson's group was already out on the road ahead of him, yet I knew he would be in good company among the thousands of other cyclists braving the rain. Nan and Doug rode out in the storm too. Later in the day, Nan was hypothermic and entered a building to get warm. Thankfully she experienced no long-term effects.

Elise was still recovering from the bad road rash she'd received in her serious wreck the same day of my mishap and would also be riding SAG, as we called the support vehicles, short for "support and gear." As we rode along in the backseat of the pickup, Elise asked me how cycling helped my Parkinson's. I explained to her that, given the right conditions, I slept better, and sometimes my handwriting was better. At that point we came to a stop in

Members of the Pedaling for Parkinson's team gather at the RAGBRAI finish line.

the parking lot of a convenience store. I jumped out and jogged across the parking lot, with no assistance from trekking poles.

"And sometimes, it's just like this and I can run!" I called to her from in front of the store.

Elise had the most amazed look on her face as she observed me running. When I returned to the truck, she said, "I'm going to do my research on people like you. Would you mind if I ever referenced you personally?"

"If that helps, of course I don't mind. Please feel free to contact me."

On day seven we said our goodbyes to the Pedaling for Parkinson's team and pulled out of our group camp for the last time.

Charlie and I arrived in the final town via the SAG vehicle. We chose this because the route included a very steep downhill with a sharp curve. This created a safety issue, one we didn't want to attack that day. Our transport driver parked the trailer, and we hopped on our single bikes to pedal the last mile. Although the group had spread out on the final leg of the ride, a large number of team members managed to collect at the Mississippi River. Somebody snapped a team picture, and then we officially concluded the ride by dipping our front tires in the Mississippi.

Charlie and I sat in our lawn chairs by the equipment trailer, watching other teammates roll in as we waited for my cousin Patty and our pickup and camper to return for us. Chomping on convenience-store pizza, I reflected on the week and realized that, as with my first Camino, I wanted a do-over—or maybe a do-better. My conditioning had not been that great. Hearing the voices and having the panic attacks had been really unnerving. Whenever we got to a pass-through town, I'd parked my exhausted and overheated self with the bike and depended on Charlie to bring me food. I missed out on a lot of the small-town fun.

I quizzed some of the lady riders in the group as they prepared to leave.

"How can I get stronger? What do I need to do to ride better next year?" Frank answers came back.

"Lose weight."

"Ride intervals on the trainer."

"Build endurance."

"Strengthen core muscles."

I was determined to return the next year a better rider. I wanted to be in control of my emotions, chase away the fake voices calling out to me, and take some of the burden off Charlie so he could enjoy more and be able to be a better contributor to our team.

My cousin Patty brought our pickup—Gertrude—and camper around to where we were waiting, and I climbed into the backseat. My head hit the headrest, and immediately I was asleep. Nan and Doug's van had been parked nearby, but we didn't see them before we left. When I woke, I felt bad having not said goodbye or thanked her for the opportunity to participate.

One stop on the drive woke me up for a hamburger at a mom-and-pop place, and then I was asleep again. When we arrived at Patty's home, I staggered sleepily into the house, sat down on the couch, and fell back to sleep. I wrote about it later in my blog:

I fell into one of those deep, deep summertime afternoon sleeps. Cousin Patty and Monte have a great sleeping couch!

Drifting up into occasional consciousness, I caught movement outside the window. Between the trees I saw bicyclists wearing the black-white-and-orange cycling kits of the Pedaling for Parkinson's team. Shaking this vision out of my eyes, I fell back into the comfort of the couch and within seconds was back into deep sleep. When I woke again, it was dark. I peered out to see the twinkling headlights of dozens of bicycles coming down the blacktop road outside the rural Iowa farmhouse. I rubbed my eyes and looked again. The twinkling headlights I'd seen along the edge of the roadway had turned to fireflies lighting up the evening sky.

For days after the completion of our ride across Iowa, my mind was filled with scenes from RAGBRAI.

Chapter 15

RAGBRAI Two:
Training for Another Big Ride

IN JANUARY EACH YEAR, THE DIRECTORS OF THE REGISTER'S ANNUAL Great Bicycle Ride Across Iowa hold a big event to announce the route and the overnight towns of the ride. When this announcement was made in 2015, Charlie and I registered for our second ride with Pedaling for Parkinson's. As part of our commitment to this ride, we planned to train harder and purchased our very own tandem bike. The bike was the same brand as the Big Yellow Mosquito Eater, Co-Motion, and made in Eugene, Oregon. We had it built to our specifications and with couplers, which allowed the bike to come apart and be placed in two suitcases for traveling. We had it painted the University of Oregon colors, green and yellow. It weighed almost thirty pounds less than our borrowed tandem. It was a head-turner, as far as tandem bikes were concerned.

The RAGBRAI training blog suggests cyclists get one thousand miles of pedaling before leaving for the ride. Charlie and I worked on endurance that year. Thirty miles became a short ride. We increased the mileage, riding several days a week. I also worked out at a fitness studio with Cindee, the owner. She took me on as one of her few personal clients, working me hard to improve my balance and core strength.

People around our community of Hermiston started noticing us. "Oh, you're the ones riding that double bike." I took this as an opportunity to share how important it is for all of us to keep moving. I told stories of our training rides. There was something unique about each of these local trips. Looks of astonishment came across people's faces as we announced that we had ridden forty, fifty-five, sixty-six, or seventy-three miles that day.

One of our most interesting training rides was on Father's Day. Father's Day in our family was usually set aside for a barbecue. Dad would don a Hawaiian shirt, straw hat, and sandals and enjoy an Alaskan Amber or two. The kids would buy their dad ties, handkerchiefs, or wallets. As they got older, these gifts turned into baseball caps, barbecue sets, and aprons. And now Loren was at college six hours away, though he did call his dad. Luke was in the stage of life when he thought his parents were dumb. Asking him to do something with his dad only brought out his sarcasm. So to keep the peace, Charlie and I spent Father's Day out riding.

He piloted our tandem bike on a sixty-six-mile ride. We rode from our house to Highland Avenue, a main street in town, then to Feedville Road, a main road out in the country, and then to Despain (which I wanted to rename Despair) Gulch. We would be returning by a different route.

Sixty-six miles can get pretty boring from the stoker's back-seat view. Charlie, in the captain's seat, had a strong, broad back that I couldn't see around. Below, the pavement whirred by under the green and yellow of Grepedo—what we'd finally had named our new Co-Motion PeriScope Torpedo tandem. On this ride I kept my mind busy by making mental lists of various items I observed in the ditch alongside the road. The lists would become conversation starters or the basis for stories I would write after the ride.

Charlie and I train on a sixty-mile group ride. (Photo credit: Goldilocks Events)

Another symptom of Parkinson's disease can be memory issues. Just as I had used a strategy for problem-solving with Linsee during our time together in France, I now relied on some strategies for myself to remember what I saw. Chunking was the strategy I chose. I made a mental picture of the category name, then placed items in each category as I saw them in the ditch. The picture in my mind was like a whiteboard that I wrote on. In the clothing category, I counted three unmatched gloves, two plaid shirts, and one pair of men's tighty-whitey underwear. In the automotive department, there were practically enough items to build a car from scratch: tires and wheels, a muffler, two hubcaps, and a license plate. The oil for the vehicle could be gleaned from drips left in oil bottles and cans discarded on the roadside. An oil filter and a beat-up air filter were there too, but miles apart. In the arena of household items, a decently preserved roll of toilet paper came into view at milepost nineteen. In the most-unusual-items-thrown-out-of-cars category, it was a tie between a yellow rubber duck and an aluminum pan holding what looked to be the dinner still cooking.

We encountered more roadkill than usual. We saw a large dead badger in the oncoming lane and three birds who'd met their demise against the windshields of speeding motorists. An unidentifiable carcass had been stripped clean by roaming carnivores. As for living creatures, Charlie saw the shadow of vultures circling. *A portent of doom?* I wondered. From my backseat view, I watched a young buck deer bounding through the ripening wheat parallel to us, as if challenging a race.

There was so much time to think from the back of the tandem bike, pedaling a consistent 12 miles an hour while we climbed toward Pendleton. Seeing these creatures made me think of other adventures Charlie and I had taken in our married life. In 1987 we'd volunteered to spend six weeks at a new mission being established by the Capuchin Franciscan Order of the Catholic Church. I believe the devil takes special offense when you are making sacrifices to do something extra good. This mission trip must have been one he was specifically interested in, as he took aim at Charlie, striking him down with a kidney stone two weeks before our flight. The devil didn't stop the Clupnys. Just two days before we were scheduled to leave, Charlie passed the stone. He was totally exhausted as I helped him onto the plane. Proving that God's plans are always better, we were asked to wait in the city of Ciudad Obregon for two days before proceeding so we could meet one of the religious brothers who was returning from California. This provided Charlie with the rest he needed.

The Capuchins planted the mission house in Yécora, Sonora, Mexico. These brothers wore long brown habits modeled after Saint Francis's robes. They traveled on motorbikes or in a one-ton pickup with several spare tires under the back canopy. Roads—or, better called, tracks—led to the small mining towns, agricultural communities, and cattle ranches. To get there we rode in an old,

I pose for a photo on our training ride on Despain Gulch, Oregon.

rickety "chicken and pig" bus, as Charlie called it. There was truth in the name, as the woman across the aisle from me had a live hen in a basket!

We were there on our fifth wedding anniversary, still years away from our adoption of the two boys. This would have been quite an adventure with them.

The bus was bouncing up the riverbed that was used as a road in the dry season when the driver slammed on its brakes. An animal had crossed the track ahead. Of course, I thought the driver was trying to avoid a collision with the creature, but when the deer bounded alongside the bus, the men evacuated through doors and windows to chase the scrawny thing. One of the men even had a pistol in a holster, which he drew as the chase began. The pathetic creature safely outdistanced the men. If these men had been so excited about that little animal, what would they think if they saw this young, healthy buck bounding in the wheat field beside our bike? This deer had not been hunted before. He was curious, not afraid. It was a game for him to run alongside us. His story might have ended differently if he had been on that road in Mexico.

When I was a little girl, I liked to walk up to where the road past my house cut through some banks. Drilled into the sandy cliffs were holes of different sizes. The smaller holes, I knew, were birds' nests, as I could watch little birds coming and going. But the larger ones, I never really knew. I thought maybe huge snakes, or some sort of rodent. After Charlie and I saw the dead badger in the road, we pedaled the tandem through a cut bank similar to the ones up the road from my childhood home. Charlie pointed out a living badger coming from its hole. I could feel him tense up. "Let's get out of here!" he hollered and pedaled like crazy…leaving me no choice but to pedal with him. I wasn't sure a badger could catch us, but with those sharp teeth and claws, I wouldn't have wanted to be its prey.

The vultures circling overhead as we pedaled along were certainly looking for some dead thing to scavenge upon. They didn't look anything like a more familiar scavenger, the seagull. I detested those white-and-gray birds. The name *seagull* implied they belonged at the sea. That may have been true at one time, but I'd seen them hundreds of miles inland, hanging around open-air dumps or on school athletic fields. They were quite aggressive when it came to food. Once, at a rest stop in California, one took a sandwich right out of my hand. Today the vultures made me think of seagull experiences when I was little. As a young girl, I would go commercial salmon fishing with my dad. He paid for a charter for as many of us five kids as wanted to go. As the boat returned to port from a day's fishing, the deckhands cleaned the fish. Seagulls had caught on to these easy pickings and squawked and pooped as they hovered over the boat. The deckhands threw unwanted parts and pieces of salmon in such a way that the seagulls made acrobatic dives to get their dinner. The provided entertainment overshadowed the mess and noise brought about by the birds.

Back from daydreaming, I looked again into the ditch beside the road.

Judging by the number of empty pint whiskey bottles of one brand on a two-mile stretch, someone besides me was in despair on Despain Gulch Road. Was the driver getting up the courage to go to work or to go home? Hopefully they had continued on to arrive at their destination safely.

Charlie had been anticipating our turn left onto Highway 37. The wind hit him head-on, and we both pedaled with all we had to get up the steep incline. Then we hunkered down and held on against the gusts, gliding to the bottom of the hill and up the next one. The hills were much like the rollers of Iowa and good practice. The Cold Springs grange came into view, a much-needed rest stop. I anticipated sitting on the steps to eat my lunch, but as I dismounted and headed that way, I saw that it had been turned into someone's private home. We sought shade under a sparse tree on the corner of the property and ate a Father's Day feast of baked potatoes with taco sauce and boiled eggs.

Father and son riders from nearby Pendleton, also taking a Father's Day ride, stopped to chat. Seeing the young man with his father made my heart sad. *Our boys should be here with their dad.* I remembered a time when Luke was two and Loren was almost ten. We'd gone camping on the Snake River above the Hells

Canyon Dam with the Berka family. Jeremy, who walked with us on the Camino, was their youngest child. There were grandkids and friends and other kids they had met at the campground all playing together.

The older kids had started a contest to see how far they could get on their bikes from riding down a hill into a shallow swimming area of the river. Later that day, Luke got on his trike and was cruising along at full steam down the grassy hillside, headed for the river too. Charlie took chase and swooped Luke off his trike, and both of them tumbled laughing to the river's edge. Loren saw the fun and jumped on top of Charlie and Luke, and they all rolled into the river. Those were the memories I wanted Charlie and the boys to think of on Father's Day.

The riders turned back toward Pendleton, and Charlie and I pedaled down Cold Springs Road. Our next stop was at another familiar landmark, the Brachers' farmhouse. The Brachers were well-known in our community. Mr. Bracher grew wheat and later held positions on school boards. Mrs. Bracher became a teacher when her children were grown up and was also a wonderful role model as a 4-H leader and community volunteer. They were not home, but, knowing they would've welcomed us, we napped on their shaded lawn and refreshed our water supply from an outside spigot.

Seven or eight miles from the Brachers', we passed Hamen farms, which marked the start of a long downhill grade to the Columbia River and Highway 730. It was 2:57 p.m. when we pedaled into Hat Rock State Park, desperate for something other than water to drink. The little store there served as a restaurant, a grocery store, and the camper registration. The sign on the door indicated the store was open until three. We dismounted the tandem, and Charlie checked the doors. They were locked up tight.

Charlie is good at getting what he wants, and he went nosing around for someone who could get us something cold. He found the cook out back of the building and procured two bottles of Gatorade. We sat at a table out front of the store. The drink tasted so good. It had been a long ride but a good one. I was sore yet felt like I still had enough energy to get home. Charlie offered three different routes back. I was starting to debate the pros and cons of each route, when he said, "Just get on." After a quick spin to the boat launch bathrooms, back we went to Highway 730.

The sky to the west was growing dark. Impending storm clouds and sore butts compelled me to order the most direct route home: "I think there's a storm brewing. Let's hightail it home on Diagonal."

"Yes, Madame Admiral." From that point on, Charlie referred to himself as the tandem captain. "But Carol is the admiral," he'd say.

The paved shoulder on that road extended about twenty-four inches from the car lane. The semitruck drivers slowed and gave us a lot of room. Other vehicles screamed by at 55 miles per hour or faster. Four-wheel-drive diesel pickups were the noisiest and scariest passing vehicles. RVs pulling boats were less than mindful about the four-foot safety margin that Oregon requires drivers give bicyclists. To distract myself, I again searched the ditches alongside the road. This stretch contained the typical litter of fast-food wrappers and used diapers.

Home at last, I took a quick shower, downed my PD medications, and fell fast asleep. I woke up from the sound of my own snoring and heard someone entering the house. Charlie didn't get a wallet or a tie or barbecue tools for Father's Day that year, and neither his wife nor his kids made him dinner. He got take-out barbecue ribs and chicken and scrumptious salads from the supermarket deli. When he called me to dinner, I literally bounced out of bed, skipped down the hall, and presented myself with a big gesture. "Ta-dah! You are witnessing the effects of forced exercise on the symptoms of Parkinson's disease."

"But I just saw you crashed out on the bed!" He was astonished.

* * *

On July 5 we started early on what would be a seventy-three-mile RAGBRAI training ride. It was to be the longest, hardest ride of our training. After the completion of this ride, we would ride shorter distances. Then we would rest from cycling during the week it would take to drive to Iowa. It was warm in the morning. By afternoon the air temperature was over 103 degrees. Pavement temperature was quite a bit higher than that. The basalt cliffs on one side of the road reflected the heat right down on us. I grabbed a water bottle from its holder on the bike frame below me. Expecting cool refreshment, I gagged as the very warm, almost hot, water streamed into my mouth and down my throat. I felt sick to my stomach, my heart was racing, and my face was beet red.

"Charlie," I said, "we need to find some shade."

He pulled Grepedo over into the only shelter around: a couple of small trees by the side of the road shading the narrow, rocky shoulder. I found an old beach towel in the saddlebags and put it down to cushion me from the rocks. Charlie removed the roll of toilet paper we carried in a plastic sandwich bag and propped it under me to protect my head. The lukewarm water I poured on my back and neck provided little relief. Charlie laid the bike down and crouched in the shade. I worried about the safety of where we'd stopped, as the bend in the road blocked the view of oncoming motorists. However, the coolness I got from the shade was enough to stop my racing heart and return my face to a healthy hue of pink. A slight breeze drifted through the trees. I fell asleep.

After a brief rest, I sat up on my towel at the edge of the shoulder. I looked at Charlie and myself. We looked like we'd wrecked. The bike was off to one side, halfway in the ditch. Charlie was sitting back on his heels, looking totally disgusted. I wondered if any cars would stop to see if we were okay. One did. The only vehicle that we met in over twenty miles turned around to check on us. I almost asked for a ride to town. But I wasn't hurt or ill, just hot. There would be harder days ahead, so it was best to be prepared with as much adversity as possible.

After this break in the only shade around, I felt rested but not at all refreshed. We rode on, stopping every few miles to drink the warm water. There were some hills, and we pedaled up just fine, but the pavement was broken up and potholed in places. The strategy on a tandem is to carefully calculate your speed on the downhill run so that the momentum carries you up the next hill with less work, but Charlie didn't dare let the bike run its full speed downhill, as hitting a hole could wreck us. *We would have cooled off some at the higher speed*, I thought. *And it's fun to go fast.* Disappointing as it was, I respected Charlie's safe handling of the bike.

When I first met Charlie, he'd rented a small house just outside of Echo, a tiny hamlet near Hermiston. It was on the Ramos family ranch, and he'd since kept his connections with this family. My weak voice squeaked out, "Charlie, find a Ramos house with some good Ramos people and some cool Ramos water. I want Ramos trees and Ramos grass. I want to lie out on their lawn and get cool."

Nan Little, Charlie, and I smile on the way to our second RAGBRAI.

Soon we were at old Joe Ramos's house, and Charlie cycled us up the gravel drive to the lawn. I struggled to get off the bike and immediately found shade and lay down. I almost fell asleep sprawled out there, but I was lured inside by a glass of cool water and the promise of a place to lie down in front of the window-mounted air conditioner. "Sis" Ramos brought me a pillow, and Jean Ramos West brought me more water. I slept with arms and legs splayed out on their cool carpet.

I thought I'd recovered enough to make the twenty miles back to Hermiston. The micro-climate changes throughout the agricultural areas on the Meadows route saved us. We pedaled along Echo Meadows Road and turned onto Stanfield Meadows, passing by irrigated farmland until we reached the Buttercreek Highway and Space Age truck stop. Here Charlie suggested we stop at the A&W for a burger, but I almost threw up all over his back. Home sweet home, that's where I needed to be.

Finally we were on the home stretch. We had the tradition of counting the last five telephone poles to the house, and then I would dismount the bike across the street and walk while Charlie took care of the bike. I walked myself into the house. This girl with Parkinson's disease—who had ridden with her husband seventy-three miles of challenging terrain in excruciating heat—walked into the house, took a shower, and fell asleep. No glory, just grit.

The reward came a little later. I didn't remember telling him what I wanted to eat, but a quiet, nudging voice said, "Your egg flower soup and Pepsi are in the kitchen." Usually it was pizza I craved after a ride like today's—pizza and ice-cold draft beer. What planet was I on when I requested egg flower soup and Pepsi? I hadn't had either of these items in years. My body must've been calling out for salt and sugar, because that was the best post-ride dinner ever!

* * *

In mid-July Charlie and I started our journey to Iowa for our second RAGBRAI. It was a small Pedaling for Parkinson's team that year. Our Ford F-350 pickup was going to be pressed into service to pull the bike trailer, so we would have the camper with us to sleep in the whole way. I was thrilled. We offered to take Nan Little's bike out to Iowa. She called and asked, "Can I ride with you too?"

The adventure began the first night, when I had put in the wrong address for the KOA and were driving around in the dark. Nan offered advice, Charlie was tired and ticked off, and I felt stupid. We found it to be one of the loveliest RV parks ever. Old-fashioned lamp poles lined the streets, and from them hung baskets of flowers. The restrooms were sparkling clean, and each shower had a grab bar and a shower chair. *This should be the model for RV parks around the country*, I thought. Charlie's brother Allen flew in from Albuquerque to drive the truck and trailer while we rode. Nan and I took over the camper each night as our sleeping quarters. For me, these sleepovers were an opportunity to see firsthand how another person lived with Parkinson's disease. And, of course, I was thrilled to sleep in the camper instead of a tent! Nan recognized how much stronger I had become since we'd ridden RAGBRAI the previous summer, and I felt proud of my hard work. Working out at the gym two mornings a week, riding the stationary bike all winter, watching my diet, and including interval speed work on Grepedo had worked!

Nan had just published her book, *If I Can Climb Mt. Kilimanjaro, Why Can't I Brush My Teeth? Courage, Tenacity & Love Meet Parkinson's Disease.* Nan was no longer just Nan to Charlie. He would only refer to her as "the famous Nan Little." The book shares the life lessons she learned while adventuring around the world as well as those she learned at home to tackle Parkinson's disease. I was touched to be mentioned in the book and pictured in a photo.

What a great time Charlie and I had on the ride. There were no flat tires, no serious accidents, and my anxiety attacks were minimal. Grepedo fit us well, and with its lighter weight than the Big Yellow Mosquito Eater, the climbs were easier. The smaller Pedaling for Parkinson's RAGBRAI team provided better opportunities for camaraderie too. One night we planned a tandem christening ceremony, in which any tandem team who wished to participate showed off their bike, told its name, and explained a story about it. Then they were "blessed" with bubbles from the sidelines. Some of the stories were sentimental; others were hilarious. In all, it was a great RAGBRAI for the Clupnys.

Charlie and I leave the church after Mass in Kingston, Iowa. (Photo credit: Tim Gallagher, *Sioux City Journal*)

When Charlie and I had such great experiences at this point in our lives, there was always a little sadness in our hearts. Our boys weren't with us. Loren had graduated from college a few months before. He'd found his partner, Alex, in his second year at the University of Oregon. Both of them had graduated high school the same year, but Loren was slower in deciding his major and took another year of college to get his bachelor's degree. During that time Alex had signed up for Teach for America and moved to New Orleans to teach at a high school. It was a challenging time for the two of them to be apart. When Loren graduated that June, he chose to attend the sociology department's morning ceremony and, in the afternoon, the Lavender Graduation. The Lavender Graduation was arranged by the LGBTQ community at UO and was very personal. Mentors or friends spoke on behalf of each student. It was awesome to hear what Loren had

Loren and Alex smile for a photo in Bandon, Oregon.

accomplished in his involvement with this group. After the ceremonies we had a celebration gathering in Eugene with Alex's parents and brother, Charlie's mom, and Loren and Luke.

While Charlie and I pedaled across Iowa, Loren came home to spend time with Luke. They found a friend to keep an eye on our house and animals—it could be a chore with two cows, two horses, two dogs, and two acres of pasture to irrigate. Luke took a few days off from his lifeguard job at the local pool, and the two brothers joined friends on a camping trip. It helped us not to worry about them so much, knowing they were together and having a good time.

Chapter 16

The Way to Discernment

THE TWO YEARS AFTER MY SECOND CAMINO WERE AMAZINGLY TOUGH on the family front. We moved my dad to Hermiston and watched his health decline, until he finally passed away on December 14, 2014, at the age of ninety-four. During that time I had many physical and emotional challenges. Exercise helped with the Parkinson's, and life challenges helped me to keep everything in perspective. I had a good dose of both, and I thought I was moving along quite successfully.

I'm not sure if there was an unnoticed, slow progression, or if it happened overnight. One day I was doing fine, and the next I felt like the disease smacked me hard. There was no letup.

I experienced insomnia most nights, which I tried to take advantage of to develop many friends among the sleepless people with Parkinson's who frequent social media sites. Because of my medication combined with not sleeping at night, the daytime sleepiness had me falling asleep while talking or typing and, unfortunately, while driving! My tight glutes and hamstrings kept me walking slowly and sometimes shuffling my steps. Dyskinesia, involuntary movements of my trunk and head, had started. Charlie especially noticed it when I sat across from him at the dinner table. He told me I looked as if I was weaving back and forth in my chair. Dystonia, uncontrolled movements of my hands and arms, caused my hands to get stuck in odd positions.

The medication would wear off too early, and I had to take more. Bad cramps in my legs and feet would hit so hard, I screamed. I had unexplainable pains in my forearms, the sides of my legs, in my quad muscles, and searing down the sides of my calves. My feet had a tingly, dry feeling that no amount of lotion could comfort. My brain was so scattered, I couldn't follow a recipe, balance the checkbook, complete a project, or finish my thoughts. Sometimes I stuttered on words. They seemed to be blocked from coming out of my mouth, like someone was strangling me. I gurgled up sounds. The volume of my voice was quiet, and my air support for speaking ran out before I could finish a sentence. Sometimes I had trouble swallowing.

I saw Dr. Hiller for my semiannual appointment in April of 2015. I described the increase in odd symptoms and the development of these newer problems. After her examination she sat quietly for a moment, as if she was gathering her thoughts. Jumping into the silence, I said, "So, am I ready for DBS?"

I'd been reading about deep brain stimulation surgery, which was gaining popularity as a treatment for Parkinson's disease. It seemed appealing during a time when my medications and exercise didn't seem to be managing my symptoms as well as they had originally.

"You're getting there. Let's talk about it at your next appointment in November."

"Yes!" I did a double-pump gesture with my arms. Charlie had a big grin on his face.

The previous summer, my friend Carol had wanted to walk the Camino to honor her seventieth birthday. In an unfortunate accident, she broke some bones in her leg, which nullified her plans but not her dreams. Carol was a spunky, faith-filled woman. Her joy of life poured out in just the right amount to fill you up, and that gave me hope.

Recovered from her injury, she was ready to prepare for the Camino Frances in the fall of 2015. I mentioned that, if she could put up with me, I would come along. It was possible that I would not be able to keep up, though. With my current symptoms, I didn't know what Parkinson's disease had in store for me. I did know the preparation would challenge my mind and body. Having traveled this route before, I had the knowledge to get her started, and I was quite familiar with alternative forms of travel via bus or taxi. It was agreed—we would walk the Camino Frances in September of 2015. Parkinson's was not going to stop me.

On my first Camino, I had been introduced to a man who had walked from his home in Austria to Los Arcos, Spain. He knew he had Parkinson's, yet he had not sought out the assistance of a specialist for his treatment.

I asked him why.

He responded in his best English, "I want to come to know this Parkinson's first."

I blurted out, "Your quality of life will be so much better when you get some treatment."

I realized at that point that I had misspoken. Who was I to decide what his quality of life was? He had made it by foot from Austria. Perhaps his walk on the Camino was a time to decide his next move in attacking the disease. My time on this, my third Camino, would become a time of discernment for me.

* * *

In the course of planning, I felt a strong need to invite my friend Maryhelen. The unique thing about this friendship was the connection we had before ever meeting. Her aunt Loretta (actually her dad's cousin, but they called her their aunt) had been a dear friend of my parents and filled in for my godmother at my baptism. I remembered Loretta telling me about her nieces in Fossil, Oregon, and that she wanted to take me to ride their Arabian horses. Later I met Maryhelen as an adult at a church workshop, not knowing there was any connection. A few months later, Loretta passed away. Maryhelen and I were both surprised to see each other at the funeral in Walla Walla. We put it all together: Loretta's nieces were Maryhelen and her sisters! The connection sealed the friendship. Maryhelen and I had shared some interesting adventures, including climbing Mount Adams and Mount Saint Helens and taking a trip to Bosnia for a prayer gathering during a time of political and military unrest. We didn't see each other often, but when we got together, we reconnected…at the funny bone. She'd be the perfect addition to this year's Camino family.

Maryhelen flew with me to Paris, and together we rode the high-speed TGV train to southern France. Carol and her friend Ann were to meet us at a hotel in Burlada, a suburb of Pamplona. Maryhelen had a little over two weeks to walk before she had to return to work. We went to Saint-Jean-Pied-de-Port, the starting point for many pilgrims on the Camino. I wanted her to see the city and to get to walk a bit of Napoleon's route. Luckily I had reserved two beds, because, as we learned at the Pilgrim's Office there, the lodging options in Saint-Jean-Pied-de-Port were full. We found our albergue and got into our room to find we were the only women assigned there. The rest of the occupants were men, and they had left us two top bunks. These were rickety metal bunks with no ladders, and we'd have to climb the frames. None of the men offered to trade, or offered help of any kind as we struggled into our bunks. We were across from each other, and I could tell by Maryhelen's face that this setting with all these men was not comfortable for her. Traveling two Caminos prior to this one, I had already adjusted to the coed housing, but the bunks were my sticking point.

Lights went out, and the guy below me kept getting texts. *Bing, bing, bing.* I looked over at Maryhelen and made the choking sign. She made a gesture like she wanted to lynch him. I burst into laughter and had to bury my head in my pillow so as not to disturb the twenty other inhabitants in the room, most of whom were already snoring.

The next morning we found coffee and churros while we waited for a ride from the baggage transport company, Express Bourricot. Piled in between backpacks in a mini-delivery van, we survived the ride up to the statue of Vierge d'Orisson, a statue of the Virgin Mary that watches over the valleys far below. From there, Maryhelen and I walked to Roncesvalles and checked in at the abbey albergue for the night. It, too, was overbooked, and we slept in the overflow trailer camp down by the creek, where Luke had played three years before. The next morning we caught the nine o'clock bus to Pamplona, and I thought of Linsee and how sad I had been to end my walk with her there.

* * *

Carol—who had nicknamed herself the Other Carol—had invited her friend Ann to come along. We were to meet Carol and Ann that afternoon at a hotel in the suburbs of Pamplona.

My online friend Karen came from Saint Paul, Minnesota. We'd gotten to know each other when I'd answered her questions on a Camino website forum. We corresponded over the summer and discovered we shared a similar itinerary and timeline. She was in Pamplona, where my group was meeting up. I invited her to join us, and within a few hours, she found us at our hotel. I was happy knowing that this fine person would be in our merry band of walkers.

That evening I asked everyone to come into my room for a chat before we set out. I felt it important they know about my disease and medications. I also wanted to apprise them of safety considerations I would be taking, as my slow movements made me vulnerable.

"I've had Parkinson's disease for about eight years. I take medications that help with my symptoms. If I'm ever hospitalized, please tell them about these medications and that I must have them on time. The strenuous walking I've been doing in preparation has helped mitigate some of the symptoms. Generally I have tremors in my right arm and sometimes in my left. I take slow steps, and my right arm does not move well, so sometimes I'll ask for help getting my pack on. Otherwise I don't expect any special treatment from any of you guys. Oh, and my emotions are affected by where I am in the medication cycle. So if I started crying for apparently no reason, you can ask me about my meds." I handed out cards with my medication and symptoms.

"I try to be extra aware of my surroundings. I feel, as a woman with a disability who moves slow and doesn't have a great handle on the language, I am vulnerable. I won't wear headphones to listen to music, so you are going to have to put up with my singing. When I withdraw cash from an ATM, I'll ask one of you to come help me. And I won't have more than one drink outside of the place we are staying and never accept a drink bought for me."

Heads nodded, and comments were made that these were good safeguards for all of us to consider.

My safety notes were done, but one final thought occurred to me to share. "Oh, and one of the reasons I'm going on this walk is to take some time to think about a brain surgery to help with the symptoms of my Parkinson's. Please keep me in your prayers as we're out walking."

After our fellow pilgrims left the room, Maryhelen hung her washed clothes around in hope they would dry by morning. The sight of socks and underwear hanging on lamps and trekking poles caught my funny bone. Laughing hard at ridiculous things is great therapy. I had finally settled down to sleep when Maryhelen got up to say something out the window to the merry partiers singing below. I stopped her, not wanting to cause trouble with the locals. At about four a.m., they stopped the serenades, only to be replaced by garbage trucks coming through the streets. I had pretty much given up on sleep and made up a song about the garbage trucks. To the tune of "The Lion Sleeps Tonight," I wrote:

In Pamplona, the city of Pamplona
The garbage trucks come at night
Oh oh oh
In Pamplona, the city of Pamplona
The garbage trucks come at night

A crash a bam a crash a bam
A crash a bam a crash a bam
A crash a bam a crash a bam
Away they go…

I entertained myself for another hour by adding verses to the song and giggling about how stupid they were. The streets outside quieted as the sun came up. I fell asleep. Then the vibration of my phone alarm told me it was time to get up. My laughter resumed as Maryhelen collected the clothes she had around the room. In need of morning coffee, she was not humored by my laughter or by the garbage truck song. We packed up our gear and scouted for coffee.

Joining up with the rest of the group on the street, we started walking west along the bronze Camino markers implanted in the sidewalk. Burlada was on the east of Pamplona, and we would have to pass through downtown and on to the other side before enjoying the countryside. A bus stopped beside us, and the Other Carol asked the driver if the bus was going into the city of Pamplona. The driver nodded, and we hopped on board. In the center of the city, we got off and changed to a bus we could ride to the outskirts of town. There we would meet the Camino, thus avoiding the miles of walking through the urban area of this large city.

My walking was slow. But, unlike the first Camino with Charlie, I walked more consistently. I didn't have to stop so often to adjust my pack or my shoes.

The Camino was crowded with so many more walkers than I'd experienced in my past walks. With a group of five wanting to stay together, we had to plan ahead and reserve lodging. At first I took this responsibility, but I felt a lot of stress in this role. Karen

I pose with my 2015 Camino walking partners in Alto del Perdón in Spain.

recognized this and eventually took over, with the assistance of the Other Carol, who had spent a lot of time with Rosetta Stone language lessons in preparation for the trip. I was relieved of that pressure.

We climbed up to the Alto del Perdón, where metal cutout pilgrims—from old times to more recent—became the backdrop for photographs. The notorious rocky backside took longer than it should have for me to get down. With lodging reserved ahead, we didn't worry about our pace.

Some days we walked as a group—Carol, Ann, Maryhelen, Karen, and I—chatting and singing together. Often Ann's long legs took her quite faster than I could manage to walk, even at my best, so I didn't get to know her well. I could always spot her in a crowd, though, with her green floppy hat and front and back arrangement of packs. Other days we walked individually or with *peregrinas* (female pilgrims) outside our original five.

One day we slipped up in our planning as a group. Without really deciding where we would spend the night, we started walking. Maryhelen and I got behind—actually, we were dawdling along. We stopped at a bar that made wonderful fresh-squeezed orange juice. At another spot we got some ice cream.

"That looks like Karen." Maryhelen pointed her trekking pole toward a pack-less woman running toward us.

"It is!" I responded.

She stopped up short.

"Karen, is something wrong? Where's your pack?"

"Nothing's wrong and, Carol, I know you aren't going to like this, but give me your pack."

"You're right. I don't like the thought of anyone else carrying my pack. So why do you want to?" Anger rose in me like a tide.

"We need to get you up to the village. There's a taxi coming for us. There are no beds here or for two more towns. The hospitalero called ahead to find us lodging and a cab to get us there. Hurry!"

I reluctantly let her have my pack, and this former Minnesota Vikings cheerleader hoisted it on one shoulder and ran back up the steep two-kilometer trail to the village.

"Wow. We better get going," said Maryhelen, and we both kicked in at the fastest pace I could go. When we got to the village, I was sweaty and tired and lay down on my back on the cool pavement in the shade of the village church. Soon the cab showed up and took the five of us women and a sole man to the last beds in Los Arcos. This gentleman had terrible blisters, and I volunteered Maryhelen to repair them. I made a running commentary of her actions, like I had done with Linsee the day I'd scrambled down the scree hill, which put me into hysterical laughter. I finally had to stick my head in my pillow because I couldn't get control, and she was trying to do an act of mercy for the poor guy.

*   *   *

On the trail, I'd often randomly break into song, and it didn't matter if I knew all the words—I would make them up as I went. One day, Maryhelen and I were walking along singing "The Happy Wanderer", "Val-de-ri, Val-de-ra, Val-de-ri, Val-de-ra-ha-ha-ha..."

We came around a corner and were met by a group of women standing by the side of the path singing, "Valderi, Valdera."

"Aha. You ladies know this song. It's your turn to sing the next verse."

"We don't know this song," one spoke up. "We have been walking in front of you, and that's all we could hear: 'Val-de-ra-ha-ha-ha,'" and the rest of the ladies joined in on the chorus. Maryhelen only had to look at me, and I burst into laughter, leaning over to hold my stomach, as the group of pilgrims marched ahead singing over and over, "Val-de-ri, Val-de-ra, Val-de-ri, Val-de-ra-ha-ha-ha..." I thought about catching up to them to teach them the verses, but thought better of the expense of energy it would take to do so. Besides, they were having too much fun imitating us by singing the chorus.

*   *   *

Frómista, Spain, is nearly the halfway point on the Camino from Saint-Jean-Pied-de-Port to Santiago. It was here that Maryhelen left us to return home to work.

She had made me laugh until my guts hurt, and now we wept in each other's arms. I watched her walk up the hill to the train station, where she stood for only a few minutes before boarding the train to Madrid. From there, Maryhelen would catch a flight home to Oregon.

Now I needed to catch up with Carol, Karen, and Ann. I shared a cab with two young people from Australia who were walking the Camino before moving to England, where they hoped to find some kind of work to sustain themselves until their next adventure. Because of my early morning taxi ride to Carrión de los Condes, I was one of the first in line for a bed at the Santa Maria albergue. The good sisters who extended their hospitality to pilgrims could not save beds for my three remaining travel companions, who were still out on the trail. I remembered this albergue was known for exceptional care of the pilgrims, as this was where Sister Lucia had treated my infected, blistered feet. There was a shared meal, a time for everyone there for the night to talk together and sing, a blessing, and exceptionally clean housing. I left my pack and went searching for a place for my friends to stay. The town was full! Finally I found a reasonably priced room with three beds on the fourth floor over a bar. I never ceased to be amazed at where one could lay their head.

Chapter 17

Divide and Conquer

THAT NIGHT I RECEIVED A MESSAGE FROM KAREN: *YOU SHOULD KNOW Ann and Carol are discussing their itinerary and going on by themselves.* The four of us met the next morning for a coffee, and Carol and Ann explained their plan. There were specific places Carol wanted to see. She felt she couldn't travel to my must-see locations and also get to hers in the time we had left. This saddened me, yet I'd known from the very beginning of planning that splitting up was an option. The four of us took a cab ride to Sahagún, where there were more options for transportation. Ann and Carol left by bus to Astorga, and Karen and I caught a train to León.

León, Spain, is a lovely big city. I was entranced by storefront displays of shoes and lovely autumn clothing as we walked through the center of the city. We found our hotel on a backstreet near the cathedral. Learning they had a laundry service, Karen and I decided to send all our clothes to get cleaned. We put on our pajamas, bagged everything else up, and handed them off to an employee with the expectation that our clothes would be returned to our room in a little over two hours. We napped and snacked and messaged our husbands as two hours went by.

At three hours, Karen called the desk. At four hours, she braved going out in her pajamas to talk with someone. We found them about six hours later, still damp, in a basket in a public area of the basement. Back upstairs, we hung our clothing around the room to dry. Dressed in the least wet items, still pondering the unsolved mystery of our wet clothes in the basement, we headed to people-watch in the nearby plaza. A late dinner from a Mexican place—the only restaurant still serving food—filled our bellies.

The next day Karen and I caught a city bus to the outskirts of León and found the Camino as it took off across the countryside. Walking along, we met up with a group of English-speaking pilgrims. The Canadians, Americans, and Australians had joined together serendipitously and were happily chatting as they walked along. We connected with Janet, a retired nurse who was interested in how I was doing with Parkinson's. Another Canadian woman, Mary Jo, was a retired second-grade teacher. That night we were split up by our separate lodging facilities. We said our goodbyes with hopes of seeing our new friends farther along the path.

Astorga, the chocolate capital of Spain, was our next night's stop. At the municipal albergue, Karen and I were assigned to a room with four bunks and a couple from Germany who was celebrating their fortieth wedding anniversary. They spoke absolutely no English to our absolutely no German. In the great way conversations can occur on the Camino, we asked if they wanted some privacy. What we thought they told us was something like, "Heck no, we've walked twenty-five kilometers and have been married a long time. We'll go to dinner and sleep well."

The next morning we joined a couple of different women from the English-speaking group on the early morning trek through the streets of Astorga and out into the countryside. We could barely see the yellow arrows painted on pavement, street signs, and curbs to guide us out of the city. I had walked this way on my previous Camino, and I remembered the places to turn.

We passed the modern church and pondered the tile artwork depicting a blindfolded woman holding out a chalice and host as if she was offering it to us to partake. A little farther there was a small roadside chapel and the well of living water in the middle of the church. The legend is that a drowning boy was saved here by his mother's pleas to Jesus. There was a tap on the outside of the church where we could fill our bottles with this living water.

There were many legends along this trail that I didn't necessarily believe or even understand. Yet they are part of the lore of the region and are meant to inspire or entertain.

The little group of women banded together, and we walked across the countryside and farmland into the rolling hills. As I had experienced with Linsee on the Chemin du Puy, pilgrims often bare their souls to complete strangers on the Camino. Knowing you'll probably never see the person again and that they don't know anyone you know makes it easier to share. I should not have been alarmed to hear the topics discussed. However, the stories told by those walking around me still broke my heart: abuse, alcoholism, divorce, addictions, infidelity, death of a child, illnesses, parents or siblings who had died too young. I only listened to the conversations, but all the events in these women's lives seemed to fall on my shoulders. Sadness weighed me down until I could bear no more.

Reaching out with my trekking poles helped my stride become longer. Walking quickly now, I moved ahead of the group. The trail left the roadside and entered an oak forest. A fence ran alongside the trail on the right and a highway on the left. Woven into the fence were crosses: big and little, of sticks and branches,

Passing pilgrims have woven crosses in the fence just before Rabanal del Camino, Spain.

cloth and yarn. There were so many crosses, there was no room to add new ones. As I passed those crosses, I mentally added the sorrows I'd heard that day to those burdens already hanging.

For some reason the crosses made me homesick, and I so wanted to hug Charlie and the boys. Missing my dad and my mom, I placed my sweet memories of childhood at the foot of the crosses. Picturing the faces of friends who were supportive in my fight with Parkinson's, I said their names, and in my mind I had a prayerful image of offering up any sorrows they might have and placing them on those crosses. Then the forest opened up, and the trail headed back toward the highway. At the feet of the remaining crosses, I placed the joys and celebrations of births and graduations and anniversaries of the past year. I placed my love for Charlie and Luke and Loren.

I finally walked into the tiny village of Rabanal. It seemed to be a gathering place for people walking the same time frame as me. Pilgrims I'd met along the way were there. They called out to greet me as I walked past their tables, already lined with empty beer glasses.

Physically the ability to move at a faster pace was exhilarating. The thought crossed my mind then: *Maybe I don't need DBS. If only I could move this well every day!* The day was one where many of my Parkinson's issues were mitigated by good rest, excellent food, and the marching west that I was doing each day. I felt revved up and running on all cylinders. It had been quite a long, gradual climb in the September heat, and I did it!

Checking into the albergue took just a few minutes. Karen, Janet, and I found beds near each other. The bunks were very close. There was a man in the bunk drawn up against mine, so I created a curtain with my sarong and sleep sheet for a bit of privacy.

The kind hospitalero took my laundry to be washed. Karen hung my clean clothes out on what seemed to be the community clothesline across the street and up a hill. Then I celebrated the great day by having beer and ice cream.

Lights went out at about nine p.m. I was in a dead sleep when suddenly I woke with a strange feeling that someone or something was very close to me. The man had rolled over, but so had I! Our faces were within inches of each other's, separated by only my sarong curtain. Then he snored! The exhalation of a stranger's snored-out breath so near me was unthinkable. Oh my, I had to move. I didn't know where to go. I grabbed my phone for a light, and I tiptoed out of the sleeping dorm. I was just a bit disgusted and wanted some privacy. The only private spot was a tiny bathroom hidden under some stairs behind the hospitalero's desk. So I hid out in the bathroom, sending email messages to Charlie and the boys.

Charlie and Luke, Do you remember our experience in Rabanal?
I am there tonight but in a different albergue at the beginning of the
town. Tomorrow we are climbing up to Cruz de Ferro. I didn't know
how to tell them about the sleeping situation, so I did not.

I heard shuffling around outside the bathroom door. I opened
it slowly to see people getting their backpacks ready. It was only
about four a.m.!

I whispered, "Why are you up?"

"Sunrise at the iron cross."

Returning from my refuge in the bathroom, I saw that the
man was still very close to my pillow and was still snoring.
The bunk above me was empty. Up the bunk I went. There were
only supports to climb, no ladder. Shimmying myself up there
took a lot of upper-arm strength and, I was certain, also made a
lot of noise. But I was in peace there and, as usual, fell asleep as
the morning was getting light.

The dorm emptied out before six a.m. They had good reasons...some because it was expected to be hot that day, and the
other pilgrims because they wanted to be at the Cruz de Ferro to
see the sunrise. Karen and I took our time, which was good because
I didn't want to see the snoring man again. Janet joined us too.

The rocky trail guided us steadily uphill through a forest and
then above the tree line. Black biting flies and the sweltering sun
contributed to the difficulty of this climb. I could spot Cruz de
Ferro above a small mountain of stones. As was the tradition,
we left the stones we had carried from home. I sat for a while
and pondered where the stones Charlie and I had left here in
2013 might be.

After a bit of quiet time at this marker, Janet, Karen, and I
discussed the downhill. It was extremely steep, and it would be
tough on us whether we walked down on the paved road or on

the path. Then I saw it! Tacked on a post was the phone number of Taxi Luis! I remembered him fondly as my favorite taxi driver from my 2012 Camino.

He arrived within just a few minutes of our call. Taxi Luis drove us down the narrow, steep, and winding road at breakneck speeds in his new Mercedes van.

Trying to speak to him in Spanish was a trial, as he corrected almost every word I said. I don't think he understood when I tried to ask if he remembered me. That was fine because this ride was just as adventurous as the one in 2012 had been. There were pilgrims on foot or on bikes around almost every sharp turn. Luis took his hands off the wheel to wave at the locals and gesture as he spoke. This terrified Karen and Janet in the second seat of the van. I held on tight, my mantra being the same as whenever I would ride a roller coaster: "Breathe, Carol, breathe. Breathe, Carol, breathe." And at the end of the chant: "Enjoy the adventure. Enjoy the adventure."

It is a two-day walk from Cruz de Ferro to Ponferrada—Taxi Luis drove us in less than thirty minutes. Karen and I found lodging in a lovely hostel; a room with two beds, starched white sheets, fluffy towels, soaps and shampoos, and *a blow dryer!* Janet had a room nearby. We met up to tour Ponferrada's well-preserved Templar castle and afterward enjoyed an Italian dinner. I was in Camino heaven that night.

Janet walked on by herself from Ponferrada. Karen and I wanted to visit O Cebreiro, the wonderful mountain village where Taxi Luis had dropped me off on the 2012 Camino. Lodging was full at this popular pilgrim/tourist spot, so we reserved a room in the modern village about five kilometers away on the steep highway below O Cebreiro. We had no idea of the fabulous food we were about to eat as we walked into the nearly empty dining room. An English-speaking couple seated at the table next to us suggested we order *caldo gallego*, a specialty from the Galician region, for which this restaurant was famous.

From there, the conversation continued. Another Carol had entered my life. The woman at the next table, Carol Elizabeth explained that her older sister, Laurie Dennett, was the author of *A Hug for the Apostle* and a well-known advocate for the Camino. Laurie had a house nearby and had started a tranquility garden with a labyrinth. Carol Elizabeth told us details of her sister's work on Camino projects. My head was full, and my tummy too! They offered us a ride up to O Cebreiro, and as we got out of the car, they told us to be sure to visit the *pallozas*.

I had noticed these thatch-roofed stone dwellings on my last visit, but I was not aware that the public could go inside. The Celtic people who'd settled here some fifteen hundred years ago had been resourceful and developed these dwellings to survive with their animals through the violent storms of winter. Inside, there was a giant fireplace that had seats in it. I saw a ladder to a loft that appeared to be a sleeping area. A large opening on the left led to a place for animals—I imagined that the animals both gave off and received warmth, but the smell must have been atrocious.

Back out in the bright sunlight, I saw the sturdy stone church across the plaza. This church is one of the oldest on the Camino Frances. I spent some time in the coolness of the side chapel, praying from the same pew where Charlie and I had sat in 2012. There in front of me was a reliquary housing the altar linens and chalice from a Eucharistic miracle. I felt a strong spiritual presence in this place.

At four a.m.—why was it always four a.m.?—the next day, I said goodbye to Karen. I was so appreciative of her companionship, and it brought tears to my eyes to part with her. She was on her way to Sarria to walk the final hundred kilometers to Santiago and receive her Compostela, the certificate of completion of the Camino de Santiago. Receiving a second certificate was not important to me, and the walking was fatiguing me. I waited for the bus in the cold, dark drizzle. It arrived full of sleeping passengers. I climbed into one of the few open seats and was on my way to Santiago to decide what was next.

The bus arrived in Santiago just after daybreak. I walked downhill from the bus station and found my hotel, about fifteen minutes from the Cathedral of Santiago de Compostela. The hotel had my room ready and was willing to let me in! After getting cleaned up and having a wonderful buffet breakfast at the hotel, I decided to attend the noon pilgrims' Mass at the Cathedral. Walking from my hotel to the cathedral, I wished I had a companion. For a city, this street was eerily void of cars and people.

There were apartments behind those ancient doors that lined the streets. From somewhere up above came the most marvelous smells of breakfast being prepared. *Do I hear a baby giggling? That is certainly the fresh odor of fabric softener. I hear some food sizzling in a pan.* These sounds and smells of home life made me terribly homesick.

I came to a busy street crossing. Waiting for the traffic light to change, I glanced ahead to assure myself this was the same way I had walked to the hotel earlier that morning. There were a few steps to go down and a very slight turn to the right before continuing on the empty street. Carefully stepping down the stairs, I turned onto the street that led directly to the cathedral. There was a woman standing there. *Where did this woman come from? She wasn't there a few seconds ago.* She looked tired and dazed as she glanced between her map and the name of the street posted high on the wall.

The *Botafumeiro* is launched during the pilgrim's Mass. (Photo credit: Karen Lewis)

"Are you lost?" I asked, taking for granted she probably spoke English.

"Yes. Which way is the cathedral?"

"I'm going that way. Come walk with me."

She introduced herself as Carol (yes, another Carol). Carol was from Libya and had left Geneva at four a.m., the same time I'd parted with Karen that morning. Between a visit with her mother and a trip for business, she was suddenly compelled to go to Santiago, quite a distance out of her way. She had booked herself a flight into Santiago for a one-day pilgrimage and would be leaving early the next morning. She explained she was a member of the Catholic Oriental Church, an Eastern or Byzantine congregation in full communion with the Roman Catholic Church.

I walked stiffly and slowly, using my trekking poles. Carol matched my slow pace without comment. We talked about Parkinson's disease and the possibility of future treatment with DBS. She was fascinated by my explanation of the technology.

We arrived at the large square in front of the cathedral. Even though it was her first time in Santiago, Carol appeared to know how to get everywhere, except to the cathedral itself. She guided me directly to the pilgrims' entrance to the cathedral, where we saw a huge line of people waiting to get in. Instead of going to the end of the line, she led me right up to the door and inside. None of the people who'd been waiting even looked at us. The security guards at the door made no comments, as if they hadn't seen us. I folded up my trekking poles, and she took my hand. Without hesitation to even look around, she led me to seats facing the altar in a section directly behind some diplomats. We sat through a beautiful Mass, and at the end of the Mass—probably in honor of the diplomats—the *Botafumeiro* flew.

The Botafumeiro is a giant thurible, a sacramental object of the Catholic Church, where incense is burned. It takes eight trained men holding the thick hemp rope to set it in motion. The Botafumeiro picks up speed as it swings like a pendulum above the pews in the church. The smoke rises, carrying the prayers of the congregation to heaven. It is a highlight of the pilgrimage.

As the Botafumeiro completed its overhead journey, Carol took my hand and guided me around the church, again with confidence as if she had been there before. She stopped at the sign designating the beginning of the line to see the statue of Saint James. In spite of crowds of people in the church, there was no line! We climbed the stairs and hugged the big bronze statue from the back.

I asked her, "What's next for you?"

"I am going up on the tour of the roof of the cathedral and then to the museum."

"I'm so thankful I met you, and I really appreciate you helping me around the cathedral."

She took a selfie of us. We hugged goodbye, and I lost sight of her in the throngs of people leaving from the Mass. I went outside and sat again in the plaza in front of the cathedral. Watching pilgrims taking their last steps on the Camino, I thought about how people come into our lives for a reason. Then I really started to wonder about her. *Was this just a coincidental meeting, or was it part of a divine plan?*

I was in Santiago de Compostela by myself now, wondering what to do for the week before my flight home. I called Tracy Saunders, owner of the Little Fox House in A Coruña, a retreat for pilgrims who need some transition before returning home. Tracy was going away, I learned during our conversation, and the Little Fox House was in the care of Gwen Van Velsor, a gourmet cook. There was space for me, so I booked a room starting the next night. Tracy had me go to her website for directions. If I was familiar with the area, the walking directions might have made sense. There was no figuring it out for me. With no paper handy, I wrote down the address on my hand, hoping someone I would meet could help.

The next day was to be my travel day. I awoke before the alarm from a dream about chasing pigs off Maryhelen's porch.

My hometown newspaper *The Hermiston Herald,* had an article about my Camino walks.

The thought of that made me laugh as hard as Maryhelen often did! After a luxurious hot shower (careful to not wash off the address written on my hand), I checked with the hotel desk to see if there was an availability for the next weekend, when I'd be on my way back to the airport and Oregon. They reserved the same room for me! I taxied to the bus station for transportation to my next stop in Muxia—then, as best I could tell from my research, I would still need to walk eighteen kilometers to Carantoña. The information office at the bus depot was open at that early hour. I asked there and found an afternoon bus that would drop me in Vimianzo, closer to the exact location I needed. Now I had a whole morning to waste away. I went to a bar where I was served a café con leche grande, a small honey-covered croissant, and a shot of OJ. It cost one euro!

I walked downhill about four blocks from the bus station to a point where I could see pilgrims scurrying along the Camino path to make the noon Mass. I posted myself in a spot on the street above. Leaning on a rail, I watched, and at ten thirty I spotted the Other Carol and Ann walking a fast pace to the cathedral. The expression on Carol's face when she heard her name called from above was priceless. She looked all around as I moved toward her. We met at the intersection, where we hugged and had a quick exchange of greetings and well wishes. We promised to meet up on Friday in Santiago.

I walked slowly up the hill and back to the bus station, where I positioned myself on a hard bench for a two-hour wait. My bus pulled in just on time. I showed the bus driver the address written on my hand, and he nodded. I took the front seat so I could watch for my stop. Local people got on and off the bus in villages and along the road. I was the only pilgrim. When the final rider disembarked, the bus driver looked at me, put his hand on the radio, cranked up the music, nodded, and put his foot to the pedal. I now knew what Karen and Janet had felt like in the back of Taxi Luis's van. There was nothing to do but go with it. I convinced myself I would be fine and sang along with American tunes from the seventies and eighties. Like Taxi Luis, this guy had driven his route a million times. I was safe.

Arriving in the town, he announced its name. I didn't recognize it, but it had to be Vimianzo. He pulled my pack from underneath the bus and I hoisted it to my back. The waving bus driver hopped back in his seat and drove down the street, around the corner, and back the way we'd come. I had no idea which way to start walking. Two women were lounging in a little park near the bus stop. I showed them the address on my hand. Both shook their heads and gestured with four hand movements away from their bodies. One gestured like she was holding a steering wheel.

"Oh. Taxi?" I said.

"Yes." They nodded. I saw the word *taxi* painted on the road near the bus stop, but no taxis were parked there. Across the street a grandmotherly woman was standing in her doorstep. She greeted a young boy with a hug and a kiss and shooed him inside. Then she started waving to get my attention. She gestured *walk* with her fingers and pointed one way, and then another. Walking down the street in the direction she indicated, I looked back to see her nodding approval. I turned right, looked back, and she was still nodding. Her motions led me into a bar full of men! Putting this all together, I realized it was siesta time. The grandma had been waiting for her grandson to come home. The men were in the bar for their afternoon break, and the taxi driver was in there somewhere too. I felt the eyes of the men on me as they looked me up and down, settling on my boots.

Calling, "Taxi? Taxi?" I was met with head shakes. I started to walk out, but the bartender had heard me and came around from another room. In a mix of Spanish and English, he told me to go back to the bus stop and a taxi would soon be there.

"Can I call one to come now?" I asked.

"No. Go wait." He held the door open for me.

Grateful for confirmed transportation, I left the bar, and as I turned the corner, the grandmother was still there, watching for me. When I nodded my head, she put on a great smile and clapped her hands. The taxi soon arrived. I used my broken Spanish to ask him if he knew the address on my hand. The taxi driver looked at me and responded in perfect British English, "Yes, that is the house of Tracy." He then drove me four kilometers—the four hand movements of the women in the park, I realized—to the Little Fox House.

There were four women staying at this house. I was over twenty years older than the eldest, almost a generation between us. Their life experiences were far different from mine. Each had had several different careers. After growing up working in my parents' drive-in restaurant, I'd had the same employer for the next thirty-one years of my life. Each woman was a wanderer, and I loved listening to stories about their life journeys. Alise was from Latvia, the only one of the group not having roots in the Pacific Northwest of the United States. Gwen was originally from Portland, Oregon. The two others were from Bend, Oregon, and Seattle, Washington. After a dinner prepared by Gwen, we drank wine and played a game called Questions until we could not keep our heads off the table.

The days were comfortably quiet. It had been a long time since I could just sit with no place to go and nothing to do. Alise, Gwen, and I ventured out one day on a hike to a lighthouse. Gwen disciplined herself to write every day. Her travel memoir, *Follow that Arrow: Notes on Getting Here from There*, would come out in 2016. On Alise's final day at the Little Fox House, we walked with her on a country path to a neighboring village. She bought us coffee, and we sat around the table talking for a long time, no one wanting to say goodbye. When I hugged her, I held her extra long and whispered, "If you come to Oregon, I will take you on the tour of your life!"

From the Little Fox House, I visited Finisterre and Muxia and ran into the Other Carol and Ann on the return bus to Santiago. On our last night in Santiago, Carol, Ann, and I found Karen and joined together for a farewell dinner. I knew I'd see—or at least hear from—these women again.

My train to Madrid was scheduled predawn, so I requested a taxi to the station. As I got on the train with the other pilgrims, I couldn't find my seat. The conductor directed me to first class. I'd mistakenly bought a first-class train ticket to Madrid, so I basked in the luxury. In Madrid I booked myself into a business-class hotel and ordered room service. The hotel shuttle delivered me to the airport the next morning. From there I made it home without any significant issues. Those twelve hours in the air seemed like forever.

Charlie and Luke met me at the Portland airport with smiles and flowers, and I hugged them like I would never let them go.

I marveled that I'd completed this trip without any major difficulties. My flights, lodging arrangements, and travel decisions all went as planned. I felt accomplished. I had headlined this trip as a decision-making time, and my decision was to go ahead with deep brain stimulation surgery, should I be eligible. The trip confirmed I was physically fit enough to endure the surgery and I had the desire to maintain that level of fitness.

Chapter 18

Medical Treatments on the Horizon

THE POSITIVE EFFECTS OF TRAVEL AND THE CONSTANT MOVEMENT OF walking on the Camino could not be replicated at home. My Parkinson's medication began wearing off each time before I was scheduled to take the next dose. Dr. Hiller prescribed entacapone with hope that it would extend each dose of Sinemet. It did nothing but turn my sweat, urine, and tears yellow and cause red marks on my arms. She added amantadine to my medication regimen, and it made my legs swell and lacy patterns form on my skin.

The November appointment with Dr. Hiller came up on the calendar. Charlie and I drove to Portland and parked in the all-too-familiar OHSU underground lot. After Dr. Hiller's check on my motor skills and the various questions that were part of the semiannual evaluation, I brought up the issues I was having with the medications.

She listened carefully and said, "It's time to consider another treatment, deep brain stimulation."

Yes! I almost yelled it. Charlie was up out of his seat.

She continued, "It's better to get the DBS surgery done sooner than later."

"By *later*, what do you mean, doctor?"

"Two or three years down the road," she said as she typed notes into her computer.

"And sooner?"

"Within three months."

"So, you're saying I need this surgery done *now*?"

"Yes, you'll have better results if you do it now." She spun her computer chair around and looked directly in my eyes. "The overall process takes about six months. It begins with you undergoing speech, physical therapy, neuropsychological, and neurological evaluations. You'll have a complete medical examination. These evaluations determine if you're eligible for the surgery and also serve as a baseline to measure results.

"In the first stage, the neurosurgeon will place two probes in a predetermined spot in your brain and run wires to the back of your head and down your neck under the skin. This surgery will have you in the hospital just one to two days. The neurostimulator will be placed in your chest, below your collarbone, and the wires will be connected in an outpatient procedure a few days later.

"When you're recovered from the procedures, about a month later, you'll return to have the power pack activated and the system tuned to its best potential. The tuning usually takes three visits about a month apart. When this is completed, we don't need to tune you up so often."

She warned me, "The surgeon will promise you the moon. Don't go into the surgery expecting a cure. You will experience improvement—we just don't know what that will be like for you. This is brain surgery, and it's not without possible dangers." She then read me the list of side effects and possible complications.

I looked her right back in the eye and said, "Let's do this thing. I am not afraid!" I looked at Charlie in the chair next to me. He was nodding.

"Why don't you two think about this more and talk it over. Do more research and talk with other patients who have the DBS."

Charlie and I talked more during our three-hour drive back to Hermiston. We realized that I was going on Medicare in February. I sent an email about it to my doctor and heard back immediately that it might be in our best interest to wait until then.

As that week after my appointment progressed, I felt worse. The dyskinesia was picking up, especially in the evening. I had periods of significant stuttering and word-finding issues. As a speech pathologist, I found these speech and language difficulties quite concerning. Friday rolled around, and I felt so uncomfortable inside my body that I knew *now* really was better than *later*. I called my current insurance and talked to one of their advisors, who explained more about the evaluations I would undergo and what my current policy would do for me. I was impressed with the agent's knowledge about the procedure.

"It would be good to get going with some of the preliminaries, and Medicare would pick up when you become eligible."

I messaged Dr. Hiller that I was ready. I got a message from the neurology rehab department at about four p.m. that same afternoon. Dr. Hiller called at five to ensure I knew she'd ordered the tests. I expected nothing more as we headed into the weekend. Sunday morning my phone was turned off. When I turned it on, there was a message from OHSU in regards to scheduling. Sunday evening at eight thirty, there was another message from Dr. Hiller asking if the schedulers had called. *Do these people ever take time off?* I wondered.

Within a week I was scheduled for all the evaluations and procedures.

                                    * * *

When I announced to friends and family about the possibility
of DBS surgery occurring in the near future, they had a lot of
questions as to my level of fear. It was similar to the "You look
so good" comments. People didn't know what to say.

"Aren't you afraid to have brain surgery?" was the most common question.

"Actually, no. I'm more afraid of the alternative. I have nothing to lose here." I really didn't. I had a better chance of feeling
better with the surgery than relying solely on medication for
treatment.

I made it a goal to hold back sarcasm with anyone who questioned my personal medical decisions. *Be nice. Be nice*, I repeated
to myself. There were more comments of "how scary" than I could
count. I could not be more excited about this procedure! The idea
of improving my mobility was so awesome! My fascination with
all things medical helped me seek knowledge and understanding.

Of course, the what-ifs did enter my mind. *What if the desired results don't happen? What if there's an infection? What if the
surgeon slips and botches it up? What if I come out of this with a
brain injury? What if I die on the operating table?* I allowed myself
a short period of time to think about these what-ifs. I decided to
go for it, to trust the scientific discovery God had given Dr. Hiller,
the researchers, Dr. Burchiel the neurosurgeon, and his surgical
team. I convinced myself that, even if something went wrong,
the doctors would learn from it, and it could turn out to be positive for some patient in the future. In my decision I committed
to being positive, exuding a peaceful attitude, and developing a
sense of humor about the entire process.

* * *

There was a nice paved walking trail near my house. I chose this for exercise over the strenuous trails of the butte or the lengthy river hike. One afternoon while sauntering along the trail, I told that day's walking buddy all about my upcoming DBS procedure. Her response was, "Cool!" At that very moment I wanted to clone her. She had it right. I needed people to acknowledge, comment, agree with, and encourage me. But *not* to feed the fears.

* * *

The travel day to Portland for the first of the evaluations started out bumpy. It seemed as if I had just fallen asleep when I heard, "Carol, we overslept." It was six a.m. Charlie and I had planned to be on the road by then. The clothes and other items I needed for my appointments were scattered around the bedroom where I'd left them the night before. Charlie's clothes needed to be packed, and he hadn't even started on that project. The horses and dogs needed to be fed. My husband, who was meticulous about his hygiene, would not leave the house until he had brushed and flossed his teeth. I was really ready to scream at him, but it would take too much time to be in a fight. We had three hours, twenty-two minutes to get to my appointment in Portland. Generally, it took us three hours to get to the outskirts of Portland. I hated to be late!

Today there was an additional factor causing me stress. I had been told not to take my medications for twelve hours before the evaluations, and I felt anxious over how my body would react without medication. Our big Ford F-350, Gertrude, could really move fast when it had to—and with the driver's cooperation.

I urged Charlie to put the pedal to the metal, but he kept driving right at the speed limit. *Can I commence screaming now?*

No matter the weather or the season, it's always a beautiful drive west through the Columbia River Gorge and into Portland. This time I ignored the scenery outside the truck window and worried. We made it across the I-5 bridge in downtown Portland with a perfectly negotiated turn toward Lake Oswego, then another turn back toward the South Waterfront and the OHSU Center for Health and Healing.

All my life, I'd felt like I needed to control time. When I couldn't control it, it was like being on the back of the tandem bike with my anxiety starting to rise. Charlie dropped me off at the door and maneuvered the big pickup down into the crowded parking garage. He thought to leave it to the valet parking to find its space for the day.

I used my trekking poles to get me into the building quickly. A placard on the wall by the elevator read *First Floor Speech Therapy.* As I walked in, I realized my mistake. This was the wrong speech therapy. The office I stood in was rehabilitation therapy, and I was supposed to be at the Northwest Clinic for Voice and Swallowing. There was a big difference between the rehab therapists and the voice evaluation specialists.

I was redirected back to the elevator and to the third floor. The receptionist greeted me by saying, "Did you bring your paperwork along?"

I wanted to say, "If I had been sent paperwork, I would have had it done."

After all the years in working in special education, I had developed a fetish with perfect paperwork. Instead I stuck with my promise to be positive and use humor, so I responded with a polite, "No. I didn't receive any paperwork."

She handed me a pen, a clipboard, and a pile of papers to fill out. *Why am I here? How many surgeries have I had? Do I smoke? Drink? Drool? Am I a professional singer?* The questions seemed endless and not always appropriate to my situation.

Before I could get to the last page, the evaluator—a speech-language pathologist—called me, and I followed her into a small, sterile-looking room. She directed me to sit in one of those funky ear, nose, and throat doctor's examination chairs. It looked like a fancy upright dental chair.

She said, "Oh, I see you brought paperwork." After briefly paging through it, she continued. "You're already a patient here at the hospital. We know all of this. Just fill out the last page." Before I could laugh at the irony, she continued, "We don't have time to do this now, so you can do it when we're done with the evaluation."

She put a microphone up to my face and kept the distance from my mouth consistent by an unappealing metal space bar. An intern came to observe. *An intern.* In my former professional life, I had courted many speech pathology interns or intern wannabes while trying to recruit individuals to the profession to serve our rural schools. It was amazing how quickly I could slip back into that mode.

"Where are you from?" I asked. "Where did you go to school? What's your area of specialty? Do they pay you good here? Wanna come out to visit eastern Oregon? I'll show you around, buy you lunch, and offer you a job." I was on a roll. Charlie had made it inside and was directed to this examination room just in time to hear the last of my drilling this poor intern.

The evaluation room was now full of speech pathologists. Both the intern and the evaluator expressed their delight that one of Oregon's former premier speech pathologist couples was in their exam room. I hoped to get special treatment and maybe a Tootsie Pop at the end of the evaluation, but the mood of the room returned to business.

Then to the voice evaluation. I was surprised to see that the evaluation itself remained the same as it had been from the beginning of speech pathology. Only the tools of measurement had changed.

The examiner passed me a piece of paper. "Read the Rainbow Passage," she said as she pointed to a paragraph on the paper. The Rainbow Passage was commonly used with adults during evaluations of vocal quality, rate of speech, and articulation of speech sounds. At one time in my university training, I had used it so much, I had it memorized.

"Give us a one-minute narrative about your hometown."

"I was born in Walla Walla, Washington, on February 14..."

"How long can you say ahhhh?" the examiner requested.

"Ahhhhh..." I responded, holding the sound for several seconds.

"Let's hear your range...pitch from low to high, high to low."

Her laptop spewed out charts and graphs.

"What?" I asked. "No oral exam? No hearing evaluation?" These were components we always completed in school-aged evaluations.

"No," came the response. "This is the voice lab. We can schedule those evaluations through other specialists if you'd like to have them done."

My results would be shared with the entire multidisciplinary team of evaluators to determine my eligibility for the DBS procedure. I was reminded the test results would also be used as a baseline to measure changes resulting from the surgery.

As I returned to the waiting room to finish the last page of the paperwork, I heard the intern say to someone, "You know that couple that just left? They're both speech-language pathologists. Aren't they cute?"

I couldn't help but smile.

I'd survived the voice evaluation and now was on to examination number two. It was a physical therapy evaluation, and it was challenging. First there was an interview about my activity. The rest included observations of this Parkinson's patient off medication behavior. I started to feel the effects of having had no medication for twelve hours.

"Cross your arms and stand up. Stand with your feet together, eyes open. Now eyes closed. Do it again standing on a cushion. Do it again standing on a slant board. Walk the line as fast as you can. Now walk slow. Walk at your normal rate and turn your head right. Now left. Walk while counting backward from one hundred by threes."

"One hundred, ninety-seven..." I started.

"Turn around as fast as you can. Now turn the other direction. Stand strong. Don't let me push you over from the front, from the back, from the side, now the other side. Sit down. Let me jerk your arm this way and that. Now the other arm. Now your feet. Okay." The physical therapist stopped to clean her hands with alcohol wipes. "Now touch your finger to your nose, then my finger. Now the other side. Touch your thumb and pointer together as fast as you can. Other hand. Flop your hand on your lap like a fish out of water. Now the other hand. Let me see how flexible your neck is." She manipulated my neck in all possible directions. "Okay, we're done. At this point I would usually talk to you about exercise, but you're doing everything I would recommend already. That's why you are doing so well with your symptoms."

"Thanks."

"Come back tomorrow on your medication. After that evaluation, we'll summarize the results for you."

I was exhausted as we left the physical therapy department and entered the huge lobby near the elevator banks. We found some unoccupied chairs there. Charlie got me a cookie and some coffee at the nearby coffee stand. Just as he sat down next to me, he popped right back up.

"There's Dr. Hiller." He walked toward her as she came around the corner from the elevator.

She was wearing a baseball cap! I loved that she was wearing a baseball cap! I got up without my trekking poles and made it over to where they stood chatting. The hat added a very human side to the businesslike white coat I usually saw in the exam room. We exchanged smiles and hugs, and she had to be on her way. I finished my treat, and Charlie and I went on to our friend's house where we would stay the night.

In the morning I took my medications as usual. I started off at the physical therapy department to repeat the previous day's evaluations *on* medication. It was the same silly directions. The largest difference I noted was that my pain level was diminished. The lead physical therapist and intern astutely noted there were marked differences in my movement patterns. I learned that the movement and motor skills that responded to medication, as measured by the off-medication and on-medication observations, were the areas that could potentially be improved by the DBS surgery.

After a short break for another cookie and coffee, I proceeded up the elevator to the neurology department for my neuropsychology evaluation. Charlie parked himself in the waiting room.

The neuropsychological evaluation was all verbal and pen on paper. It was held in a regular department examination room, to which they had added a hospital bed tray for a desk. I was just happy to not have to answer on a computer screen.

If there was a stereotype for a psychiatrist, this gentleman fit it. Thin face, glasses, receding hairline, white shirt, cardigan sweater, narrow tie with a tie clip. He addressed me in a very formal manner. The examiner demonstrated his professionalism by following testing protocol exactly as he should. I commented that I was familiar with these types of evaluation procedures, and I wondered how it was for him that I cared so much about his technical skills. Having spent my career administering standardized measurements, I understood what he needed to do to be sure the results were valid.

By the end of this examination, I was again physically and mentally drained. But the day was not over yet. We were to meet Dr. Burchiel.

Charlie and I settled into the exam room. Seeing the red-script embroidery on the doctor's white lab coat helped me get the pronunciation of his name correct. The stern, deep-set eyes and gray goatee gave him the appearance of a scientist. Dr. Burchiel carried himself in a very confident manner. He spoke to us about his background, the procedure in general, and his sincere efforts to assure patient comfort before, during, and after the surgery. He brought out example models of the probes, the wires, and the neurostimulator that would be placed in my body so I could hold them and feel their weight and flexibility.

After answering all our questions, he said, "Your evaluation results will be discussed amongst the team. I'll be speaking with Dr. Hiller within the next week, and the decision will be made about your candidacy for the surgery and the exact location in your brain where we want to place the probes."

In my research about the DBS procedure, I had learned that my surgeon, Dr. Kim Burchiel, was among the nation's leading surgeons for this procedure. He'd studied under the French neurologist and researcher Dr. Alim-Louis Benabid, who had developed the technique. Dr. Burchiel became the first neurosurgeon in the United States to use DBS to treat a Parkinson's patient. Since then, Dr. Burchiel had performed DBS more than a thousand times. This was a reassuring number.

I was most pleased that Dr. Burchiel had pioneered asleep DBS and that it would be performed on me. I had read about the asleep vs. awake procedure and spoken with patients who had experienced each. Those who had been awakened—brought out of anesthesia for a short time—during the surgery had been asked to demonstrate different movements. This helped the surgeon determine the most effective placement of the lead—the electrode inserted into the brain. After doing many awake surgeries, Dr. Burchiel had discovered there were two locations in the brain that responded to the placement. From that time on, they had used high-resolution scans taken a few weeks before the surgery and live pictures from the CAT scan during surgery to place the lead with exceptional precision. In his opinion there was no need to bring the patient to consciousness and then return them to the anesthetized state. "Just as Dr. Hiller had reported, Dr. Burchiel's current methodology was to place two leads into the brain during the first surgery, which usually took under three hours. The patient was released from the hospital after a night of observation and returned a few days later for a pacemaker-sized device called the neurostimulator to be placed in the chest, most often on the left side and beneath the collarbone.

As I looked further into this surgeon's work, I found a valuable resource called the Parkinson's Disease and Movement Disorders Program on the OHSU website. The webpage reported, "What our results say is that asleep DBS is as safe as awake, and has fewer complications—and the accuracy of the electrode placement is the best ever reported," which furthered my confidence that I was at the right place for my surgery.

This webpage also noted that Dr. Burchiel especially enjoyed guiding patients through the DBS process: "In the nearly twenty-five years since I first started performing DBS surgeries for patients with Parkinson's or essential tremor, I've seen the remarkable difference that it can make in patients' lives."

Dr. Burchiel had won global recognition for his work. He and his colleagues had conducted extensive research on DBS, publishing at least fifty articles in periodicals such as the *Journal of Neurology*. The list of his honors was extensive. I felt secure that the surgeon in charge of my case was held in high regard by the medical community.

Chapter 19

Deep Thoughts for
the In-Between Times

Everyone thought I had an awesome attitude. I appeared positive about everything in my life. People told me I "inspired" them. But, darn, I had some very dark moments. I felt like my need to spread a message of hope should outshine any darkness. Sadly, I was not always hope-filled.

One day when I was really down, I wrote a blog post about exactly how I felt:

> It's getting dark. The moments I am in light are slipping away. Daylight all around me, I wake up in darkness and go to sleep in darkness. The disease that entered my body eight, nine, ten, twelve years ago... It affects how I respond to the darkness around me. And it invades my being and dims the light within. At times I am trapped, unable to respond to the darkness, to create light in my own heart. I want to take action. The body does not move. I want to fully partake in the communion of my church, but I struggle to reach the altar rail. I want to play music, sing praises, acclaim the power of God within me. I cannot strum, I cannot sing, I have no voice. My affect is flat.

Pain has me spiraling down. Continuous pain. My body does not sit still even for the pain. I weave and move and shake. Tears stream down my cheeks, and I don't know why. I cannot control them. Reaching out for comfort, I travel paths beaten down by lack of healing and continued heartbreak. My paths take me to the refrigerator, the liquor closet, the internet, to past relationships with family, friends, and lovers of forty years ago...to memories of places where my strength and health abided...where I ran, and played, and rode, and threw, and hit, and caught, and raced. I can't do these things anymore. Terrible darkness. You have me.

Locked down in my bed by depression and apathy, I remembered a lesson I had learned once long ago, before the disease.

Charlie and I had taken eleven-year-old Loren and four-year-old Luke on a bicycling adventure on the Hiawatha Trail in northern Idaho. This fifteen-mile trail had been reclaimed from the rail bed of the Hiawatha, a passenger train that traveled from the Pacific Northwest to the Midwest in the time before the automobile ruled. I had actually ridden the Hiawatha train with my dad on a visit to family in Iowa when I was a little girl. I had vivid memories of that train ride and still told stories of how I had ordered my eggs sunny-side up and over easy in the dining car and how we sat on the track for hours after a collision with a farm implement.

Charlie, the kids, and I slept in our camper the night before the bike ride and then drove into the forest to find the trailhead. Loren was old enough to ride his bike. For Luke we rented a tagalong that attached to Charlie's bike frame. Luke had handlebars, a seat, and pedals all his own. We knew we needed lights, as the ride started at a very long tunnel. However, we were not prepared for what was ahead.

We hadn't thought of needing taillights, and we had only two headlights, which were mounted on Charlie's and Loren's bikes. When we entered the tunnel, it was pitch black. I followed the sliver of light in front of Loren as best as I could. My equilibrium was messed up. I couldn't keep the bike going straight, and I even rode it into the gutter. I got soaked by unseen waterfalls. Frightened, I knew I needed to keep going or I would lose the sliver of light that was Loren. But I wanted to stop and get off my bike. I was ready to seek refuge in the gutter and shiver in the dripping water.

Then I saw it. A tiny light. I was so glad. I knew that if I kept my eye on this one light, it would lead me out of this darkness.

Hmm. I correlated this bike ride with the darkness of the past few weeks. I'd gotten sucked into the darkness. *I was not prepared!* The dark days, the darkness of our world, the dark sadness of those around me, my own darkness pulled me down…down to the gutter of that dark, seemingly endless tunnel.

But a light came into the darkness. It was a tiny light, but it grew. I saw it over a manger, guiding peoples of all nations, faiths, beliefs, and orientations. Travelers throughout the ages have followed the light. And it reminded me of the tiny light I had to move toward. My inner light of Christ and the Holy Spirit, placed there by the Father. I had forgotten, from lack of practice, how to reach for the Light.

I added the tunnel story to the blog post, and then expanded it with:

> To prepare oneself, to always be ready, to go into automatic mode when the situation arises. Practice. When you practice that riff of the guitar over and over a million times, then when you are on stage and excited and nervous, you can play

it. When you practice catching the throw into home, then when the runner is coming in ready to slide and take you out, you can catch it and tag her. When you practice prayers and praying and meditating, then when you need to pray, you know how. When you practice healthy eating habits and you are tempted by sodas and cookies and candy and cake, they don't taste good to you anymore. When you practice patterns of movement and strengthen your body, you will get up from your fall when no one else is there to help you. When you keep your mind alert, you will plan appropriately for the event and see the obstacles you need to avoid. These are my headlights (and of course taillights) to keep me prepared for the next dark tunnel.

Charlie, the boys, and I had come out of the long tunnel into the blazing sunlight of a September afternoon. We were blinded by the brilliance we saw and had to collect ourselves and recall what we had just experienced before we could ride on down the trail. Like I was doing as I wrote my blog—and later, this memoir—in real life. I had been in a place of suffering from my disease, which I had allowed to take me to a dark place.

Thinking back on that blog post later, I paused to recollect: I'd come out of that darkness by picking up the guitar; remembering the outs I had tagged at home and the basketball game where I hit four three-pointers in a row; reaching for carrots and water instead of pop or candy; receiving the sacraments of my church and reciting the ancient prayers; going to work out; riding my bike; walking; connecting with friends…a whole chain of lights. Next time the darkness hit, I would be ready to move.

At church one Sunday, the reading from the Gospel of Luke had Jesus convincing some fishermen to take him on their boat just a little way from shore. From that short distance offshore, the mob of people who'd been following Him could hear Him as His voice was carried across the water. While on the boat, He noticed the empty nets. (This passage drips with symbolism.) The fishermen who transported Him were weary from fishing for hours. They had caught nothing at all. Jesus had them take their boats out a little farther and then go deep with their nets. They brought in so many fish that their boat almost sank, and they called to a nearby boat to come and get some fish too. These fishermen who were all told to "go deep" became fishers of men: Jesus's apostles.

Another day at church, I felt very emotional. I was hyper-aware of people around me. My medication was wearing off, and the dyskinesia started in. My torso weaved in and out like I was grooving to music, but there was no music playing during Father Maxwell's homily. I had never been this bad in public. A few tears worked their way out of my eyes as I tried to hold them back, and then they just kept on coming.

I thought about going deep. *What does that really mean?* In football it's sprinting as hard as you can down the field, giving it your all, and then receiving the pass. For the soon-to-be fishers of men, it had meant trusting someone they hardly knew. Even though they were weary and downhearted from unsuccessfully fishing all night, they were willing to take this stranger's word that they would find fish if they cast their nets again, if they went deep. Their tired and empty souls were replenished. *Ahh, I am starting to get it.*

My home church is Our Lady of Angels in Hermiston, Oregon. (Photo credit: Father Daniel Maxwell)

I looked at the people sitting around me and saw so many instances of those who had cast their nets into the deep: people who had invested in relationships, who had raised their families, who had taken the risks, who had worked extra hard and had received. Kristi, in front and to the right of me, lovingly rubbed the back of her adult daughter Jillian, who experienced a disability. This mom had gone deep for her girl on so many levels, beginning at a very young age. She had been parenting this child for over twenty-five years. She was not tired, at least not in a way that showed when she rubbed her daughter's back with such calming love. It touched me.

The couple next to me, Dale and Shannon, had been married many years and had kids the same ages as Loren and Luke. They loved and supported each other in different ways now, as the kids moved on into adulthood. They had not only run the deep pattern but had also dug deep into their hearts to keep living and demonstrating their love. It touched me.

At the front of the church was the group of catechumens. They were studying the Catholic faith and would be baptized in a little over forty days from then, at Easter. They were going deep as they cast their empty nets out into unknown waters. They, too, were trusting someone they were just getting to know: Jesus. He guided them to treasures ahead. Soon their nets would overflow. That they were making this commitment, I was touched.

The director of this study group, Kay, took the podium and offered prayers for each individual. As she did so, she looked at each one—really looked deep into their eyes. From where I was sitting several rows back, I felt the love she had for them. It was absolutely radiating from her. She had gone deep in her spirituality and had received the bountiful blessing. She had called to nearby boats to come join in the catch. I was touched.

As I started to leave the church, Shannon helped me out of the pew. Donna took my hand in hers and greeted me warmly. I tried to catch up with Eileen, who also had PD, but she cruised out the door with her walker. If I had caught her, I would have missed seeing this: A young son from the family that was giving her a ride that day, Benedict, gently placed his hand on the middle of her back as he guided her to his family's vehicle. He had seen his dad do this with his mom, for sure. He already knew about going deep. I was touched.

I wondered, *What do all these examples of going deep mean to me as I prepare for brain surgery?* Lent would start that week with

Ash Wednesday. From childhood we Catholics remember the tradition of having the sign of the cross placed on our foreheads with burned palm ashes. We try to experience a small amount of suffering by giving up something. Right then my nets felt light. Quite empty. *What if I try something different? What if I go deep this Lent…trust this friend Jesus as he tells me exactly where to put my nets…and when my net overflows, show others they can go deep?*

I focused on keeping healthy in my mind and body, being well practiced so I would be prepared for anything.

A few weeks later, I visited a classroom-sized chapel in a medium-security prison not far from my home. I'd obtained clearance in advance, and the volunteer coordinator was there to greet me and assist me through the metal detector—where I had to remove my shoes, belt, and glasses before the alarm would stop—and help me complete other check-in procedures. She read me a statement about my expected behavior as a visitor and of the possible risks involved in visiting this facility. Then we passed through security checks and doors until we were outside, walking across an open area to enter the building holding the chapel.

After clearing two more security doors, we turned down a long, wide hallway of highly polished cement. I thought, *Walk in the middle where the cameras can keep a close eye on you,* somehow thinking this was a safety measure, maybe learned on a previous visit to this prison or some other correctional facility in the area. We entered the last door and waited in a small hallway while the Baptist service came to completion. I watched the security procedures as one congregation left and the other entered and prepared the room for the next service. I felt safe, even comfortable, trusting that any one of these men would protect me should an incident occur during my visit.

I had been invited to participate in the week's Mass by the prisoner's Catholic Bible study. Charlie had been participating in the Bible study as a religious volunteer for sixteen years. He'd often shared bits of our home life with the men, so they knew about my travels and also my struggles with Parkinson's disease. In anticipation of my upcoming DBS surgery, they'd requested to pray for me in person. How could I refuse?!

Taking a seat, I folded my hands and placed my thumbs to make a cross, as Charlie and I did when praying. The room filled with male voices singing hymns and chanting the prayers of the Mass in English, Latin, and even Greek. The men prayed for each other, for families, for those without families, for the sick, for those in isolation. Then Father asked them to raise their hands and pray over me as he spoke a blessing.

At the completion of the final hymn, each man came to greet me. One by one they offered words of encouragement and hope and promises of prayers during my surgery and recovery. These men, who had turned to God since their incarceration, made this moment and this place sacred. With their gentle souls and contrite hearts, they lifted my heart and my being in prayer.

Charlie and I left the chapel area as the last of the men were getting a pat-down check by the officers. The walk on the hallway's highly polished cement floor seemed shorter. Soon we were outdoors, and I breathed in the brisk night air and felt the chill wind against my face. I was free. The high walls, the razor wire on top of the fences, the locked doors were behind me. But the sacred moment, the prayers and blessings, I hadn't left back in the prison chapel. The men had given me that gift to take with me.

Chapter 20

Counting the Days to Surgery

I GOT IN THE CAR AND DROVE TO THE HIGH SCHOOL. I PARKED MY car in the first available spot, quite a distance from the door, grabbed my stadium seat, and made my way into the gym and toward the bleachers to sit by retired teachers Mary and Chris and watch the game. I was trying to act okay. I had trouble maneuvering the bleachers, but I finally sat down. My hands and legs did fantastic tremors the whole first half, and I had to flag down a friend to help me out of the building when the game was over. I was quite stiff and was afraid that I would fall if I was bumped in the crowd.

The saying goes, "If you have seen one person with Parkinson's, then you've seen one person." That is to say, each Parkinson's patient is unique in the symptoms they present.

Parkinson's disease has such a variety of symptoms, and you are reading about some of mine—some very observable and many that you might not even notice. The less noticeable in most PD patients are the nonmotor symptoms. Through my adventures and in everyday life, I had experienced depression, anxiety, apathy, irritability, difficulties in planning and carrying out the plan, slow thought processes, language problems, dementia, and hallucinations. To all of these—which I experienced at one time or another—I have to add pain.

By the time the DBS surgery was close enough for me to begin counting down the days, I had been dealing with a great deal of pain. I had PD pain, but it was complicated by sciatica. I poured on the physical therapy exercises I'd learned from a very gifted clinician, had weekly therapeutic massage from the best around, worked with a knowledgeable and observant personal trainer, and stretched and bent, and drank lots of water and ate well, and the pain decreased. Then an ear infection, inflamed throat, a huge change in barometric pressure, and a great big windstorm, combined with me attempting yard work plus a dose of apathy seasoned with an added measure of depression—all of this put me in the recliner for a few days, and *yowza!* I was back to square one for pain and depression.

It would have been easy to sit and hurt and be depressed. But I remembered my discussion with God on the Meseta in Spain—I had promised I would "do something good" in this world. Doing good required I move and show up, and that meant I had to be healthy.

When I was physically well enough, I went to work out. Cindee, my physical trainer, was intuitive and supportive, and, yes, she gave me hard things to do because she knew when I completed those exercises I felt so much better about myself.

After one workout, I guzzled lots of water and headed to my next appointment about six blocks away. I was welcomed by Mary, who'd studied hard and long to become a therapeutic massage provider. As I entered, she was sitting at her desk with a huge book in her lap, reading up on massage techniques for people with Parkinson's.

These specialists, along with medical staff, made up my team.

I'd learned from them that I could not let up on how I ate, how I moved, where I let my mind go. I had to keep it up. I was thankful for the support I had from these professionals.

* * *

One morning I woke up at one a.m. with *the most terrible* headache and feeling quite ill. I was not prone to headaches, so I knew this could not be good. I took a blanket to the bathroom and nested near the porcelain throne, feeling the cotton mouth of impending doom. Rather than lose the contents of my stomach, I fell back asleep there on the bathroom floor and slept solid the rest of the night, right through to seven forty a.m.

I became aware of the time and thought, *There's something I'm supposed to do this morning!* Then I remembered. Charlie and I were supposed to be down the road at the radio station for the *Odds & Ends* program at eight a.m. No matter how crappy I felt, I had to show up. I managed to make myself presentable and got in the car.

Before long we had the big recording studio microphones in our faces and were telling Erik and the listening audience about the event the next Monday at six p.m. in conference room two at the hospital. My friend Nan Little would be there to talk about her book, and we were quite excited.

The next Monday rolled around, and I drove to the airport to pick up Nan. That afternoon before her talk, I spent quality time with her. I wanted to know these things: If she had not been diagnosed with Parkinson's disease, would she have climbed Kilimanjaro, trekked to Annapurna base camp, visited Machu Picchu, cycled across Iowa five times for RAGBRAI, hiked, skied, kayaked? Would she have met me?

She turned the tables: Where did this PD journey take me? If I had not been diagnosed, would I still be working? Would I have made five trips to Europe, three of which were long-distance walking treks? Would I have cycled across Iowa, not once, but twice, in the middle of summer, or logged hundreds of miles at home training? Would I have taken up tai chi, started to kayak, put a punching bag up in my garage? Would I have met all of these kind and wonderful and smart people who were my friends and health care providers? Would I have met Nan Little if I had not been diagnosed with Parkinson's disease?

The physical sensations I felt from PD were annoying, yet I lived with them. It was a choice to take my meds, to eat reasonably, and exercise hard. It was just as possible to ride across Iowa with PD as it was to stay home with PD. It was always my decision how much I wanted to put into fighting the symptoms.

The big, stormy rain cloud does hide a silver lining. I was amazed at what I had accomplished. I was amazed at what my friend has accomplished. It became obvious, if I hadn't known it before. It was a choice we made each day…to move.

* * *

I overheard my husband tell a friend that I was anxious and nervous about the DBS surgery. I wished I could say I was anxious, nervous, excited, or scared…or any emotional feeling at all. Actually I only felt physical sensations: trembling hands, inner tremors throughout my body, extreme stiffness and tightness and the pain that went with them, and a sore hip. At that moment, it was difficult to stand up straight, and I was going to regret getting in bed, because there was just no comfortable position.

Will I feel joy, relief, or happiness—or any emotion—after the surgery?

Will there be a change in the physical sensations with no emotional counterpart?

I just want to feel!

* * *

I went out for a drive one late winter day. Coming around the corner on my drive home after stopping to visit friends, I noticed the scenery had changed dramatically. Brown grass and gray sagebrush had been replaced by circles of green winter wheat shooting up blades from rich, dark soil into bright, warm sunlight. In the distance the silver line of the road ahead drew west, meeting the clouds on the horizon. I was almost home from my day's excursions, and I was tired.

I had visited three different friends who were hurting and engaged them in this conversation:

Can we draw good from…
the losses in our lives?
when your spouse leaves you?
when you receive a diagnosis of a life-threatening illness?
when you grieve the death of your child?

I thought there must be a point in the grieving when we leave the desert's winter landscape behind. When we turn the corner to see new growth and a ribbon of silvery highway that leads us away from here, to there.

In separate conversations, all agreed that some good comes from the bad. I summarized it in my journal that night:

It would not be worth the pain except that
hearts have been touched,
warmed to compassion,
strengthened with courage,
motivated to action.

On the day after the spring-forward time change, things started to be tougher for me to do. I would have liked to say that the change did not affect me. I also would have liked to think that the wind did not affect me, nor the change in barometric pressure when a weather front pushed through our area. That day, we had all three. Charlie said it was my trifecta. I wished I could win money, but I was not coming out on top of the betting game. I knew I had to do what I'd practiced. This started by moving.

Charlie tried to have a conversation with me about what I wanted to do that day. I told him, or thought I did, but he was giving me some odd looks. Then he said, "Having a conversation with you is like trying to herd cats on the Hermiston Butte."

What did that mean? Maybe I sounded like this:

If words were cats… You are out walking your cats. Some of them are on leashes. The big cat sees a rodent, the black cat is scared to death and hugs close, the young cats don't follow trails, and those stray cats we picked up on the hike turn this way and that and totally have their own agenda. The cats, like me, may never quite get to where they are supposed to be…the end of the story.

Suffice it to say my communication skills were demonstrating the disruption caused by Parkinson's disease.

I reminded myself that time changes throw everyone off just a little. Young children may take a while to adapt. We all enjoy a bit more daylight, yet it throws the dinner schedule off. It threw my medication off by an hour. Charlie hadn't adjusted and brought the med box around; I let him know I was on top of this one. I could suffer through one hour and get back on schedule with the time change.

* * *

The surgery date was drawing near. Life was mundane and usual, but in a nice sort of way. I wanted Charlie to go on a bike ride with me. By the time we were dressed for the possible rain, it had arrived. Good thing we had the gear, because it rained hard and we rode hard.

Where we lived, if it rained the wind blew. The wind blew hard. Really hard. We were home walking in our driveway when big gusts hit, almost knocking me to the gravel.

Inside, I was stiff and sore and tired as I fell asleep on the couch. Like so many times when I'd fallen asleep early, I woke up at midnight and was wide awake until five thirty a.m. I looked at the computer screen the entire time. I made no decisions, bought nothing, read nothing, wrote nothing. What a waste. Falling back to sleep, I started having cramps in my toes, then my calf, then my hamstrings. Charlie, who somehow knew I was in trouble, arrived on the scene with my medication and the cramp-relief pills.

I slept until nine, woke, then back to sleep…awake, asleep, and finally up at noon. The wind was still up; Charlie was gone; I felt wobbly.

I set out to put the laundry away. While doing so, the top closet shelf came down on me, taking the next shelf and all the clothes to the floor. It was a mess. But I was not hurt. I gathered everything up, replaced the shelves, and started putting the clothes away, when the darn thing fell again. Apparently I needed stronger little brackets, as the current ones were bent. Sitting there on the floor, under a pile of clothes that had escaped the closet, I had to grin. I started to giggle. *No one else would see the humor in this mess,* I thought. *Or would they?*

The pile of clothes from the shelves was left on the floor. My iPhone was near a comfortable couch. I started to type a blog post, and then an error notification popped up. *How can there be an error on my iPhone?* There had been no opportunity to save. I lost what I had written. Determined, I turned on the computer, opened the blog, and there it was…everything I had written. Relieved, I fell asleep right there with my head on the keyboard.

Survival with good humor is the key, I had written—with an image below it that read: *"It's only brain surgery," said no one.*

Chapter 21

The Big Day: DBS Surgery

THE CLOCK ON THE WALL TICKED THE MINUTES OFF SLOWLY. My scheduled surgery time had passed over an hour before, and I was still waiting in the pre-op. Pre-op didn't provide much privacy, the patient areas being separated only by thin curtains that didn't even reach the floor. Eavesdropping on the other three patients as they went through their preparations helped me pass the time. They had been wheeled out one by one to their assigned surgical suites. It had been quiet for some time when the whisking sound of surgical slippers on the tile floor alerted me that someone was approaching. A gloved hand whipped the curtain aside, and a figure, completely gowned and masked, entered my tiny space. The figure paused at the end of my bed for a moment, staring at me.

Then I heard, "What are we going to do with that hair?" It was a woman's voice speaking from behind the surgical mask. Perhaps she had been in earlier to introduce herself, but now I did not recognize her voice or have any idea why she was asking about my hair!

"Excuse me, what did you say?"

"I said, what about your hair?"

I am here for a deep brain stimulation procedure, a treatment for my Parkinson's disease, not another haircut, I thought.

"Isn't it short enough? I took a poll on social media, and all my friends love this style." I had known the incisions would affect my hairstyle, but how, I was not sure. In preparation for this surgery I had gradually shortened my hair from shoulder length to a bob, then to the current pixie style. I'd had fun along the way as I'd posted pictures of glamorous women with the hair I desired and allowed my friends to have input through voting. Diane, my hairdresser, had complied by cutting my hair to a likeness of the winning hairstyle.

"If we leave it like this, when you get out of the surgery, it's going to look like a three-year-old took scissors to it while you were napping."

"What do you suggest?" I asked.

"Shave it off."

"Shave it off, now?"

"Not now. When we put you under."

"Who will do it? Dr. Burchiel?"

"Never," came the reply. "He's a brain surgeon. You don't want *him* cutting your hair. I will do it myself."

I had to do give this some thought. "Come on, Carol," I muttered under my breath. *It's just her sense of humor. You promised yourself you would remain positive and lighthearted.*

"Um, thanks," I said to the mystery nurse.

The gloved hand parted the curtain behind her as she backed away, and she was gone, leaving me wondering, *Should I have asked her to wax my eyebrows too?*

All alone again in my patient preparation room, waiting my turn in the surgical suite, I started to doze. I was startled by the entrance of another masked-and-gowned staff person, who also whipped the dividing curtains aside. I recognized this teenaged-looking figure as the anesthesiologist who had been in earlier to gather pre-surgery information.

"Surgery is ready for you. Are you ready for surgery?" he asked cheerfully.

I was! I was also fairly calm and cool, having decided in advance I was going to control my emotions during this process. When anxiety started to creep up, I chased it back with the controlled breathing I had been practicing. I was also able to dig deep and draw from a sense of humor that had been all but taken away by the disease. Being wheeled out of the pre-op area and into the surgical suite by Dr. Alex Something, the sixteen-year-old-looking anesthesiologist, was my first opportunity. He assured me he was far older than sixteen and had passed his anesthesiology boards. Before I could ask him to pull out his wallet and show me proof of age and his medical license to put me to sleep and wake me up, we'd arrived at the surgical suite. This area was prepared specially for patients undergoing deep brain stimulation surgery.

"Here we are," said the young Dr. Alex. "This is the surgical unit where we do the DBS."

I looked around. The room was much larger than I had imagined, with different machines and stations throughout. The giant CAT scan looked like a donut hanging on one wall. There was a table of instruments nearby, and I was glad to recognize some similar to those Dr. Burchiel had shown me during the pre-surgical consultation. I also spotted the leads that were to be implanted in my brain in the area of the substantia nigra called the globus pallidus, GPi for short. The MRI I'd had a few weeks before and the live CAT scans were to target the exact trajectory into my brain for the placement of the leads. The continued plan was that I would spend one night in the hospital in the neuroscience intensive care unit and then go home, 180 miles away, for the weekend. When I returned five days later, the neurostimulator would then be implanted.

As if my life were flashing before my eyes, I imagined this huge life-changing event that was to happen very shortly. I would wake up in recovery somehow different. I took a big gulp of air at that thought, but I couldn't dwell on it for long. Before they could operate, I had to answer: "Tell us your name, your birthdate, and what we are doing for you today."

My internal monologue ran with that: *Dr. Alex will put me under. Mystery nurse will shave my hair and sterilize the heck out of my scalp. The techs will put a big cage on my head to hold it still. Then the docs will peel back a portion of my scalp and drill a hole. Somebody who really knows their stuff will overlay the MRI scans and the current view the CAT scan was providing. One of the docs will put the lead on an instrument, where it will be inserted at just the proper trajectory into the hole until it reaches the GPi portion of my brain. Some of the other docs will hook up wires and tuck them away for the next step in five days. Another doc will get to practice their sewing while closing up that hole with dissolvable stitches. The complete process will then be done again for the other side of my brain, with the hole drilled about four inches away. Yet another doc will get to practice stitching to close that up. The stitching had better match! The cage will be removed. I will then be wheeled to recovery. The attendant there will wake me up and serve me a cheeseburger, onion rings, and a peanut butter milkshake.*

My real response was, "I'm here for deep brain stimulation."

"Good. That's what we're here for too," responded one of the voices.

"Hey, I want to know all your names," I called out to the people working in surgery. I spotted that familiar body shape and gloved hand, and I really wanted to know her name, as she had the barber position for the day. I found out that she was the lead nurse in charge of the surgical unit.

"Alex—you already know me."

"Andy."

"Sara."

"Mary."

I heard the responses from various corners of surgery.

"And that guy over there"—a technician pointed—"is the Medtronic rep. He'll be taking care of the devices."

"Where are the docs?"

"They'll be right in," Dr. Alex, forever sixteen in my mind, responded.

"Okay, you guys. I know your names, and I expect you will be doing your very best work today. This surgery is ultra-important to me. I am praying for you all."

"I am going to give you some more oxygen now," Dr. Alex said, and suddenly it got really quiet and dark. I was under anesthesia.

* * *

I had a sense of someone standing by my bed—a figure in dark-blue scrubs.

"Hi, Carol." *Oh my gosh!* It was my neurologist, Dr. Hiller.

I announced her presence to the room of postsurgical patients in various stages of consciousness. "Hey, it's Amie Hiller! My doctor is here. Hi, Dr. Hiller. I just had brain surgery!"

"Just thought I'd check in and see how it went. Gotta go." The figure in blue scrubs was gone. I drifted back off into a state of anesthesia-induced semi-unconsciousness.

Someone was wrapping a band around my arm. It startled me.

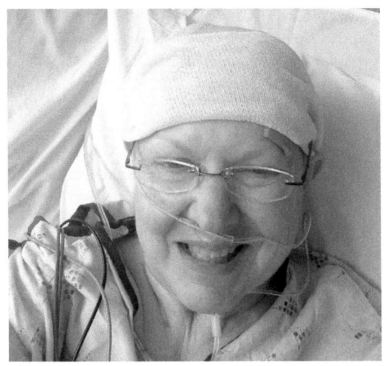
I take a post-surgery selfie.

"Was that really her?" I asked the person checking my blood pressure.

"Who?"

"Dr. Amie Hiller."

"I don't know."

Later I thought, *Well, shouldn't they know if a stranger appears in the recovery room?* But in my then semi-sedated state, I enthusiastically voiced, "I know it was my doctor. Dr. Amie Hiller was here. I am sure."

I was wheeled out of recovery and into the neuroscience intensive care unit. My head throbbed terribly, yet I felt quite hungry. Charlie and the boys were the first to stop in to see me, and they caught me taking post-surgery selfies, so we got a family photo too. After a brief visit with my guys, I was allowed to have some pudding and some water. That did little to nothing to curb my hunger, so I requested another round. Managing to keep everything down, I then requested real food. My request was granted with a cheeseburger and a soda. I started to munch away and apparently fell asleep, as a nurse later told me she'd come in and seen me with the burger in my hand propped near my mouth.

I needed to use the bathroom, and no one seemed to respond to my call button. My door was open a slight bit, and I called out to a passing nurse. She got an assistant to accompany me and unhooked my oxygen.

"Help her back to bed when she's finished," the nurse said to the assistant. "They're coming to check our charting, and I need to get back to it."

The young nursing assistant was helpful in getting me back to bed, and then she left and closed the glass door tightly behind her. She hadn't hooked up the oxygen.

Other than the headache, I felt well. There were patients in this unit who required much more care than I, so I tried not to be too needy. But the nurses who had been in hourly to take my vitals seemed to disappear, and I knew I should have the oxygen. I hit the button, and kept hitting it, but nobody came. There was a paper cup on the little table beside my hospital bed. I drank the water and waited until I saw someone go by—then I threw the cup so it plunked against the closed glass door. The nurse opened the door and picked up the cup, then started to leave.

"Excuse me," I called.

"Yes? Do you need something?"

"Am I supposed to be hooked up to oxygen and these other monitors?"

"Let me take care of those things." She quickly hooked me all back up and left without another word.

A doctor came in at five a.m. to check on me, and then another set of vitals was taken. I fell back asleep but was awoken when my door slid open. It was time for the rounds with the teaching physicians. I didn't really know who were the doctors and who were the students. They gathered up in a tight group just outside my door; all had white lab coats and clipboards or tablets.

In my half-asleep state, I heard a report: "The patient in number nine is a fifty-eight-year-old female who underwent a deep brain stimulation procedure for Parkinson's disease at 13:30 yesterday. The patient remained under anesthesia the entire procedure, which was completed at 16:15. She tolerated the procedure well and was sent to recovery. After awakening, her only complaints have been a severe headache and a sore throat, which have been managed with extra-strength acetaminophen. Appetite is good, and she is eating solids. Vitals are stable, with an exception of blood oxygen in the low range."

I could have told them why that was!

"When levels improve and she has completed the PT instructions, she will be released to her home. Return Monday for completion of the procedure with implantation of the neurostimulator in day surgery."

Chapter 22

Recovery

Loren and Luke bought me a red skullcap to keep my head warm and the bandages covered up.

"It matches your red car," Luke said as we piled in for the trip back to Hermiston. I slept most of the way through the gorgeous Columbia Gorge this time.

After being home for a few days, I was ready to go out. Charlie packed up my guitar, and we went to Pendleton, where there was a bluegrass music jam every Saturday afternoon at the Great Pacific, a favorite wine and coffee spot. Playing familiar songs and fiddle tunes with my friends Anne and Ron and a host of other musicians was a great boost to my mood.

Knowing I was stretching the terms of my recovery by being out in public for so long, I called it an early evening, and we headed on home.

I had just settled into my chair at the dining room table when the doorbell rang. Charlie got up to answer, and I heard a brief welcome to the guest, and then a familiar voice… And it rolled through my memory banks… Someone from church? One of my hangout buddies? A teacher friend? Yeah, that was it. The person at the door was someone I knew from my years in the field of education. *Give me just a second*, said my mind. *You know this person.* My brain got in the groove. Thought processes were reconnecting around the wires and probes, which were welcome intruders in my brain.

The call I made to my brain switchboard was instantly transferred to a classroom in the old Armand Larive Middle School building. I got a picture in my mind: The students are in a special needs classroom, and they're making cute and useful items that will be sold to make money for other classroom projects. I hear the cheery yet soothing teacher's voice, a voice you can sit and listen to for hours and never grow tired; her life's wisdom embedded in the stories she shares.

She's at my house, right now, standing at my door. It was her, that amazing teacher who knew instinctively how to make learning real and functional. And I could not think of her name.

I had seen this teacher only a handful of times in the years since we'd worked together in those classrooms at the old Armand Larive, the ancient walls almost crumbling in around us. Our paths had crossed here and there, and although I had always enjoyed the crossings, they were too few and too short. *What is her name?*

My sister Beth was sitting across from me at the dining room table. She had just come from the living room, where she had been reading pieces of my writing.

"Carol, you expressed your spirituality in your writing and demonstrate your faith by your actions."

Wow, what could I say to that?

Charlie was by now fully engaged in a conversation with the person at the front door while Beth and I continued on. She'd read the part about the day on my first Camino when I'd had the major meltdown and yelled at God.

"That was when Charlie and I were walking the ribbon of road that led us across the Meseta in Spain," I said. "God told me, 'Do something good!' It seemed simple. But as time went on, the 'do something good' statement was too open-ended. I needed direction. I had to ask, 'What do you mean, God? What specifically do you want me to do?'"

"You're a lot like me." Beth ran her fingers along the edge of the place mat. "I'm a person who deals better in concrete directions too."

I explained to her how specific direction hadn't come, so I'd decided to be a do-gooder and support what was put in front of me. I had continued raising money for Parkinson's disease research, which was the top priority. "But I didn't like to ask people for donations." We both laughed.

The money raised so far had been a good thing. Riding with Pedaling for Parkinson's had helped me physically, and the dollars raised in the sweltering heat on the Iowa back roads in July of 2014 and 2015 had helped YMCAs set up programs for individuals and small groups to use stationary bikes as part of their own Parkinson's treatment plans.

Along with doing good, I realized I needed to take care of myself, physically and emotionally. My doctor had ordered physical therapy, and a new connection was made. As the physical therapist walked me out of the office after one session, I asked if she thought there were enough local people with PD to start a support group. She responded that a group was very needed. She and Charlie and I got together and discussed a proposed time, place, and content of the gatherings. We hung posters around town and placed an announcement in the newspaper that we would meet in a hospital classroom the first Monday of the month. Eight people came to the first one. We were thrilled.

Charlie and I were invited to a Parkinson's support group facilitator training offered by the Parkinson's Resources of Oregon. This group provided us with the comfort of an overseeing body. PRO had numerous resources, ideas for meeting content, and even a social worker who helped patients with challenging needs.

Before I left for the third Camino, our group had outgrown its small space at the hospital. We asked the bowling alley if we could use their party room, and they were most gracious to accommodate us. Lunch was available, which I felt drew more people out. There was never a time when we could not find an interesting topic to discuss. Some meetings we had guest speakers, others we watched a video and discussed it, and sometimes we just broke into small groups and talked about our challenges. It was good. I could add it to the list of good things God wanted me to do.

Sitting there with Beth, overhearing Charlie still chatting with the person at the front door, I recalled that I hadn't considered my writing to be one of the good things God had suggested. Apparently it fit in the scheme of things, though.

One spring afternoon I had ridden my bike to my friend Brandi's house. Brandi was about fifteen years younger than I was, and her wisdom reached beyond all ages. Sitting on her front porch with our feet up on a low wicker table, sipping from glasses of ice tea, I asked, "I've been writing mostly about positive experiences. But there's darkness in my soul too. Do I write about this? I mean, Parkinson's is a crappy disease. Yet I don't want anyone to think I'm negative or having my own pity party. I want to do good stuff."

"Carol, life is not all diamonds and roses. We need to hear about your struggles and how you get through the difficult times. You inspire us."

The last phrase—"you inspire us"—got to me. I did not see myself as an inspiring person.

Brandi had given me permission; I could write the good and the bad.

So I'd written more. I'd sought out meaning in the mundane. I'd taken those journeys—of mind, spirit, soul, and body—and I began writing about them. The stories I shared on social media and in my blogs were being read. I did not know just how far the stories traveled.

Without planning for it, it was these stories that seemed to be doing the most good. I exposed my heart and soul, and now my brain, to the world so anyone who took time to read the stories may see my hope. There is hope in the miseries of daily life and in the pain and inconvenience of significant disease. There is hope that we will move beyond the physical, where we experience the discomfort of our human weakness and illness, and into the spiritual, where we move beyond pain into freedom and peace.

Beth's connection with my words emphasized that my writing was doing good. I smiled at her.

The teacher at the door was now making her way to the table, and Beth moved to give her space. The woman had a bag for me. In the bag was a beautiful crocheted prayer shawl. She had made this—*for me!* Accompanying the prayer shawl was a card with a big *Thank You* on the front and a letter inside that she asked me to read later. As soon as she walked out the door, I opened the letter while Beth watched me curiously.

Carol,

I'm sure you are asking yourself, "Thank you? Thank you for what?" Well I want to tell you...

Thank you for the inspiration you have been to me throughout your struggles with this disease.

Thank you for sharing. We've all watched and followed you along as you have tackled your condition with such force and dignity. I've been in awe of you in the way you've been able to openly share your struggles and victories.

Thank you for your courage. You've helped me to face my personal battle with less self-pity and more proactive decisions. I've learned to research and keep asking questions. In the past I've been very passive with doctors when I've had medical issues but thanks to you...no more!

Carol, this shawl may seem kind of old and "rockin chairish" but that is not the intent that is meant. It is meant to let you know that you are loved. As I crocheted this "prayer shawl" for you, I prayed. I prayed each time I picked up the hook and yarn. I prayed for your healing. I prayed for your comfort mentally, emotionally, and physically. I prayed for your family. I prayed for your doctors and nurses, for their wisdom and caring.

Carol, I love you and will continue to pray for you as you make this journey.

Your indomitable spirit is precious.

God's Blessings.
Andrea

Andrea—that's her name. My mind felt relieved, and I made another picture in my mind, this one not of her classroom but of her knitting. As her strong, weathered hands slowly stitched, her lips moved in prayer for my well-being and healing. In the course of her prayers for me, she received her own healing. *Isn't that the way it goes?* I thought. *Do something for someone else and you also experience the blessings?*

I wrapped myself in the shawl. It was warm and soft and comforting, and so very full of prayers and love. So true to form for this teacher, who made the *practical* into the most *meaningful*.

Beth looked at me across the table, her eyes moist with tears, as were mine.

* * *

On Easter afternoon we drove back to Portland for the next day's surgery to have the neurostimulator implanted.

I have heard this device called many things: neurostimulator, generator, battery pack. Most often I called it the "little box-shaped thingy in my chest." It is the powerhouse of the DBS. From this small device, electrical stimulation is delivered to both sides of the brain to help relieve Parkinson's symptoms throughout the body.

The day-surgery patient-preparation rooms were identical to those in neurosurgery: thin sheets blocking the view but nothing else. The curtain was whipped aside, and there was the young anesthesiologist, Dr. Alex. I was ready to tease him again.

"It's my favorite teenage anesthesiologist," I said.

"You're back. Glad to see you, Mrs. Clupny. We're ready for you in the surgical suite. What? No IV yet?"

"Who's supposed to put it in?" I inquired.

"It could be any number of people, but for right now it's going to be me."

"Dr. Alex, tell me the truth. Do you put in IVs on a regular basis?"

"Yes, Mrs. Clupny. I've put in thousands of IVs. You can be assured that I will do a good job."

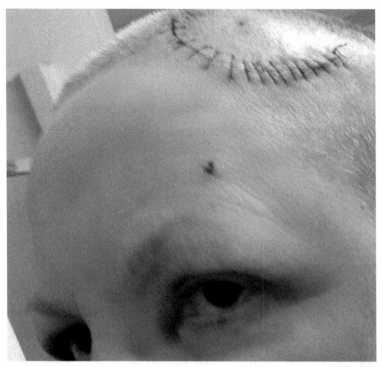

The stitches dissolve on their own within a couple weeks of surgery.

Dr. Alex put a rubber tourniquet on my arm, and I showed him the vein that always worked. With the needle, he proceeded to miss the vein and had to start over with the IV. What luck for the poor Dr. Alex! I didn't say anything, as I was anticipating just the right moment to get him. Finally he took the brakes off the bed and pushed me out of the pre-op area and around the corner to a short hallway.

"Are you carrying your medical license in your wallet, Dr. Alex?" I started in on him.

"No, it's on the wall in my office, right next to my Eagle Scout Certificate." He was on to me.

As we entered the surgical suite, I called out to the surgical staff, "Showtime!" They were busy making the last preparations for my implant. "Hey, you all need to be on top of it today. This surgery is really important to me. I will be praying you do your best work." I clasped my hands in fervent prayer, careful not to disturb the IV. "And I will especially be praying for Alex, who seems to be having a hard time with IVs today."

This brought out a roar of laughter from the surgical crew.

Before long I was on the surgical table, where oxygen was attached and monitors were connected. Young Dr. Alex's masked face leaned down toward me. In spite of my teasing, he continued with his professionalism. "Mrs. Clupny, breathe deeply and start counting down from one hundred."

I started to mouth the words, "By threes? Ninety-seven...," joking about the physical therapy tests I'd had to take. No words came out. I was down the deep, dark hole of drug-induced sleep.

* * *

During the pre-surgery consultation, Dr. Burchiel had shown me the neurostimulator and the wires that would be running under my skin. I was surprised that the box looked so big and felt so heavy. He pointed out the location on my body and how the wires would connect with the probes in my brain.

"That is in the vicinity of bra straps," I commented.

"Most women adjust well."

"And I backpack. What about my backpack straps?"

"You may consider a different type of pack if it bothers you."

My thoughts at this time were: *Gee whiz, these brain scientists and neurosurgeons came up with this great procedure and worked with engineers at Medtronic to create this magnificent system. It seems clunky and without consideration of differences in men's and women's anatomy. Why is this?*

These thoughts went unexpressed. Like with many medical procedures, I took it as the way it was going to be.

* * *

During the day-surgery procedure, the team placed the neuro-stimulator under the skin on the left side of my chest, just below the collarbone as I expected. They connected it to the wires that ran from the side of my neck, to the back of my head, to the leads in my brain. They closed up the little pocket with six or seven self-dissolving stitches. I woke in the surgical suite, and in my post-anesthesia fog, I thought I saw several green-robed people with masks and hairnets gathered around. I heard them saying, "This is the woman who rode her bike across Iowa?"

"Yeah, and walked on that Camino de Santiago in Spain."

"You mean the one in that movie *The Way*? That's fantastic."

And then I was out again.

Chapter 23

The Tune-Ups

Luke traveled to an overnight lacrosse tournament in the Portland area. Charlie and I were so proud that he was playing on the varsity team, and we traveled to watch the games. We returned home, thinking he'd had a great weekend, only to receive a call from the athletic director.

It was reported that Luke had been in possession of marijuana in the hotel room he'd shared with three other athletes. The school needed us to come in for a suspension hearing on the same day that I had an appointment to get the neurostimulator turned on and programmed. I *could not* miss this appointment at OHSU, and the high school did not want to reschedule. Due to this unforeseen event, Charlie would have to stay home and deal with this situation.

After some thinking and following my problem-solving format, I looked at the resources available and my options. Rose and Art were the answer. Rose, my sister's husband's sister, and her husband, Art, lived in Troutdale, Oregon, just east of Portland. I'd lost count of the number of times Charlie and I had stayed at their home.

My plan was to drive myself to their house the day before the appointment so I could take as many breaks as needed. Rose and

Art would help me negotiate traffic across Portland to OHSU for my appointment in the morning. Desiring perfect driving conditions heading out of eastern Oregon, I waited for the wind to settle a bit and headed out in the afternoon. When I arrived, I treated Art and Rose to dinner. With a belly full of pasta and spumoni ice cream, I hit the hay, so to speak, in the familiar guest bed.

In the morning Art drove me to my appointment, and I invited him into the exam room to witness the event. Dr. Hiller swooped in as usual, but this time with a first-year med student, also named Art, on her heels and a small tablet-like device in a zippered pouch in her hands.

Dr. Hiller looked at the locations of the incisions on my head and commented on the job well done by the surgical staff.

"Dr. Hiller, my only point of discomfort has been the neurostimulator."

"Hmm." She noted that it was also a "job well done" and "many people have this device quite more noticeably protruding," which I took to mean, *There are folks out there more uncomfortable than you, Carol. Buck up.*

That was the end of that complaint. Dr. Hiller expertly ran her handheld programmer through its paces and checked out my implanted device. Then she started working on which of the leads were to be used. She asked me what symptoms most bothered me, and I commented, first, stiffness and rigidity, and second, tremors. She took my right hand in hers and, with her other hand, started manipulating my right wrist and arm to make it move almost as if I was throwing a softball.

When I looked over at my friend Art leaning against the wall, and then to the future Dr. Art, their faces showed astonishment as they witnessed a rigid shoulder, elbow, and wrist moving freely.

I started to feel really odd—that was the only way I could describe the feelings, as I had never felt these sensations before. Dr. Hiller had forewarned me to comment immediately on any strange feelings I had. Before any word left my lips, though, I experienced bright flashes in my right eye.

"Um, Dr. Hiller?"

She looked at me and quickly used her handheld device to turn the amps down until no secondary effects were noted and my wrist and arm were quite flexible. She completed that adjustment, and went through the process again, and my tremor disappeared.

Next was the left side. I was asked to flick my fingers, and as she amped up, my cheeks began to feel like I had been shot full of Novocain.

"Mmm, momer, mimma?"

"What are you feeling this time, Carol?"

"Mi moamamama mot?"

Again she adjusted her handheld device, and my speech returned to normal. I was asked to flick my fingers again, which were sometimes most wonderfully coordinated and other times an uncontrolled mess of fingers tangling with each other. Soon that setting was reached, and I could flick my fingers without difficulty. I was asked to demonstrate walking for the doctor and med student. I did well, but after sitting for a while, my sciatic nerve wanted to act up. I couldn't show them what I felt I could really do.

Then Dr. Hiller asked me which medication I would prefer not to take anymore. That would be Ropinirole, which I had judged to have the adverse side effect of obsession with computers and food and a cause of the hallucinations. We made a plan to delete this drug and also to decrease the Sinemet. The good doctor carefully recorded all the settings and told me not to leave town for a day, to be sure I was okay with the new settings before I was too far away for adjustments. We made plans for the follow-up appointments. Before I left, she demonstrated my personal hand-held device, which would be used for regular device generator battery checks, powering up, and settings changes.

Dr. Hiller had worked with me for only about ninety minutes to change eight years of symptoms. The tremors were gone. I could swing my arms, reach around to pull my sweater on by myself, and bend down to the floor to fix a loose shoelace. I walked confidently out of the exam room and easily reached the button to call the elevator.

During the drive back to Art and Rose's house, Art kept saying, "That was amazing. Absolutely amazing." It was. There was no denying it.

I woke up early the next morning and had a busy day running errands and shopping until I finally left Troutdale around three p.m. No naps. I drove home wide awake, comfortable, and confident in my driving. At the rest stop, getting out of the car was not a struggle. I was up, out of the car seat, and walking. *Oh my! Way cool!*

I knew the process was going to take more time before I would see its maximum potential. But truly, it was amazing!

A few days later, I marveled that the sky was a perfect shade of gold through my windshield. Driving up Rieth Ridge on I-84 west out of Pendleton, I knew what I was in for. Twelve years of commuting to work had taught me about the beauty and challenges of driving into sunrises and sunsets. When I arrived at the top of the ridge, the gold reflection of that sun would hit my bug-splattered windshield. It was going to be more challenging to see.

But I did see. I looked at the huge, golden sun as it dipped into the horizon. There, those dark mounds, my mountains, the volcanoes of the Cascade Range. Far left was Mount Hood, its triangular summit reaching toward the heavens, and directly ahead I saw the first mountain I'd ever climbed, Mount Adams. I'd loved it so much that a few years later, I'd climbed it again. Slightly north I saw Mount Rainier and recalled one of the coldest and most magnificent nights I'd ever spent outdoors, our tent dug into the snow at 10,000 feet, glaciers glowing white in the full moon.

Today was a golden day. Some time spent with friends. A day when I drove my car by myself with music blaring. Driving on familiar mountain roads that in times past had led me to skiing, hiking, and work locations. The hillsides were green—the greenest, richest green that breathes of new life. The sky was an indescribable hue of blue. The snow-covered Wallowa Mountains in the Eagle Cap Wilderness were still as white-capped as their descriptive name.

I feel now. I feel emotion, I thought. Joy, happiness, the giddiness of a young girl on a spring day. I *felt* more than I had felt in the last ten years.

Parkinson's disease had stolen my affect, but now, I was feeling it return. It started in small ways: fingers moving on guitar strings, smiling and laughing at jokes, speech with volume and vocal inflection, telling a congruent story, jogging down the long hallway in our house, driving my car for four hours and not needing a nap. Other abilities returned too, like saying hard things out of anger instead of hiding behind anxiety, sobbing desperate tears, screaming, then talking, and then laughing over life.

* * *

Charlie was with me when I returned to OHSU a month later for the second tune-up session. Dr. Hiller was not available, and another young doctor performed the programming. He took his pen and drew out on the paper covering the examination bed how the process of DBS works in the brain. He'd make adjustments, and different amounts of current would be sent to the active probes. He'd maybe even activate more of the probes. I knew this, as Dr. Burchiel had explained that my progress with this device could be like peeling an onion: more layers and layers of improvement could be revealed as the settings on this device were tweaked. Over time, I would discover movements that I had forgotten I was able to do. Again I left Portland feeling like a different person.

* * *

The next programming was scheduled for a month later. Rushed, we were thankful the traffic on the freeway down the Columbia River Gorge was moving well. The medical assistant called me into the exam room, and suddenly I became very self-conscious. I was going for the third programming of my deep brain stimulation neurostimulator, which meant Dr. Hiller would be up close and personal. There had not been enough time to find a breath mint to take care of my tuna breath.

I had sent Charlie to forage through the nearby café and the coffee shop for something to eat. He made an excellent find and brought back tuna on a bed of greens. I wrapped the tuna up in the lettuce and ate it sandwich-like right there in the crowded waiting room. Glancing up from my grazing, I realized that other patients were watching me and probably smelling the tuna also, and maybe my feet. That was another issue. I had chosen the wrong shoes. They were old Keen brand Mary Jane sandals.

They'd felt loose that morning, probably because they were so old, they were broken down. So I'd put on a pair of white socks. At some point in the day, I noticed Charlie was wearing mid-calf white socks with his Keen hiking shoes and shorts. It was then I realized how ridiculous my white socks looked with my Keen Mary Janes.

Taking off the socks required taking off the shoes. When the shoes went back on my feet, they were loose again without the socks. I asked Charlie to assist with tightening the buckles, and it was then he noticed and commented on their smell. Oh well, time to go into the examination room.

Dr. Hiller whisked in with her now-second-year medical student, Art, in tow and got right to business. I was sure she didn't care about my breath or my feet, unless we figured some way to relate those two things to Parkinson's disease.

The first thing I realized—and she realized—was that I had not followed the instructions to take my meds as usual. I was a twitching mess. So I took them immediately. She arranged for me to come back after her next patient to continue the programming.

Medication in effect, I returned to the exam room about forty-five minutes later. While she was turning knobs and punching in numbers on her handheld unit, Charlie told her about my recent adventures with the Parkinson's women's Sprint Triathlon relay team.

I had teamed up with two other women with PD for a relay in Moses Lake, Washington. Charlie was super proud of me, and I couldn't blame him for wanting to brag. It just wasn't the right time! I had not planned to say anything about this event. I wanted her full attention to be on the programming. Dr. Hiller acknowledged Charlie's comment with a smile, and then it was back to business. For the third month in a row, I left OHSU better than when I'd walked in. Life was good.

Chapter 24

How It Worked: Four Examples

Bike Ride

We came downhill through the trees at a pretty fast pace. Moss-covered trees in the old-growth forest near the Columbia River whipped by. Or rather, we whipped by them. It was beautiful there, and peaceful. If only we'd just ridden slow enough on our tandem bike—Grepedo—to enjoy it.

"How fast?" I shouted at Charlie, his ears just about twelve inches from my mouth.

"Twenty-eight," he shouted back.

Usually I was screaming, "Faster! Faster!" But this time, one hundred days since the brain surgery and still recovering, I said, "Okay, let's slow it down a bit."

Day one of our thirty-fourth wedding anniversary adventure found us riding from Mosier to Hood River and back. There were many hikers and cyclists out on the beautiful day, as it was also Father's Day. The views were outstanding, and the Mosier Twin Tunnels were fascinating. The trail surface itself was well-manicured asphalt. We had both hiked and ridden this trail. It was familiar and not too challenging. We didn't go too fast or too slow. It was a just-right kind of day.

Charlie and I celebrate our thirty-fourth wedding anniversary with Grepedo on the Historic Columbia River Highway.

Pedaling on the Historic Columbia River Highway 30 was a great adventure to add to our anniversary list. As we'd planned this trip, we thought about anniversary adventures past and wished we had made some sort of paper record. Charlie and I reminisced and decided that of all the anniversaries, this pedaling trip rated right up there with backpacking in Europe, living in the mountains of Mexico with the Capuchin Franciscan missionaries, climbing Mount Adams, climbing Mount Saint Helens, camping at 10,000 feet on Mount Rainier, walking the Camino de Santiago, working at summer camp with a hundred high school kids, and getting a tattoo of the Parkinson's tulip.

Many sections of the old highway have been restored to paved hiking/biking trails. Other sections are directly adjacent to the freeway. Concrete dividers separated us from traffic, but not from the roar of trucks and cars speeding along the interstate.

Some portions of the historic Highway 30 are still used for auto travel, and we rode those cautiously with tourists in their RVs creeping by us on the narrow, shoulder-less sections.

Day two started at Ainsworth State Park, as we turned Grepedo's nose east toward the Cascade Locks. Not knowing this trail, we were surprised by the challenges of our own abilities. The first surprise occurred shortly after starting out in the glorious sunny morning. On a downhill glide, I wanted to rest a bit, so I gave my request. "Right down. Right down, Charlie, right down!"

He shouted back, "Well then, *you* put *your* right pedal down!"

The front and back pedals on the tandem are meant to move together. With his directive, it dawned on me: our pedals were not synced up. My right leg was down on my right pedal, but his right leg was up on his right pedal. Once discovered, it took little to convince either of us that we needed to stop and fix it. The bike path opened into a parking lot, and a kind couple who had ridden their mountain bikes to this trailhead were just locking them to explore one of the trails on foot. They watched a moment as we struggled to get the bike situated so Charlie could examine the chain linking the pedals. Luckily they offered us assistance. The man helped Charlie take the chain apart, while the woman and I held the bike and saw to aligning the pedals. Within a few minutes, we were happily pedaling east again, and they were hiking west.

The old highway has beautiful cement guardrails, some original and some reproductions. Bridges over small creeks lead to views of waterfalls not visible from the freeway. We rode over the car tunnel near Bonneville Dam and enjoyed momentary quiet—traffic sounds from I-84 encased in the mountain below. When we reached the other side, the noise leaked out on the bike path as we picked up speed. Pedaling farther east along the interstate, we suddenly came into some hairpin turns.

"Hold on!" yelled Charlie. Grepedo's disc brakes whirred as Charlie's strong hands pulled hard to slow us down. I wondered how cars had made turns on this highway. Our tandem was a bit longer than a regular bike, making the tight turns even more challenging. I was not sure I had ever been the stoker through these types of steep downhill spirals. Charlie expertly guided us through, and I held on, leaning as he did.

Riding behind Charlie, my view was limited to the sides. I seldom could see over or around his broad back to view what was ahead. He was taken by surprise, too, when we bounced over the first set of tree roots. *Wham!* I hit the seat hard on the way down, and the neurostimulator implanted in my chest took a big bounce against my skin. It hurt for the rest of the ride and several days after.

Charlie started calling, "Bump!" when he could see them. If we went into glide mode instead of pedaling, I could use my legs as additional shock absorbers. Some of these roots were marked with a very slim bit of white paint, almost like the line of a white felt-tip marker. I felt I should buy the historic highway society some bright-yellow paint that should be applied with a twelve-inch roller, to be seen far enough in advance that the captain can warn the stoker. I didn't think they were thinking of tandems when they were preparing the old highway for cyclists, though.

We found this to be true after the *Stop, Stairs Ahead* sign appeared on a tree next to the path. We did stop, dismount, and struggle to get the bike's wheels in the bike-wheel groove while we held it upright and negotiated the steep set of stairs ourselves. How had the cars driving this segment of the highway gotten down this steep part? There were no remnants of highway to give us a clue.

At several points, we rode under the freeway and through small tunnels much like the familiar one that leads to Multnomah Falls from the parking lot. We pedaled under bridges following the creek beds. There were many steep climbs, but unlike the rides in Iowa, we could not see them ahead so we could build up speed. It was darn hard work. We hadn't thought we'd need to train for our anniversary ride, and neither of us had pedaled much lately, and of course, we were not twenty anymore.

Stiff and hurting, and the area below my collarbone bruised from the bump to the neurostimulator, I got off the tandem in Cascade Locks, our turnaround point.

"I am not riding this back!"

"Okay, how do we get back to the truck?" Charlie said, seemingly disgruntled at my choice.

"We hitch a ride."

"I am not hitching a ride," was his response. He was like that, making snap judgments about the safety of an idea before he had explored the options. I didn't help him out, as I often thought aloud without framing it as a suggestion. Charlie went into a coffee shop to use the restroom, while I called a friend, Tricia, who lived near Hood River.

"Can you come get us and give us a ride back to our truck?" Luck had it that she had a little bit of free time and agreed. Charlie came out of the coffee shop.

"Hey, there's a guy in there who said he would give us a ride!"

"Cool, but Tricia is going to save the day."

We were so glad not to ride Grepedo on that trail back to our truck. We left that for another day. Maybe.

Our marriage has been an adventure of ups and downs and all-arounds. Isn't that how it goes? Neither of us could have ever imagined I would be struck with a progressive neurodegenerative disease like Parkinson's. We would hope that our pedals would always be in sync, but sometimes they are not. Smooth cycling paths with no climbs, bumps, hairpin turns, or bike stairs would be desirable, but realistically, smooth paths are nonexistent. Marriage is about working together, pedaling hard, taking the bumps, and leaning together into the tight turns as they come and then relishing those downhill glides.

Charlie and I have managed to hang together; sometimes it's been harder than hard. Sometimes I have wanted to get off that tandem event called marriage and walk. I am sure Charlie has felt like this too—just throw the bike down and walk. Walk in opposite directions. But we didn't. We are committed to work together, for life.

Bluegrass and Baseball

I had only attended a handful of bluegrass festivals in my life. Not that I didn't want to go to more. Life just had its way of getting in the way. A bluegrass festival is an event sponsored by some entity, such as a local bluegrass group, a traditional music society, or a town. Most often the attendees pay for a wristband that allows admittance to the main stage area to listen to various headline bands or attend music workshops. There are open mic sessions, band scrambles, and usually a Sunday morning gospel music hour. Attendees camp out at fairgrounds, on football fields, or in parks. My favorite part is the campsite jam sessions. Musicians wander around with their instruments and stop to listen to circles at different camps with hopes of being invited to play. If you're lucky enough to be hanging out with friends already, others come join you. I like that best.

Each festival I'd attended had its own flavor, which contributed to distinct memories for me. Although I played guitar, I

I play rhythm guitar in a bluegrass jam.

reminded myself that I had not started to play bluegrass until after I was diagnosed with Parkinson's disease. There had been days when I picked along with the group at breakneck speed, and others when I sat with my arms hugging my guitar close to my chest because my hands and arms wouldn't cooperate. A guitar amplifies sound in its big body. Being able to hug my guitar brought comfort to me and soothed the extreme frustration I felt when my brain could not make my limbs work.

One festival, I played with group of people I didn't know. As the evening slipped away, I asked the time and was told ten minutes after nine. *Wow!* It seemed later than that. Later I realized they must have wanted me to stay around because it had actually been ten minutes before two a.m. Another year a rowdy group started singing "Dead Skunk in the Middle of the Road," and other groups in the vicinity joined in the chorus to serenade the coyotes (and any nearby skunks). One festival's location had wonderful biking trails, and pedaling won over picking, as I put over seventy miles on the odometer. My good memories went on and on.

The summer after my DBS surgery, my trip to small-town Fossil, Oregon, on July 3 for its annual bluegrass festival provided more fodder for pulp. I loved that I drove myself. Charlie and I had diverse interests—he used to come to festivals with me, but then he became more involved in his own activities. That was one reason we bought the pickup-camper combination, as I could manage that type of recreational vehicle myself.

Bluegrass Junction was tuned in on my satellite radio, and I arrived about when I had expected and just in time for my friend Maryhelen to get off work. We visited the McMasters' guitar booth, where Maryhelen and the McMasters caught up on old times. McMasters had lived in Fossil before moving on to Hermiston. What a coincidence! While listening to the stage bands, we were entertained by a Hula-Hoop artist who danced beautifully to each song...with her Hula-Hoop. When the bands and the Hula-Hooper finally took a dinner break, Maryhelen and I wandered away from the McMasters' guitar booth in search of dinner. That was when I spotted them—two men playing catch.

I watched them toss the ball back and forth as memories flooded my brain. I could feel the ball burn in my glove when I'd played catch with a younger Luke. I could remember when I had first known something was wrong—I'd thrown the ball for the dogs, and it had gone about five feet. My fielders glove still felt like it was an extension of my hand after playing softball from March to October for so many years.

Setting any inhibitions aside, I picked up my trekking poles and walked directly to the men. I introduced myself and explained I hadn't thrown a ball in many years. When I saw them playing catch, I wondered if my recent brain surgery had improved that function. As Dr. Hiller had completed the first programming of my DBS in April, she'd manipulated my right arm, which had included some throwing-type movements—movements that, until I saw the men playing catch, I had not thought of attempting.

The gentlemen, Leif and his dad, Pete, appeared quite surprised at my request, yet they were willing to oblige. My hands were really shaking as I put my left hand into Leif's glove and took the baseball in my right. I was worried that I could not throw, or that I would "throw like a girl." But I felt it. I felt the motor memory kick in. I threw it directly into Pete's glove. *Smack.* Pete threw back, and I threw the next one harder.

"Have you played some baseball in your life?" Pete asked me. It felt so natural, like I had just played just yesterday.

"Many seasons of softball," I replied.

Ten throws were enough. We talked a bit more. Now Leif and Pete had a story to tell about playing catch with a fifty-eight-year-old woman with Parkinson's disease at a bluegrass festival in Fossil, Oregon, and I had another thing to thank God for—another gift of movement that had been returned to me.

At this point in my recovery, I had not gained enough coordination in my hands to keep up with the fast-paced bluegrass music on my own guitar. But that was fine with me; discovering I could throw a ball was amazing enough.

The Horse Ride

There was no doubt in my mind that my spouse would do anything for me. After a day of looking through all our financial paperwork, balancing five checkbooks, and paying the bills, Charlie was brain-dead. Neither of us were in the mood to cook, so we went out. I found some grilled veggies for me and sweet-and-sour chicken dinner special for him.

As we were driving home, he asked, "Is there anything else you need done tonight? 'Cause I just want to go to sleep."

It was selfish of me, but my body just felt like I could do this. "Yes, there is one more thing tonight. I want to saddle up one of the horses and get on."

He sighed and said, "Okay."

We pulled into the driveway as the beautiful July sunset colors were escaping from the sky. He caught the horses, brushed them, and checked their hooves. I grabbed a saddle and dragged it out to the horses, not recalling that someone else had used it. The cinch was too short, and the stirrup length needed to be changed. I didn't notice until Charlie threw it up on the old mare's back.

I looked at Charlie's exhausted face, and I pleaded, "I really want to get on tonight." He carried the saddle back to the tack room.

By that time the colors had completely faded from the horizon, and the big light on the back of the shop came on to illuminate the scene.

"Okay, let's do this thing," he said as he returned with the adjusted equipment.

He saddled the mare with the saddle I'd last ridden in, years ago. Positioning the mounting block perfectly, and with Charlie tightly holding the reins, I put my foot in the stirrup, grabbed a hunk of mane, and sprung up, swinging my bad right leg over the cantle. Muscle memory brought my leg down where it automatically found the stirrup and slipped in. I had made this same maneuver thousands of times over my years of riding.

I rode around our little dry lot for ten minutes maximum. Up on the back of this mare I'd purchased nineteen years ago, I felt on top of the world. She responded to my leg pressures to move forward, turn, sidestep, and back. It felt good, natural, like before PD, when I had ridden daily.

Charlie helped me get off. It was easier than I expected. I was glad for his close proximity and watchful eye—I didn't need to get hung up where I dismounted. We worked together to put the saddle away. As he locked up the shop, I headed for the house, thinking, *Tonight of all nights, I had a whim to get on a horse, and this tired guy made it happen.*

Charlie had always been there for me. He supported my goals and had done so much to make things happen, even when he may not have agreed. His signature on the greeting cards he gave me through the years included the phrase *your greatest fan.* That he was, even as I fought the progressions of Parkinson's disease.

I Ran

It was a girls' trip to beat all girls' trips. In the first week of August 2016, my husband's youngest sister, Maryrose, and I met in Portland to start a weeklong camping trip. Our first stop was the Portland International Airport, where we were to pick up Alise, who was flying in from her home country of Latvia. She was taking me up on the offer I'd made her the previous September when we'd said our goodbyes in Spain: "If you come to Oregon, I will take you on the tour of your life!"

The fun started immediately, as Maryrose and I made a sign so Alise could recognize us—actually I was worried about recognizing her. We drove by the passenger pickup area, flashing the sign out the window and laughing hysterically. The third time around, we saw her. My abrupt turn of the wheel put two wheels up on the curb. The hysterics continued as we pulled Alise into the vehicle and I drove off pretending all was normal.

Taking the interstate east into the Columbia River Gorge put my exhausted and excited friend into a state of ecstasy. What fun it was for me to point out the natural beauty of a place I could take for granted. We arrived at the campground at dusk. Fortunately, there was no tent to set up, as we had the big truck, Gertrude, and the deluxe Arctic Fox camper. We would be glamor camping—glamping.

We visited waterfalls, orchards, and Mount Hood, and then we drove to the coast. Kayaking, bicycling, hiking, beachcombing, campfires, singing, and laughter made the trip pass too quickly. I remember just about every moment of every day of that trip. But there was one short period of time—maybe just about an hour—that will forever stand out.

It happened to be Alise's birthday. We met up with my bicycling friend, Anne, from Hermiston, who owned a little house in Garibaldi. Anne took us touring in her car, which was much more spry than Gertrude. We found a beach where there were no people. I understood why as we opened the car doors to the freezing wind. It was here, where the sand met the waves, that the reality of my life with Parkinson's met the changes my body was starting to show with each DBS programming session.

The sand was firm and so very smooth to walk on. The water was numbingly cold. I walked knee-deep into the surf to soothe the pain radiating from my back down to my calves. Although I wished for relief, the DBS had done nothing for this pain. When I could no longer feel my toes, I retreated a bit away from the water and walked on the firm black-sand beach. As I moved toward the jetty, I searched for pools among the rocks where I might spy sea stars and anemones or maybe a small octopus left by the outgoing tide. Finding no sea life of interest there, I turned north and faced into the wind. My skin freshened to the

My friend Anne and I head towards the water on the beach where I ran. (Photo Credit: Alise Avota)

crispness of that wind, and suddenly I felt the difference. There had been a huge change in my body since the DBS surgery, but suddenly there was more. I felt so strong, so wild and free.

Every muscle inside screamed: *Run! Run away from the incoming waves that desire to freeze your bony ankles. Run into the wind until it sandblasts your face and burns your skin. Run in circles, with your arms reaching out and hands wide open as to touch the air and grab the moment. Run with your back to the wind so it pushes you faster and farther. Feel* alive *as the chill ocean breeze tousles your hair and reaches through seams and zippers and buttonholes in your clothing. You are not cold. You are alive!*

So…I ran. I truly ran.

I had so missed running. Running had always been a part of my life. I'd run track in high school, played basketball and softball. I quit any attempts to run after I started falling, shortly after my diagnosis. On the stormy day on the last Camino in 2015, my body loosened up enough to let me do a half jog along a gravel road and again on the mountain trail the day prior to reaching the iron cross. But neither of those runs was anything like this day on the beach.

Absorbed in the moment, I didn't see that my friends were headed back to the car. They told me later that they had turned to the beach to call to me, but what they saw silenced them. They saw my body freed from the symptoms of Parkinson's. My friends stood watching as I ran and twirled and skipped and sang. They were surprised, believing, pleased for me. I had no sense of time passing. The beach belonged to me.

Anne came back down on the beach to tell me, "The girls are freezing and heading back to the car." I walked with Anne up through the dunes to parking area, where Maryrose and Alise were using the car as a windbreak.

"We saw you," they called to me when I was close enough to hear.

"I ran, didn't I?"

"Yes, you ran."

Acknowledgments

My life with Parkinson's disease requires I have help. And this memoir would not have been finished without assistance from friends and experts. I loathe asking for help. Yet so much help found its way to me, and I am overcome with gratitude.

Help arrived first from the Parkinson's community in the form of inspiration. I learned quickly about the phrase "use it or lose it." "Keep moving and keep engaged" was more advice I heard from those who had more experience with the disease. I am grateful for the friendships I have forged since my diagnosis. And to the researchers, my doctors, therapists, trainers, coaches, and all who care about and for people with Parkinson's—thank you.

Then came encouragement. I want to thank acquaintances and friends who, after reading my adventures in my blogs and social media posts, asked for more. Without their constant prodding, my stories would never have evolved into *The Ribbon of Road Ahead*.

To Ali McCart Shaw of Indigo: Editing, Design, and More, I owe oodles of accolades. She confirmed what my readers said—yes, I had story to be told. Then she assisted me with turning the bits and pieces of writing into a memoir. Thank you. Thanks to

Vinnie, Olivia, Kristen, and Dehlia, also of Indigo, who used their expertise to design and put the book together.

Kristel Barry and Amanda Mills Woodlee read the early drafts. The keen eyes and thoughtful suggestions of these young women were of immeasurable value in developing the manuscript.

For her technical assistance, thanks from my heart to Alise Avota.

And my deepest gratitude to those who entered my life for a moment in time or came to stay. I can never thank enough:

- Strangers who gave me the last of their water, shared their cherries, or hopped out of their car to help me up when I fell crossing the street
- Friends who asked me to lunch, carried my kayak to the water, taught me a new tune, or cycled slowly so I could keep up

And to my family:

- My son Loren who cooks gourmet meals, mixes outstanding cocktails, and even cleans up, and his younger brother, Luke, who comes when I call him for anything and keeps my blood pressure up with threats of giving me a ride in his racecar
- And my husband who hikes behind me, pedals in front of me, and stands beside me

I love you.

About the Author

CAROL CLUPNY GREW UP RIDING HORSES, CLIMBING TREES, AND TUB-
ing down the creek. The fish would not stay off her line nor the
tales off her lips as her love of outdoor adventures grew. It came
as a blow when at age fifty she was diagnosed with Parkinson's
disease. Retired from her career as a speech-language patholgist,
she quickly became fed up with sitting in a recliner and feeling
sorry for herself. She decided to travel but needed to get her diseased body moving. Her first steps, walking out her door to the
mailbox, led to treading the pilgrimage trails of the Camino de
Santiago in France and Spain. A dusty bike discovered in the garage resulted in three rides on the Des Moines Register's Annual
Great Bike Ride Across Iowa.

Carol is active in the Parkinson's community as an advocate
and support group facilitator. She and her husband, Charlie, have
raised two boys, two horses, numerous dogs and cats, and fifty
calves on their small acreage in Hermiston, Oregon.